Advanc

Sri Raman offers a panoramic view of the history and politics underlying the nuclear standoff in South Asia and shows that the struggle for nuclear disarmament has to be simultaneously a struggle for peace and justice.

—M. V. Ramana,
Formerly of the Program on Science and Global Security,
Princeton University

"J. Sri Raman is one of India's most courageous journalists and well-known anti-nuclear activists. In this book he has ably highlighted the distinctive nuclear danger in South Asia situating it in its proper context—the historical antipathy between the governments of India and Pakistan and the more recent rise of religious extremism in both countries. This is an important and welcome contribution to the struggle for nuclear disarmament in South Asia and the world."

—Achin Vanaik
Visiting Professor in the Department of Political Science,
University of Delhi, and co-recipient of the Sean MacBride
International Peace Prize for the Year 2000.

This is an important, passionate, engaged, accessible and up to date book, raising issues crucial to the future of South Asia, home to one sixth of humanity. It forcefully exposes the mix of nationalism, nuclear weapons, religious militancy and superpower self-interest that has taken India-Pakistan relations to the edge of catastrophe."

—Zia Mian,
Program on Science and Global Security,
Princeton University.

Flashpoint is a clinical report of the subcontinent's sickness. This full indictment of the military-fascism on both sides of the Indo-Pak border will send chills down the spine of ordinary folk, just as it will move us to move on.

—Vijay Prashad,
author of *Fat Cats and Running Dogs:
The Enron Stage of Capitalism*

With over 30-years' experience as an esteemed journalist and peace activist, J. Sri Raman gives us a dynamic, astute and beautifully-written book for English-speakers seeking to understand India's and Pakistan's dramatic recent history and socio-political complexities, including the roles of the US and the "post – 9/11 era," leading to the region's current status as a nuclear weapons flashpoint with imminent global implications. This is essential reading!

—Sally Light, JD
Former Board Member, Global Network Against
Weapons & Nuclear Power in Space

Flashpoint

How the U.S., India and Pakistan Brought Us to the Brink of Nuclear War

J. Sri Raman

Common Courage Press   Monroe, Maine

ISBN: 1-56751-234-8 paper
ISBN 1-56751-235-6 cloth

**Library of Congress Cataloging-in-Publication Data is
available on request from the publisher**

Common Courage Press
121 Red Barn Road
Monroe, ME 04951

800-497-3207

FAX (207) 525-3068
orders-info@commoncouragepress.com

See our website for e versions of this book.
www.commoncouragepress.com

First Printing
Printed in Canada

Welcome, welcome, welcome
You who would do a single great deed
To bring peace to the nations of the world.
                    —Welcoming New India,
                    Subramania Bharati, Tamil
                        poet of India's freedom
                                    struggle

Contents

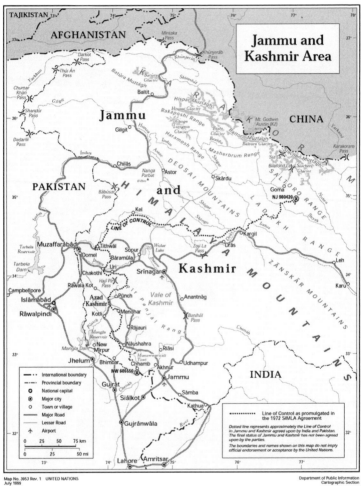

The UN map. Trouble spot for a coming nuclear war?

Preface

Who is most likely to use weapons of mass destruction next? Not Iraq. Not Afghanistan. Not Iran. Not North Korea. Forget the Axis of Evil, and turn your eyes instead to two allies of the United States of America, using their membership in the "coalition against global terror" to mount a terrifying threat to each other and the region: allies whose false rapprochement is endlessly cheered in the US media while, in reality, they have become more implacable adversaries than ever before. They are both nuclear-weapon states, with missiles aimed at major metropolitan areas, which have been waging a series of hot and cold wars, punctuated by cease fires and pious declarations of peace-making intent. They are India and Pakistan.

Readers may recall the crisis of the summer of 2002 when South Asia came close to a nuclear war. What I try to do in this book is point out to others what is so obvious to many peace activists in India and Pakistan: the nuclear kettle remains on the boil, as hot as ever.

What the region witnessed then was the result also of a new threat to world peace. A threat that has created a new world movement for peace. The central thesis of the book is that South Asia has become a particularly dangerous nuclear flashpoint because of the wider threat posed by the allegedly anti-terror "coalition."

As this book goes to the press, events in Pakistan are making the prognosis offered in these pages appear even more likely than ever before. Two attempts were made on President Pervez Musharraf's life in the space of eleven days in December 2003. These were, officially, the second and third (and, unofficially, the fourth and fifth) such attempts since 9/11, which paved the way for the US war on Afghanistan and Pakistan's consequent abandonment of its former Taliban allies. The general has blamed the attempts on the "Islamic" or "jihadi" radicals, especially the homegrown variety (as distinguished from the Arab-based al-Qaida), associated with terrorism in India-administered part of Kashmir. The incidents have come as yet another illustration of the metamorphosis of these forces of US-Pakistan creation into Frankenstein's monsters beyond easy control. Their terrorism represents today a threat not only to an individual leader, but also to millions of lives in South Asia by creating conditions of dangerous instability. These are conditions that only help the hawks on both sides, to whom, as we shall see, a nuclear holocaust is not too horrendous a prospect to contemplate. The assassination bids came on the eve of a summit of the South Asian Association for Regional Cooperation (SAARC) in January 2004, billed as a New Year event raising new hopes of peace in the region, even when New Delhi was categorically rejecting any bilaterial talk on any bilateral issue and Islamabad was equally firm in its "no" to any compromise on Kashmir. Even after the pretended beginnings of such parleys, the outlook does not warrant even a fraction of the optimism for the region feigned by the rulers of the two countries and the commander of the "coalition" of their uneasy co-existence.

The first round of talks (at the level of bureaucrats), after the famous summit, took place in February 2004 in Islamabad. Nothing much came of it except a schedule for further talks. They were described, actually, as "talks about talks."

Despite the media and official hype, the Islamabad summit was just one in a series of such hypocritical India-Pakistan "peace" moves. There is a tendency to look at any peace talk as a sign of a hopeful trend. But history and the alignment of contemporary political forces can provide a more clear-eyed assessment of the direction. The previous moves—like Atal Behari Vajpayee's bus ride to Lahore and the Agra summit—led respectively not closer to peace but to the Kargil war and the standoff-at-the-brink of 2002. In contrast, the peace moves of 2004 are different. Namely, they are staged under U.S. pressure. Unfortunately, this only makes them more of a pretense.

Perhaps this analysis seems cynical. After all, the next round of talks (again at a non-political level, but talks nonetheless), is to be held by June, after the general election in India and the installation of a new government in New Delhi. As a concession to critics, it has been promised that the future talks will also cover "confidence-building measures" on the nuclear front (which were on the agenda in Lahore as well). And didn't cross-border clashes in Kashmir slow down?

It is not cynicism but the desire to describe the conflict accurately that motivates the drive to cut through the media gloss. To cite one example, few reports describing the slowdown in the Kashmir border clashes mention a critical factor: the subcontinental winter slows them down every year. As spring returns, we will get a clearer idea of whether the melting snow will melt the peace.

The celebrated political "thaw" comes after a couple of attempts on Musharraf's life in Pakistan and ahead of an advanced general election in India. I have mentioned the outlook of uncertainty in Pakistan. In India, the party of nuclear militarism is trying to win over the peace constituency by talking of the "achievement" in Islamabad. It, however, is not abandoning its traditional, anti-peace constituency. The far Right has made it repeatedly clear (as this book reviews in detail) that it is just waiting for an electoral victory at the national level before going entirely berserk.

The fascist forces in both countries, which have kept animosities alive, continue to be active. The "jihadis" in Pakistan continue to target even Musharraf as too moderate. In India, in early January, a library of rare ancient and medieval records was destroyed by a mob because a scholar of the institute, to which the library was attached, had given an interview to the Western author of a book that was not sufficiently respectful to a Hindu warrior against a Mogul (Muslim) ruler. Trigger-happy terrorists, book-burners and makers of bombs and missiles cannot combine to usher in an age of South Asian peace.

Noticeably, the Islamabad summit talks had not touched on the nuclear issue at all. A serious review of the "peace moves" should raise an alarm: they have been accompanied by moves towards further militarization—on both sides. Media reports focus on India and Pakistan's avowed support for the Bush crusade against "proliferation." But behind the fanfare celebrating the rhetoric of nonproliferation is a harsh reality: both sides have ruled out any roll-back of their nuclear-weapons programs.

* * *

This book was the product of a dialogue that began at the height of that chilling summer between Greg Bates of Common Courage Press and the author. It was a little dialogue within a larger dialogue—between the peace movements of a developing region and the developed world. The interaction enriched the book, as it set out to answer a series of questions (listed towards the end of Chapter 1).

Grateful acknowledgments are due to the many who have made unwritten contributions to the book. At the head of the list is the unusual publisher—Greg to me, by now a friend and a fellow-activist (and also an editor of great skill and sensitivity). I must place on record also the inspiration and encouragement from several other friends and comrades. I intend no invidious distinction, when I say a special thanks to Gopal, Subbu, Shankar, Ramana, Philip, Achin, Praful, and Sukla in India, to dear Sally, Dale, Erika and the Globenet fraternity of Bruce in the U.S., to John, Terry, and Jacob in Australia, and to Satomi and others in Japan who have made a hallowed memory of the horror that was Hiroshima. My warm gratitude to Zia Mian for his kind response to the book, as also to Ejaz Haider and Arifa Noor of the *Daily Times* (Lahore) and other Pakistani friends who, too, gave me a sense of participation in a shared South Asian cause. The book is also a product of the anti-fascist campaign in India, which it seeks to introduce to the outside world. My thanks also to all those with whom I came into warm and rewarding contact in this multi-faceted campaign over the years.

I must add a very personal acknowledgment of all the involvement of Papri in all aspects of the book. Thanks, too, to Taranga and Varna who helped so much by just being there.

J. Sri Raman
March 1, 2004

...safety will be the sturdy child of terror, and survival the twin brother of annihilation.

—Winston Churchill,
commending the "balance
of terror" concept to the
House of Commons, 1955

CHAPTER I

THE SUMMER OF 2002

When South Asia Became the Scariest Place on Earth

> Only the fallen know the number.
> —Wilfred Owen, the pre-nuclear anti-war poet

The numbers were chillingly precise, to the last thousand. They were worked out on the assumption that five major cities each in India and Pakistan would be hit first.

Killed before they knew what hit them would be about 1.7 million people in India and about 1.2 million in Pakistan or a total of about three million. The breakdown: for India, 477,000 in Mumbai (formerly Bombay), 364,000 in Chennai (formerly Madras), 357,000 in Kolkata (formerly Calcutta), 314,000 in Bangalore, and 176,000 in New Delhi; and, for Pakistan, 336,000 in Faisalabad, 258,000 in Lahore, 240,000 in Karachi, 154,000 in Rawalpindi, and 154,000 in Islamabad.

The numbers did not describe the kind of deaths since they did not specify the kind of war that would cause them. What the estimates envisaged were nuclear exchanges between the two South Asian adversaries and, therefore, deaths by instantaneous evaporation in many, many of these cases.

Figures for the number of severely injured were also forecast: 892,000 for India (22,900 in Mumbai, 198,000 in Kolkata, 196,000 in Chennai, 175,000 in Bangalore, and 94,000 in New Delhi) and 612,000 for Pakistan (174,000 in Faisalabad, 150,000 in Lahore, 127,000 in Karachi, 97,000 in Rawalpindi, and 67,000 in Islamabad). That is a total of over 1.5 million. But there was no forecast for the radioactive fate of the writhing survivors.

The fate of the would-be survivors was faintly suggested by the far smaller precedent of the world's first nuclear bombing, of just one city. The survivors of Hiroshima, the "hibakusha" as they are called, include those who are still suffering and undergoing treatment over a half-century later. Exposure to radiation led to thousands of cases of instant sickness including hemorrhages and bloody diarrhea and to the development of fatal diseases including leukemia, thyroid cancer, breast cancer and lung cancer. The somewhat delayed radioactive fallout spelt a further spread of the same effects. Among the non-fatal but even more nightmarish results have been a large number of birth defects, cataracts and mental retardation among the youngest of the young.

The fallout would be compounded in the subcontinent by carcinogenous black rain in all the coastal cities with Hiroshima-like high humidity. The velocity of the summer winds and the dust storms, especially in the India-Pakistan border region, could be expected to widen the fallout. So could the explosion of nuclear bombs on the ground instead of in the air, considered a realistic possibility by experts.

These were the figures for a "limited war," involving only the largest of the cities of the two countries.

Projections for a larger lunacy were soon forthcoming. If 15 cities were victims of nuclear bombing, it was estimated, as many as 12 million instant deaths could be expected, with serious immediate injuries to about seven million. The list of cities now included Jaipur, Ahmedabad and Pune in India and Quetta and Hyderabad in Pakistan.

Like the smaller forecast, the reports of larger conflicts did not include estimates of subsequent deaths caused by urban firestorms ignited by the heat of a nuclear exchange, deaths from long-term radiation, or deaths from the expected spread of disease and starvation. The estimates also postulated that the nuclear weapons would explode on the surface and not in the air: such "ground bursts" would dig up tons of soil and spread the poisonous, radioactive debris over a large area.

A media report from the US said that the war would have "cataclysmic results," requiring vast international assistance to battle radioactive contamination, famine and disease. "The humanitarian crisis that would result would be so great that every medical facility in the Middle East and Southwest Asia would be quickly overwhelmed," said an unnamed US Defense Department official in the report, adding the anticipatory rider: "The American military would have no choice but go in and help with the victims and to clean up."

Mind-boggling as they may be, none of these scenarios was science fiction. It was reported in the prestigious, no-nonsense *New Scientist* in May 2002 that drew wide public attention to the "limited war" projections. The projections had been previously made by acknowledged nuclear experts Zia Mian, M. V. Ramana, Matthew McKinzie and A. H. Nayyar in a paper on "The Risks and Consequences of

Nuclear War in South Asia" in *Out of the Nuclear Shadow* (ed. Smitu Kothari and Zia Mian, Lokayan, Rainbow and Zed Press, New Delhi and London, 2001)[1].

The estimates about a less limited war came from at least three different sources. A reporter and a graphic artist at the *Washington Times* used the computer terminal of a Consequences Assessment Tools Set (CATS) system, quantifying factors ranging from weather and wind velocities to the warheads and vehicles and including the size and density of populations. The computer terminal was made available by the highly reputed Heritage Foundation's Center for Media and Public Policy.

Arriving at roughly the same figures as the team was an American intelligence assessment, reportedly completed in the last week of May 2002, according to what unnamed Pentagon officials told *The New York Times*. The assessment, which factored in current weather conditions, used "military judgment to guess the targets" and postulated that "most but not all the weapons" would be used.

A third, strikingly independent analysis of the consequences of a South Asian nuclear war came from the Natural Resources Defense Council (NRDC), a U.S.-based nonprofit organization concerned with the environment, which used state-of-the-art nuclear warfare simulation software. The exercise assumed 24 nuclear explosions targeting 15 cities.

"Contrary to conventional wisdom," as the analysts put it, they believed India had 30 to 35 nuclear warheads and Pakistan's 48 or so. The NRDC chose target cities throughout Pakistan and in northwestern India to take into account the limited range of Pakistani missiles or aircraft. It assumed that a dozen 25-kilotonne warheads would be detonated as ground bursts in Pakistan and another dozen in India, producing a substantial fallout. The devastation that would result from the fallout would exceed that of blast and fire. NRDC's second scenario would produce far more horrific results than the first scenario because, in this forecast, there would be more weapons, higher yields, and extensive fallout. In some large cities, it was assumed, more than one bomb would be used.

The study concluded that 22.1 million people in India and Pakistan would be exposed to lethal radiation doses of 600 rem or more in the first two days after the attack. Another eight million people would receive a radiation dose of 100 to 600 rem, causing severe radiation sickness and potential death, especially for the very young, old or infirm. Roughly divided between the two countries, as many as 30 million people would be threatened by the fallout from the attack.

While these apocalyptic scenarios of what would happen if nuclear war started between India and Pakistan may be reliable, to many they have a feel of implausibility. After all, the world has survived a half-century of nuclear deterrence where two massively armed superpowers and a host of smaller powers have not used nuclear weapons in war since the Second World War. As these forecasts reveal, the outbreak of nuclear war and the breakdown of deterrence between India and Pakistan would be suicide. In the world of nuclear deterrence, this can be read as an assurance that such war will likely never happen.

But such a view of deterrence omits the scary moments, most notably the Cuban missile crisis of 1962. Any comforting sense that this particular episode is long behind us and such escalation cannot happen again is belied by the current situation in South Asia. "Deterrence" here takes place in a context where the opponents are already at war with each other. The events in the summer of 2002 revealed starkly that beneath this veneer of stability lies the prospect of a nuclear war whose likelihood is rapidly increasing. As this book is going to press in the U.S., there are reports of a thaw in relations between India and Pakistan. Yet, as discussed in later chapters, this is an illusory diplomatic cover for a situation that is rapidly deteriorating. Just how close have we come to war and where is the situation going? This core question must be viewed both from the vantage point of hostilities between the two countries and in the context of America's developing "war on terror," a critical factor which will be later discussed at length.

At the height of a long Indian summer in 2002, stretching from March to May, the world woke up to a nuclear nightmare. But to those watching South Asia closely and longer, it came as no surprise. For a full six months beginning in December 2001, about 750,000 soldiers from India and about 250,000 from Pakistan faced each other in an eyeball-to-eyeball confrontation. No localized conflict, troops were spread along a 3,000-km border running all the way from icy Himalayan heights in Kashmir to the scorched deserts of Rajasthan and Gujarat through the war-weary plains of Punjab. Intensifying the conflict, India also placed at least five warships menacingly close to Pakistan's coast.

Far from a stable situation of deterrence, all through this period of increasingly unbearable tension, the two nuclear-capable adversaries engaged in serious hostilities which would anywhere else have been regarded as acts of war. Artillery fire was exchanged frequently, destroying unelectrified homes and hamlets on both sides of the border and killing, in ones and twos, hapless villagers of whom nobody kept a count. It was twice reported that military planes embarked on "secret sorties." Those on the ground understood that war was very likely, and began to flee, leaving villages deserted. But even for those far from the border, there was no fleeing the terrors of the standoff.

Both sides bragged about their missiles and their imminent deployment. The vagueness about details was hardly calculated to delight. India heightened the tensions of the standoff early on January 25, by test-firing its Agni (Fire) missile, capable of hitting targets some 700 km away (about 450 miles). Through the crisis Pakistan retaliated with three missile tests of its own—the 1,500-km Ghauri, the 300-km Ghaznavi and the 180-km Abdali. The first two, named after invaders of parts of medieval India from the Islamic world, reveal a war of names between the nuclear rivals: that is a subject to which we will return.

In January 2002, Prime Minister Atal Behari Vajpayee of India was reported to have authorized military use of the Prithvi (Earth) missile, even as American intelligence was stated to have caught Pakistan missile launch sites close to the border.

There was no clear word from either side that the missiles were meant for nuclear warheads. The dangerous standoff, however, did not allow anyone the luxury of dismissing the nuclear threats traded by both as mere rhetoric.

The month-long Kargil conflict of 1999—the conventional India-Pakistan war in Kashmir—took place within months of nuclear-weapon tests by the two countries. According to Indian anti-nuclear activist Praful Bidwai, nuclear threats had been exchanged no less than 13 times. Whatever the quantity of words, they were no match this time for the quality of nuclear intimidation. The directness of the threats between nuclear powers was without precedent.

Threats were exchanged at the highest levels. Prime Minister Vajpayee, none less, led the way for India. The plaster-saint politician, who occasionally pens verse or worse for peace, left no one in the subcontinent in doubt about what he meant by his call to the soldiers for "a decisive victory." Orating at an election rally in Lucknow on January 2, 2002, he shed the proverbial fig leaf: "No weapon would be spared in self-defense. Whatever weapon was available, it would be used no matter how it wounded the enemy." And the nuke-rattling continued, no matter that it failed to win that election for his Bharatiya Janata Party (Indian People's Party).

None did it in quite so casually swashbuckling a manner as Defense Minister George Fernandes. In May, even as the expert estimates of a nuclear war toll were running into millions, he was telling the media: "India can take a (nuclear) hit and hit back. Pakistan cannot."

Indian Army chief S. Padmanabhan vowed vengeance like a warrior of yore in the event of Islamabad resorting to a nuclear strike. "The perpetrator of that particular outrage shall be punished, shall be punished so severely," he thundered, "that the continuation of any form of fray will be doubtful." He took it upon himself to spell out India's readiness for "a second strike" and told the nation that there were "enough" nuclear arms in his arsenal.

General Pervez Musharraf of Pakistan did not lag an

inch behind the Indian Prime Minister. The President himself, in and out of uniform as the occasion and the audience demanded, went beyond the "any weapon" talk in an interview to Germany's *Der Spiegel*. If Pakistan was pushed too far, he warned, "as a last resort, the atom bomb is also possible." He also told his countrymen that he would go for the dreaded option if the danger arose of Pakistan being "wiped off the world map."

Resorting to similar scare-mongering, prominent minister and former chief of the country's Inter-Service Intelligence (ISI) Javed Ashraf Qazi promised: "Pakistan will nuke India if it has to save itself." Munir Akram, Pakistan's Ambassador to the United Nations, addressing a news conference in New York on May 30, delivered the threat in unreassuringly different terms: "India should not have the license to kill with conventional weapons while Pakistan's hands are tied regarding other means to defend itself." That Pakistan kept its first-strike option open was, of course, a point that its leadership found it fit to reiterate several times during the standoff.

Former army chiefs, too, jumped into the fray. General Mirza Aslam Beg of the pre-nuclear Pakistan army seemed to be making up for lost time as he proclaimed: "We can make a first strike, and a second strike or even a third." The estimates of instant and eventual deaths and destruction from a nuclear war did not impress him. "You can die crossing the street, or you could die in a nuclear war," so ran his cogently argued case, "you've got to die someday anyway." Former Indian army chief V. P. Malik eschewed such flamboyance but made a "limited" nuclear war appear little more than a fascinating game involving no human lives: "The escalation ladder would be carefully climbed in a carefully controlled ascent by the protagonists." Few could have shared this touching faith.[2]

Especially in the capacity of either side to control the escalation. Actually, the importance of this statement is not that it is likely false. Whether the ascent is carefully controlled or not is not nearly as important as the idea that there will be an ascent. Controlled or uncontrolled, the ascent up the escalation ladder would be a disaster.

Apprehensions about the standoff leading to a nuclear war included real fears about either accidental or unauthorized use of nuclear weapons setting off an uncontrollable spiral. Indian anti-nuclear activist Achin Vanaik holds that "South Asia's potential for a nuclear catastrophe is the highest anywhere in the world since the 1962 Cuban missile crisis." One reason is the primitiveness of the nuclear weapons in possession of the nuclear powers of the region. The first-generation weapons lack the minimum safeguards such as authorization locks and insensitive explosives, alleges the Movement in India for Nuclear Disarmament without eliciting any official contradiction.

The second, and even stronger, reason that nuclear catastrophe is likely is the notoriously poor safety culture of both India and Pakistan. The rate of transportation accidents in the subcontinent is estimated to be 10 times the world average. Trains have skidded off rails into swirling rivers below; civilian air accidents have included a mid-air collision of planes. There is no reliable record of road mishaps, with hit-and-run cases accounting for a large proportion of them. India acquired, in 1984, the dubious distinction of providing the venue for the world's worst ever industrial accident—the Bhopal gas-leak tragedy that claimed over 3,000 lives and has left over

50,000 long-suffering survivors (the primary responsibility for which remains, of course, with the profit-mongering US multinational Union Carbide). Meanwhile, Pakistan set a new record in peace-time military mishaps in April 1988, when the explosion of an ammunition dump in its Ojhri camp in Rawalpindi killed over a thousand people.

If the fears caused by the primitive weapons in an accident-prone setting are not enough, the situation is compounded by the total unreliability of the command and control systems. This became startlingly clear when, during the standoff, India learnt that the Prime Minister lacked the facility to make direct telephonic calls from his official plane. Even more incredible, at a time when speedy consultations might have been a matter of survival for both, almost all communication channels between the two countries were closed.

Primitive weapons, loose command and control, poor communications and closed diplomatic channels—all in the midst of an actual war—are heightened by an even more alarming factor: a geography that threatens an inescapably terrible culmination to a history of hate. As experts have pointed out, while estimating the casualties in an India-Pakistan nuclear war, the missile travel time between the two contiguous neighbors is a maximum of about 10 minutes, and a minimum of about four. Greater distance would allow for critical options—for a start an early warning system to verify that an incoming missile was indeed just that and not some other event; for a few crucial minutes to decide whether striking back was a wise countermove; for diplomatic exchange as a nuclear exchange was unfolding. But the nations' proximity pre-cludes decisions, and with weapons on hair trigger, avoidance of war becomes increasingly a matter of chance, not choice.

Events leading to the standoff were themselves cause for alarm. The standoff was a sequel to what was projected all over India as the most symbolic instance of terrorism that targeted the country. On December 13, 2001, millions watched on television as unidentified militants found their way into the heavily secured Parliament House in New Delhi and battled with Indian soldiers. While no member of Parliament or government leader was killed, the incident left 14 dead, a trail of bitterness, and initiated a massive military build-up on the border.

India was quick to claim that the attackers were Pakistanis and were sponsored by Pakistan. Islamabad, equally quick to condemn the attack, deplored India's "knee-jerk reaction."

In his televised address to Pakistan on January 12, President Gen. Musharraf himself reiterated his government's denunciation of the terrorist strike but refused to accept New Delhi's demand for the handing over of 20 listed allegedly Pakistan-sponsored militants and, by implication, any charge of involvement in the incident.

The record of both the countries and their rulers, especially in the recent period, was such that no reconstruction of the incident could be ruled out. True, Gen. Musharraf was Pakistan's acclaimed architect of the Kargil conflict that left 1,200 to 1,800 dead (the estimates continue to vary considerably even today). True, too, however, that the general and his regime have been the political targets of terrorists and their repeated outrages inside Pakistan, particularly after the imposition of an official ban on their major outfits and their funding.

But December 13 was no signal for a debate. It was the day that the hawks in both India and Pakistan were waiting for, ever since the more infamous date of September 11, 2001.

The massive military build-up on both sides of the border was almost immediate, by all accounts. Winter may have compelled a relatively slow start in the Kashmir sectors, but the early summer saw a mobilization of remarkable rapidity here.

The Indian army had been forced into a truly uphill struggle in the Kargil war, with Pakistanis capturing the vantage high-altitude points, and it was resolved not to repeat the costly folly. The tensions of the standoff grew, amidst terrorist strikes on both sides besides skirmishes and steady nuclear drum-beating. Hope, however, hinged on international efforts to persuade the nuclear enemies to pull back from the brink. By the beginning of May 2002, some wishful South Asia-watchers had convinced themselves that the worst was over and started trying to convince the world. They were silenced by militant gunfire in Jammu and Kashmir.

On May 14, 2002, within a week of a terrorist assault on bus passengers, unidentified gunmen raided a camp at Kalachuk in Jammu, housing the families of Indian soldiers posted in the region. Most of the 34 victims of the brutal massacre were women and children, and the anguished survivors shown on television stirred emotions all over India.

A reputedly restrained newspaper (the *Times of India*) declared: "Many in this country believe that...diplomacy is no longer the answer to the problem of cross-border terrorism. In their view, New Delhi has little option but to launch what a former chief of army staff (Gen. V. P. Malik) described—less than 24 hours before the latest outrage in Jammu—as a 'limited war'. Such retaliatory strikes, it is believed, will not risk escalation since their aim would be solely to inflict punishment and not gain territory...New Delhi has a pressing obligation to protect its own, with or without American help." A "fitting reply" to Pakistan was what was demanded from numerous fora across the country. It was back to the mood of December 13 for most of India and, consequently, the subcontinent.

The Jammu massacre came right in the middle of the months long riots in India's border-state of Gujarat. The minority community of Muslims was the main victim of state-supported violence here, which claimed about 3,000 lives. We shall return to the riots in a later chapter dealing with the fascist dimension to South Asia's nuclear flashpoint. Suffice it here to note that the bloodletting in this home-state of Mahatma Gandhi, the apostle of non-violence, barred the path further to a return of sanity and a relaxation of the standoff.

* * *

THUS it was that, at the height of the standoff, the question was not whether there would be a war but when. And how it would start.

The talk in India was about raids on the "terrorist camps" inside "Pakistan-occupied Kashmir" (PoK) or "Azad (Liberated) Kashmir" as Islamabad prefers to call it. Claiming "a moral and legal right" for India to attack these camps (as India had, if less directly, claimed in the international arena ever since September 11), India's defense secretary Yogendra Narain argued: "Surgical strikes are the only realistic option." The media picked up the refrain of "swift surgical strikes" and made these sound imminent. Others, however, envisaged a different scenario.

Defense analyst Brian Cloughley, a former British army colonel to have served with the UN in both India and Pakistan, ruled out a "surgical strike" since Pakistan was committed to considering even such a strike as an "act of war". On how the war "might begin, spread and possibly end," he said: "India would attack what it states are 'terrorist camps'… probably with a brigade of some 3,000 infantry supported by Indian Air Force (IAF) strike planes. Temperatures will soar to 45 degree C before the monsoon. The air force would be at the forefront as the ground along most of the Line of Control between Indian and Pakistani Kashmir is unsuitable for tanks and armored divisions. Pakistan expects a thrust and has planned to counter-attack in force while itself striking IAF bases and increasing pressure elsewhere along the border. India would have to commit more troops to extricate its brigade. Fighting would increase in intensity, with neither side able to force a conclusion. It is probable that India would then launch an attack along the international border, in the southern plains, using its three armour-heavy Strike Corps…. It is likely the IAF would achieve air superiority over the battlefield for extended periods, while its counterpart would concentrate on attacking IAF bases. Both sides would take severe casualties."

As for where this war could lead: "World leaders would try to mediate, but it is probable this would be a fight to the finish. Nobody can predict the stage at which nuclear weapons could be involved. India's defense secretary stated that India does not know Pakistan's 'nuclear

threshold'. But he said if there is a nuclear strike by
Pakistan, 'We will retaliate and must be prepared for
mutual destruction on both sides.'"

"Rarely," commented Cloughley, "can there have
been a more chilling message." It was at this nerve-racking
stage of the standoff that concerned experts began estimating the consequences of a nuclear war. What they
came up with were, or must have been, far more than cold
figures. Certainly to all those, who could put flesh and
blood on them, to whom South Asia was more than a map.
Questions must have haunted them, as the region seemed
to approach the end of history. Even if it was only a "limited" nuclear war that loomed ahead.

Would Delhi, the city of tombs and monuments, disappear without a trace? Would the fallout reach as far as
the Taj Mahal, the extravagant memory of an emperor's
love? Would Shantiniketan, the Abode of Peace, the syl-
van university founded by Japan-loving poet
Rabindranath Tagore who did not live to see Hiroshima,
be reduced to ashes in an insane war? Would Mumbai's
Gateway of India open into a world of the dead and the
living dead? What would the charred and poisoned relic of
Chennai's Marina Beach, lapped by gentle waves through
long centuries of coastline trade and temples, look like?
Would an instant kill the ages? And what of the living and
the loving? What would become of the sights and sounds
of Lahore, to the memory of which hundreds of families
now in India still remain fiercely loyal? Of the sweets of
Rawalpindi and the street cricket of Karachi? Would a
"ghazal" culture, a cult of the singer and the song, grow
again in a nuclear-hit nation?

What of the more than immediate future? South Asia

was still paying dearly for the cruelties of the colonial partition of the subcontinent in 1947, which created present-day India and pre-1971 or pre-Bangladesh Pakistan. The subcontinent had yet to live down the legacy of bitterness, leading to the very brink of a nuclear war. What hope was there for normalcy in a post-nuclear-war region? Would anything but hate ever grow on that contaminated soil?

The questions must have haunted the people of the subcontinent more than anyone else. But very few Indians and Pakistanis appeared to be asking them.

The peace movement in the two countries, of course, made repeated attempts to raise the questions. In mid-May, for example, the main umbrella organization in India stated: "The Coalition for Nuclear Disarmament and Peace (CNDP) is deeply concerned at the campaign unleashed in India for a 'full-scale war' with Pakistan and the attempts at projecting a 'national consensus' in favor of such a war. Resort to such a war to settle disputes between two nuclear-weapons states is a far from readily acceptable option. It is all the more so in view of the nuclear-weapon capability acquired by both India and Pakistan in the last four years and the fact that neither has ruled out the use of weapons against the other. The acquisition of nuclear weapons by them has only been followed by the deterioration of both internal and external security in both countries. The government of no nuclear-weapon state can be given a carte blanche in this regard and authorized to take 'any action' in the name of fighting terrorism..." The desperate plea for sanity was nearly, but only nearly, drowned by the official and media war drums. The figures, however, were frightening enough to increasing sections in the rest of the world. When former US

President Bill Clinton described South Asia as "the most dangerous place on Earth," he had just made the most uncontroversial statement of his public career. He had also spoken for the foreign missions, particularly from the Western countries, in India and Pakistan. To quote one of the many agency reports that captured the very real fear in the air:

June 2: Expatriate families thronged Delhi's Indira Gandhi International Airport last night amid intensifying fears that an attack on Pakistan by India might escalate uncontrollably into nuclear war.

France and Japan yesterday advised their nationals to leave India, following similar warnings from the US, Britain, Australia, New Zealand and Germany. The UN prepared to evacuate the families of staff from Pakistan.

The warnings came as shelling by India and Pakistan continued in many places across the Line of Control in Kashmir, the long de facto border between Indian and Pakistani territory....

Deborah Wise, a British mother of two, doing last-minute packing, said: 'I'm nervous. I'm glad I'm leaving tonight. I don't like leaving my household behind, but I can't pack it all up in two minutes.'

A member of staff with the American embassy, who declined to be named, was getting ready to leave with his children on Monday. He played down the anxiety. 'A lot of people are going off on their holidays, anyway. There's a natural siphoning off of people...this gives me a couple of weeks extra vacation.'

Others, however, believe the danger is real and urgent. 'My wife and children left this morning,' said one British company employee. 'I am very glad they're out of here. If I have to stay I may move somewhere safer than Delhi.'

At any one time there are about 20,000-36,000 British nationals in India, many of Indian origin. The recent tensions are thought to have cut sharply the numbers of backpackers and other tourists....

Shock and bafflement marked the reactions even of veteran contingents in the world peace movement. A sample was the statement from Dimity Hawkins of the Friends of the Earth, Australia (where, of course, there was entirely warranted and widespread fear of the fallout). "We have all heard the rhetoric of the threat of nuclear war ending with the end of the Cold War, but with hundreds of nuclear weapons in this region alone, the potential for nuclear war is still very real," said Hawkins. "[We have been] actively working against nuclear war and nuclear proliferation for over 25 years—this current crisis has brought us to the brink in ways not seen for a generation." The FoE called on Prime Minister John Howard and his government to use all diplomatic links at their disposal to try to assist in de-escalating this situation "between Australia's regional nuclear neighbors."

So did the peace movements of several other countries demand similar intervention by their governments. Successfully, to go only by appearances, in quite a few cases. There were a lot of diplomatic comings and goings in the region, but these seemed to make no difference except of the smallest and the slowest kind. Special hopes were pinned on the South Asian missions of high-profile Western leaders including US Secretary of State Colin Powell and British Prime Minister Tony Blair. The hopes were bound to be belied, as we shall see later. Not so, however, were the expectations of the embattled Indian peace activists from their allies everywhere, and especially in the West.

I was in Berkeley, USA, in the first half of May 2002 to attend the annual conference of the Global Network Against Weapons and Nuclear Power in Space on behalf of the Chennai-based Movement Against Nuclear Weapons. Here I discovered, among not only the peace campaigners from all over the globe but the common American people as well, a deep concern, if no detailed knowledge, about the endangered region. They were and have been, in our continuing contacts since then, full of questions.

The first and foremost of these has been about the emergence of South Asia as a nuclear flashpoint. To many, many, this has been a painfully shocking rediscovery of a region they had unwittingly come to consider a preserve of relative peace.

The lingering image was a legacy of South Asia's nuclear-weapon-free past. Of the days when nations of the region raised their voices against nuclear rivalries that could have spiraled and spelt humanity's doom.

Wars, of course, have raged in the region, but none that was ever expected to go entirely out of control. It was the Middle East, Africa and the Far East that used to set alarm bells ringing once in a while. How did the safest part of the planet become "the most dangerous place on Earth"?

The ferocity of the Israel-Palestine conflict was familiar; the fratricidal fury of the India-Pakistan hostilities was not. Hardly common was knowledge of the history and the geography that threatened a holocaust. Or of the fascism of a subcontinental species and "fundamentalism" that stoked the fires.

Then there were the special problems of understanding in the post-9/11 world. Were not both India and Pakistan on the same side in the "war on global terror"? Were they not allies now? Was the standoff actually a sequel to the September outrage? Why did the West of the unipolar world allow the standoff? What was the role of George Bush and his band of warmongers? Is it all over now? Can anything be done to prevent the return of months that shook the region and the world?

What follows is an attempt to help friends of peace find answers to these questions.

CHAPTER 2

BLOODY BAPTISM AND AFTER

The History That Threatens to Repeat Itself

> On the flowing Sind, under moonlight.
> With young Chera damsels,
> Singing in sweet Telugu,
> We'll ferry and frolic.
> > —Tamil poet Subramania Bharati, at the dawn
> > of the century, on his dream of free India

> Better than all the world is our beloved India,
> We're its singing birds, and it's our flower garden.
> > —Urdu poet Allama Iqbal, years before he opted
> > for Pakistan

The summer of 2002 was a sequel to a monsoon of over half a century before. On August 14-15, 1947, long-awaited independence came to the subcontinent, but in a form that few of its early freedom fighters could have foreseen. It was a truncated India and an even more truncated Pakistan (which translates literally as Land of the Pure) that celebrated the midnight event and waited for the morning after. Britain, renowned for its divide-and-rule dictum, had reserved the biggest of its divisive exercises for the end of its rule. The retreating colonialism resorted to a scorched-earth policy for which South Asia was hardly prepared.

Violence may not always be the midwife of history. But, there are passages of violence without which subsequent stories of peoples and countries may not make much sense. Violence of a kind that alone can explain its special consequences, otherwise beyond easy comprehension. The world has not been the same after Hiroshima or September 11. South Asia could not have been the same after the Partition of the subcontinent in 1947.

The Partition was a point of no return. It ruled out a return to the pre-Independence past. To the dreams and visions of Bharatis and Iqbals. Of the bards of the freedom struggle (like the ones quoted at the head of this chapter), who sang of a united subcontinent and a post-Independence paradise.[1] Mahatma Gandhi, launching the Quit India movement in 1942 and calling upon colonialism to withdraw without professing concern for the consequences, had declared: "Leave us to chaos." He was now coping with the chaos of colonial creation.

He faced howling, stone-throwing Hindu and Muslim mobs in Bengal's Noakhali, even as New Delhi ushered Independence in with fireworks and fanfare. The feeble, old man followed this up with fasts-unto-death which helped to bring down temperatures in some places at least for a time. It would have, however, needed many a Mahatma to prevent the Partition from heralding a history of hate that was to grow over the years to a grim nuclear pitch.

There are, of course, historians who see no colonial design in the Partition decision, no intent on Britain's part to split India. Some make the special plea that the last

Viceroy of India, Lord Louis Mountbatten, was a man in a hurry. The deadline he had set for himself (mid-1948) and for Independence mattered more to him, they insist, than what the decision might spell for the subcontinent. The plea is made despite the time he took to persuade unconvinced political leaders to agree to the Partition. One of these, would-be Indian Prime Minister Jawaharlal Nehru, after agreeing to the terms of the transfer of power, reportedly told the Viceroy: "Now I know what they mean when they talk of your charm being so dangerous."

Just how dangerous became clear soon after Mountbatten's announcement, aired on the radio, on June 3, 1947, of the plan for the Partition, envisaging a Pakistan made up of far-apart West Punjab and East Bengal and an exchange of populations. That was a green light for the grisliest rioting the region has seen.

The Partition was a point of departure. Today, the warmongers of both countries now portray the violence at Partition as a culmination of an unremitting series of religious-communal conflicts ever since the advent of Islam in India, the result of so-called "civilizational" skirmishes. But that is not correct. It was more of a belated success for nearly a century of systematic efforts by British colonialism aimed at an enduring subcontinental schism.

* * *

IN 1857, a revolt broke out. It was the "Sepoy Mutiny" to colonial chroniclers, while the subcontinental nationalists gave it a prouder label, the "First War of Independence." It was a rebellion of the soldiers and peasants and also of sub-regional chieftains of both the Hindu and Muslim communities.[2] The Hindus were represented by legendary woman warrior Rani Lakshmi Bai of Jhansi, Nana Sahib, Tatya Tope and Kunwar Singh and the Muslims by the Maulvi of Fyzabad and Bakht Khan, among others. It is strikingly significant, in the light of later developments, that the rebels of all communities and classes consciously adopted the last of the Moghuls as their common leader, their counter to the colonial rulers, a move that united Hindus and Muslims. They proclaimed Bahadur Shah Zafar, the poet-king, in Delhi as the Shahensha-e-Hind, the Emperor of India, on May 11, 1857.

Marxist P. C. Joshi saw the meaning of the moment. Writing a century after the historic event, he stated: "It was a stroke of instinctive genius on the part of the insurgent sepoys (soldiers) of Meerut when they crossed the Jamuna and liberated…the…capital of our ancient country and crowned the disinherited heir of Akbar, Bahadur Shah…The revolutionary significance of this event was universally accepted and has been characterized by Charles Ball in the following words: 'The Meerut sepoys in a moment found a leader, a flag and a cause….'" The significance was clear to Bahadur Shah Zafar. "During the siege of Delhi," recalled Joshi, "British agents repeatedly tried to transform the joint Hindu-Muslim struggle into a fratricidal Hindu-Muslim war. Even as early as May 1857, British agents began inciting the Muslims against the Hindus in the name of jihad and the matter was brought before Bahadur Shah." Joshi quoted British chronicler Sir T. Metcalfe on what followed: "The king answered that such a jihad was quite impossible, and that such an idea an act of extreme folly…[it] would create internecine war and the result would be deplorable…A deputation of Hindu officers arrived to complain of a war against Hindus being preached. The king replied: 'The holy war is against the English; I have forbidden it against the Hindus.'"

The lesson from this show of anti-colonial Hindu-Muslim unity was not lost upon the British. They set about creating a deep religious-communal divide by a deliberate policy of discrimination against the Muslims. Indian historian Talmiz Khaldun wrote: "...the Nawabs of Jhajjar, Ballabhgarh, Furrukhnagar, and twenty-four shahzadas (princes) were hanged. Muslim property was either confiscated or destroyed. While Muslims were made to pay 35 per cent of their immovable property as punitive fine (a collective penalty for participation in, and support for the rebellion), Hindus were let off with only 10 per cent. After Delhi was reconquered, the Hindus were allowed to return within a few months but the Muslims could not, before 1859.... The story was the same in other places and provinces."

It got worse. "The Muslims continued their struggle against the British—if not openly, then in daily antipathies. These took the form, collectively, of antagonism to British culture and civilization, philosophy and education, everything British. Thus in the post-rebellion period, 'while...Hindus...inspired by the arts and sciences of Europe, were experiencing an intellectual and moral renaissance,' wrote Sir Theodore Morrison, 'the Muslims all over India were falling into a state of material indigence and intellectual decay...the proportion of the (Muslim) race which a century ago had the monopoly of government, has now fallen to less than one twenty-third of the whole administrative body. This, too, in the gazetted appointments...In less conspicuous office establishments...the exclusion of Musalmans is even more complete.'"

Khaldun noted: "By the time they realized the cost of such an attitude..., the Hindus had taken long strides in education and had entrenched themselves in government services and business...This uneven development of the two communities raised the Hindu-Moslem problem. It was later to distort India's struggle for national independence. Encouraged and exploited by the British, this development eventually led to the creation of Pakistan."

The problem would not have acquired the proportions it did in the years to come—and its nuclear pinnacle half a century later—but for its false "solution" in the form of the Partition.

There is no need to deal here with the intricate details of the political process preceding the Independence of both India and Pakistan. But some major landmarks in the colonial creation of "communalism" are worth noting. Ever since its creation in the period following the rebellion of 1857, the region has struggled to get free of it without success. It is this force that now poses a nuclear threat to the subcontinent's very survival.

* * *

WITHIN 50 years of the First War of Independence, the colonial rulers scored a signal victory in the aggravation of the post-rebellion problem. The All-India Muslim League was formed in 1906 in opposition to the Indian National Congress that, in the eyes of many of the country's largest minority, had increasingly acquired the hue of a Hindu party. A defining moment in the deterioration of religious-communal relations came in 1930 when Iqbal, the beloved poet of "Hindustani" patriotism, upheld the demand for Pakistan as a homeland for the Muslims of the subcontinent. The Muslims, the most anti-British section of the population in the bitter aftermath of 1857, were now projected as the colonial masters' protégés.[3]

This, however, did not stop Quaid-e Azam (Great Leader) Mohammed Ali Jinnah, missionary leader of the Muslim League, from calling for direct action by his following to protest British plans for subdivision of provinces to create an unviable Pakistan. The action, which turned violent, did not prevent Lord Mountbatten and his men from proceeding with precisely such plans. The British had divided and ruled; they were now dividing South Asia further to make it vulnerable to neo-colonial designs. The League action gave the region a foretaste of what was immediately to precede and follow the Partition.

Here is an unsigned newspaper account of what happened after the Mountbatten radio broadcast of the Partition plans on June 3, 1947, in Delhi:

> At about 10 p.m., scores of fires broke out in the Moslem sections of the city. The town seemed more brilliantly lit than on Diwali (the Hindu festival of lights). An hour later gunfire was heard all around. I ran upstairs to the flat roof to survey the situation. I noticed an increasing amount of shooting from the adjacent kucha (residential area) where about five thousand Moslems lived. Shortly afterwards, I heard the cries of women pleading for the lives of their children. After an hour, there was complete silence. Not even cries of children. The innocent people of that kucha had all been put to death.... Now, the authorities were on the side of non-Moslems. Many fortunate Moslems were lucky enough to hastily leave their homes to take shelter in a well-protected park and avoid the Hindu mobs. When morning came,

wholesale looting started. Even respectable and law-abiding citizens could not resist the temptation. Anarchy was the rule of the next few days...."

This was a mere curtain-raiser on one of the most diabolic of human dramas, after which the subcontinent would never be the same again. The exchange of populations, which the Partition Plan and the accompanying passions did not allow to be effected in an orderly and phased manner, entailed the biggest and bloodiest peacetime mass migration in history. It lasted a little over a month and involved an estimated 18 million people and, by the time the holocaust among the "homeland"-bound was over, about a million had perished.

The tragedy is remembered in many ways, but trains have perhaps been its most enduring metaphor. The railways, cited repeatedly as one of the blessings of British rule, provided the main venue for the memory-searing violence. Ritu Menon and Kamla Bhasin, in their study of the event titled *Borders and Boundaries*, meticulously recorded the series of train massacres that took place between August 9 and September 13, 1947:

> ...by August 13, it became impossible to reach Lahore station (in Pakistan) because they were attacked en route; between August 12-18, it became a veritable death-trap and, in the rural areas, by August 15, nearly every east-bound (India-bound) train passing through Montgomery and Lahore was stopped and attacked.

* * *

IN His novel *Train to Pakistan*, Khushwant Singh quoted Nehru's famous Independence Day address in New Delhi—"Long years ago, India made a tryst with destiny, and now comes the time when we shall redeem that pledge, not wholly or in full measure but substantially..."—and added: "Yes, Mr. Prime Minister, others too had their tryst with destiny then." An unspeakably horrendous destiny for hundreds of thousands. Like the train passenger, who was pulled out and whose penis was cut off and presented to his young bride, and several other victims of much more than merely physical violence. Historian Mushirul Hasan recalled, in one of his papers on the Partition, the "ghost trains" that carried compartmentloads of "severed breasts" that kept arriving at railway stations on either side of the Punjab border.

Menon and Bhasin brought out the large part played by gender violence in the rioting that left generations seeking and plotting revenge. "The most predictable form of violence experienced by women, as women, is when the women of one community are sexually assaulted by the men of the other in an overt assertion of their identity and a simultaneous humiliation of the Other by 'dishonoring' their women..."

They were dishonored in ways that could not be easily forgotten and forgiven. They were stripped naked and paraded on the streets. They were placed in brothels. They were raped, by individuals and gangs, mostly in public. Their humiliation was often accompanied by horrendous physical torture—including beatings and, in one recorded case, by the placing of the legs of a charpoy (cot) on the woman's hands while her violator sat on it unmindful of her screaming.

The women's bodies became the battlegrounds between the two communities and the two countries in the making. Death was often the only deliverance. Say

Menon and Bhasin: "Many women and girls saved their honor by self-immolation. [In one case, they] collected their beddings and cots in a heap and, when the heap caught fire, they jumped on to it…. There is also a story of ninety women of Thoa Khalsa who jumped into a well…in order to preserve their chastity and the religious honor of their families." The victims had no protectors left on their side, either. "Men turned against their own wives, daughters and sisters, murdering them before they could be dishonored through rape and disfigurement."

It was a life-long laceration that many suffered. "Tattooing and branding [of] the body with 'Pakistan Zindabad [Long Live Pakistan]' or 'Hindustan Zindabad [Long Live India]' not only marked the woman for life, they never permitted her (or her family and community) the possibility of forgetting her humiliation. [The tattooing and branding] engraved the division of [erstwhile] India into India and Pakistan on the women of both the religious communities in [such] a way that they became the respective countries, indelibly imprinted by the Other."

The amputation of breasts "desexualized" the woman, made a "freak" of her, and denied her "the mother's natural role as a nurturer." According to psychoanalyst Sudir Kakar, noted for his studies of civil strife, this particular piece of savagery "incorporates the (more or less conscious) wish to wipe the enemy off the face of the earth." Just as, one may add, the nuke-rattling by both sides during the standoff does today.

It was to this hate-filled humiliation of the enemy's women, reminiscent of the worst of war crimes, that relatively forgettable and forgivable religious affronts were added. There were cases of non-Muslim men being forcibly circumcised; and beards were a badge of shame that it took a brave Muslim to sport in a Hindu-majority area. Pigs were slain in front of mosques and cows in front of temples, in what the Muslims and the Hindus respectively considered the ultimate acts of sacrilege, by miscreants who wanted communal mayhem.

The Partition left wounds that were not only hard to heal, but could be reopened any time and allowed to fester again by forces opposed to peace in the region. It created constituencies for politics of religious-communal mobilization, for a regional variant of revanchism, in both countries. Each had a sizeable enough population (particularly in certain pockets of concentration) of originally refugee families that would not forget an unavenged past. They and the rest of the people were not, in any case, allowed to forget.[4]

One of the two other important points to remember about the Partition is that all that rioting was not spontaneous. There were organized forces on both sides that caused the conflagrations and kept fanning the flames, that provoked one community and pretended to protect the other, and that continue to do so even today, if on a smaller scale than in 1947. Particularly noteworthy, in retrospect, has been the role played by the Rashtriya Swayamsevak Sangh (National Volunteers Corp) of India. We shall deal in some detail with the RSS and the later additions to a large fascist "family," the Sangh "parivar" as it is styled, in a later chapter.

The other fact, all too often forgotten, is that it was not only the South of India that remained free from Partition-time rioting. So, too, despite its closeness to

Punjab, did Kashmir. The territory, which was to become an intractable India-Pakistan issue, was a haven of communal peace amidst the holocaust. The subsequent transformation of the tourist paradise into a center of violence and terror, too, will need separate treatment. Examination of the transformation can illuminate important aspects of today's nuclear tensions.

EXIT UK, ENTER USA

If you go back to the 19th century, Britain was one of the major rogue states. In the latter part of the 20th century, the US is supreme in these respects…

—Noam Chomsky to Star TV
in New Delhi in November 2001

The United States has sowed…in South Asia very poisonous seeds. The seeds are growing now. Some have ripened and others are ripening. An examination of why they were sowed, what has grown and how they should be reaped is needed.

—Pakistani thinker Eqbal Ahmad (who died
in 1999, two years before 9/11 and three
before the India-Pakistan standoff)

THE India-Pakistan problem was, of course, one of British creation and its efforts to divide the conquered. But it was also one of aggravation by the historical descendant of direct colonialism. The retreating Raj had left the subcontinent broken and bleeding. No healing touch, however, was forthcoming from the New World neo-colonialism that rushed in to fill the vacuum and replaced the departing masters of the divide-and-rule game. In the decades following Partition, South Asia witnessed a steady worsening of the India-Pakistan rivalry, promoted above all by Washington's policies and role in the region.

It can be argued that the rivalry was promoted really by the Cold War, to which the Soviet Union, too, made its contribution. But the collapse of the Cold War following the dissolution of the Soviet Union did not end the hostilities, suggesting that rivalry between the superpowers cannot entirely explain the tensions. There were two other reasons for the rivalry.

What shaped the subcontinent's fate, in the first place, was the US rulers' policy of trying and making a proxy of every partner and a frontline state (against the Soviet Union) of every friendly one. Adoption of Pakistan as their ally on such terms did not serve the cause of peace and stability in either that country or South Asia. Secondly, the nuclear brinkmanship in the region is a direct result of the American adventure of the eighties and early nineties in Afghanistan, when it supported the Taliban. Both of these will be examined in turn.

An official US review of Pakistan-US relations, released in November 1996, could not have been more candid: "The long and checkered U.S.-Pakistan relationship has its roots in the Cold War and South Asia regional politics of the 1950s. U.S. concern about Soviet expansion and Pakistan's desire for security assistance against a perceived threat from India prompted the two countries to negotiate a mutual defense assistance agreement in May 1954. By late 1955, Pakistan had further aligned itself with the West by joining two regional defense pacts, the South-East Asia Treaty Organization (SEATO) and the Baghdad Pact (later Central Treaty Organization, CENTO). As a result of these alliances and a 1959 U.S.-Pakistan cooperation agreement, Pakistan received more than $700 million in military grant aid in 1955-65. U.S. economic aid to Pakistan between 1951 and 1982 totaled more than $5 billion."

"Differing expectations of the security relationship have long bedeviled ties," the review conceded. "During the Indo-Pakistani wars of 1965 and 1971, the United States suspended military assistance to both sides, resulting in a cooling of the U.S.-Pakistan relationship." There were also professed tensions over Pakistan's nuclear plans (of which more later). All this was, however, a passing phase.

"Following the Soviet invasion of Afghanistan in December 1979, Pakistan was again viewed as a frontline state against Soviet expansionism. An offer to Pakistan of $400 million in economic and security aid by the Carter Administration in early 1980 was turned down by President Zia-ul Haq as "peanuts." In September 1981, however, the Reagan Administration, negotiated a $3.2 billion, five-year economic and military aid package with Pakistan....Pakistan became a funnel for arms supplies to the Afghan resistance, as well as a camp for three million Afghan refugees."

It is an open secret that Pakistan became for more than the next decade a sanctuary for freebooting "freedom fighters" from the Middle East and Central Asia as well. This was the period that saw the US-aided build-up of many an Osama bin Laden in the backyard of Afghanistan, in the Pushtoon country spilling over to Pakistan's side of the always-notional border of a nomadic people. This was also the time that saw the complication of the Kashmir problem with the induction of non-

Kashmiri and non-Pakistani "jihadis" (crusaders or holy warriors) as well into the Valley especially after the launch of an armed anti-India insurgency in 1987.

Concern over the possibly dangerous consequences of all this was raised repeatedly even then. After issuing appropriately stern-sounding warnings every time, however, Washington found a way to evade the issue at home and actually encourage the divisive developments in the subcontinent. The review was candid enough on this count as well: "the U.S. State Department warned Pakistan, in January 1993, that on account of its alleged support of terrorist activities in Kashmir and Punjab it was being put under 'active continuing review' in order to determine whether it should be placed on the terrorist state list. The terrorist state list, which is maintained pursuant to Section 6(j) of the Export Administration Act of 1979, currently includes Cuba, Iran, Iraq, Libya, North Korea, and Syria. (When a state is placed on the terrorist list, it is ineligible for direct US aid and also denied loans by multilateral lending agencies, such as the World Bank and the International Monetary Fund.) Pakistan maintained that it lends only diplomatic and moral support to separatist groups in Kashmir and Punjab. Many of the charges against Pakistan appeared to stem from the presence of several thousand Islamic fundamentalists from various countries who went to Pakistan to participate in the Afghanistan war and who remained in the Peshawar area in 1993. Some of these fundamentalist groups allegedly have been involved in assisting the Kashmir separatist movement with Pakistan government support. Algeria and Egypt also charged that Muslim radicals based in Peshawar had been involved in anti-government terrorist activities in their countries."

The review added: "In April 1993, the Nawaz Sharif government began rounding up and deporting Muslim radicals illegally residing in the Peshawar area. Islamabad also offered full support to India in apprehending perpetrators of the Bombay bombings (during 1992), some of whom reportedly fled to Pakistan. The director of Pakistan's Inter-Services Intelligence (ISI), which allegedly had been involved with supporting militants in Kashmir and Punjab, was replaced. Extensive talks on the terrorist issue were held between U.S. and Pakistan government officials in both Washington and Islamabad. In July 1993, Pakistan was removed from the informal terrorist watch list when the State Department determined that Pakistan had implemented 'a policy of ending official support for terrorists in India.' The State Department informed the Pakistan government, however, that it would continue to monitor the situation...."

All this, emphatically, does not testify to the truth of New Delhi's oft-asserted claim that India's Kashmir problem is entirely one of external creation, of "cross-border terrorism" and little else. But, it does expose the part played by the U.S. and its foreign-policy-makers in promoting a dangerous Pakistani folly in the disputed area and exacerbating the problem. Washington was only too willing to accept anti-terrorist claims by Islamabad, which had never officially supported terrorism in India. The review is an eloquent commentary on the wisdom of expecting real peace returns from the "global war on terror" for the region chosen as its first theatre.

Close relations with Pakistan could not but spell contentious ones for the U.S. with India. By placing itself in a non-aligned position, India and its neutral position were instantly branded by American policymakers as anti-U.S. The Non-Alignment Movement, which India helped to found in 1961 and where its size assured it of a leading status, came to be seen in Washington as a hostile horde. Then US Secretary of State John Foster Dulles called non-alignment "immoral." Similarly self-righteous was Washington's characterization of a series of the 120-nation NAM campaigns. These campaigns supported Vietnam and the Palestinian liberation movements, opposed the puppet government of Augusto Pinochet that the U.S. had propped up in Chile, favored the dismantlement of the US military base in Diego Garcia, and pushed for an equitable international economic order, among many others.

Dulles had his fellow-detractors of nonalignment inside India. Righteous indignation was the response to the NAM platform from the political Right, too, in the sixties. An important constituent of this camp in India was the Jan Sangh, the parent of the Bharatiya Janata Party heading the coalition currently ruling New Delhi. Its battle cry was "genuine nonalignment" and its plea for better relations between the world's "largest and greatest democracies" (longhand for the U.S. and India). With the Cold War behind, it is little wonder that New Delhi should today be aspiring confidently to a strategic tie-up with the world's sole, surviving superpower.

We shall take a closer look at the post-September 11 regional politics later. What deserves note here is that New Delhi's hope for a new India-US deal is not one for an India-Pakistan détente as well. The then official thinking on the two sets of relation was reflected in analyst

Ranjan Goswami's think-piece of October 1998 on the subject (titled "India-US relations: A conflict-ridden past, a cooperative economic future"): "...we can look at the US's relationship with Pakistan to date and [see] why it is not in the US interest to maintain close relations with Pakistan, especially if that means distant relations with India."

Goswami had five reasons to arrive at his conclusion:

First, the demise of the Cold War has ended any need for a territorial alliance with Pakistan. The US need not worry about India's turning away from democracy, as one could argue that India is one of the most democratic nations in the world with its government changing every 8-15 months! Secondly, current US good will towards Pakistan lies in Pakistani help in repelling the Soviet invasion of Afghanistan. However, Pakistan's involvement with terrorism in Kashmir and with Sikh separatists has long been suspected. In 1992, the US threatened to place Pakistan on the list of states supporting terrorism. Pakistan reacted by channeling trade via private organizations, something that President Clinton acknowledged at the Indo-US Summit in 1994. Pakistan's Islamic fundamentalist groups are anti-American, something that is likely to spread to the general population with current sanctions. This makes cooperation with Pakistan harder for the US. Thirdly, Pakistan's backing of the Islamic fundamentalist Taliban regime in Afghanistan is not in American interests, nor is such an action in line with the American ideals of freedom and democracy. Fourthly, Pakistan seems to be in the process of shifting to a more Islamic fundamentalist state. On October 9, the National Assembly voted to amend the constitution by granting the federal government power to enact and enforce laws based on government interpretation of the Koran, Islam's holy book. This amendment allows for arbitrary government decisions that lessen Pakistan's reliability as an ally.

Fifthly, Pakistan has been soliciting nuclear technology
from China and denying doing so.

One can smile not only at the fond hope that the
Musharraf regime would stretch its support for the fundamentalists in Kabul to a suicidal point. Or, that
Washington, a staunch ally of Saudi Arabia, won't abide
by a rule by Quaran-wavers in Pakistan. Equally, if not
even more amusing, perhaps, is the assumption that
Pakistan's nuclear plans might disqualify it for a partnership with the U.S. Especially when India's own nuclear-
weapon tests in Pokharan, conducted four months before
the publication of this analysis, were expected to elicit no
such response from Washington.

Developments after 9/11 have proven again that
nuclear non-proliferation is in fact a negotiable issue to
the U.S. That, however, lay far ahead of the foreseeable
future as India and Pakistan limped out of the Partition,
with a heavy burden of hate and bitterness that subcontinental politics was not going to lighten. It would take four
conventional India-Pakistan wars before the world woke
to the South Asian flashpoint in the summer of 2002.

CHAPTER 3

WOUNDS OF WARS

From Tanks to Bomb Threats

> We will fight a thousand-year war with India.
> —Zulfikar Ali Bhutto, after he founded the
> Pakistan People's Party in 1966

> Why should we be afraid of war?...the ceasefire is not
> an end in itself...The (Indian) armed forces are fighting a
> war they are not allowed to win.
> —G. M. Vaidya of the Rashtriya
> Swayamsevak Sangh, demanding raids on
> "terrorist camps" in "Pakistan-occupied
> Kashmir," March 19, 2001

> From within the dispute between India and
> Pakistan, issues of national sovereignty and religious iden-
> tity seem worth the risk even of nuclear war, but from out-
> side there is no conceivable justification of that risk... But
> that contradiction adheres in every situation of war. From
> within a dispute, drastic action is always justified. From
> outside it, compromise, negotiation, and restraint are
> always seen as preferable to violence. The India-Pakistan
> war, in other words, is a revelation of the futility of war as
> such....
> —James Carroll, May 28, 2002

> War is a poor chisel to carve out tomorrows.
> —Martin Luther King, Jr.

> You can tell a true war story by the way it never
> seems to end...
>
> —Tim O'Brien, *The Things They Carried*
> (1990)

Until the dawn of the 21st century, South Asia enjoyed a reputation as a region of relative peace. It was grossly undeserved. No other part of the world has seen two immediately neighboring nation-states embroiled in continuous hot-cold hostilities for nearly six decades. No other part of the world in this period has been through four full-scale wars and now seems to be waiting helplessly for a fifth.

Three of these wars have been waged over a single issue—Kashmir—which has stubbornly refused to be resolved and has, by all indications, become more intractable than ever before. One of the wars inflicted a fresh wound on the subcontinent's body and psyche by leading to the break-up of Pakistan and the birth of Bangladesh.

It was the fourth in the series, however, that caused world concern of a different kind by being the first in South Asia fought under a nuclear shadow. The concern, of course, turned into alarm over the threat of a fifth, which would have been the first nuclear war of the world, had it not fortunately been averted. Until nearly the end of the 20th century, the constantly warring countries were not considered a nuclear flashpoint. But that changed with their acquisition of nuclear weapons. So far, despite allegations by the lunatic fringe from both countries, there has been no credible report of the subcontinent harboring arsenals of any other weapons of mass destruction (WMDs).

The hot wars of South Asia were also connected, like almost all other conflicts in all continents until the collapse of the Soviet Union and its Socialist bloc in the nineties, to the Cold War. The two superpowers of those times might have openly taken sides only in the Bangladesh War, but their broader sympathies were never in any doubt for most of this period. Nor was their role, especially the U.S.'s, in funding and fuelling the blood feuds in the region. It is the sole, surviving superpower that continues to play the role now, as an avowed protector of both the adversaries.

* * *

THE first India-Pakistan war broke out in 1947, within two months of the creation of the two as independent countries. In one sense, from the point of view of both the Indian and Pakistani establishments, the war was an inevitable sequel to the incomplete process of Independence and the Partition. It might not have seemed so to the Kashmiri people assigned since then the least conspicuous and consequential role in the unfolding drama of their own collective life.

Amidst the religious-communal riots that raged on both sides of the India-Pakistan borders in the west and the east, Kashmir remained a haven of peace despite its mixed Hindu-Muslim population. This was made possible in part by its long and proud tradition of inter-communal amity and tolerance. But another factor was that it was a "princely state" within the British Raj that had not opted yet for integration with either India or Pakistan. This curious situation was again one of colonial creation.

The First War of Independence of 1857 had reached

a high point as a revolt of the chieftains or "princes" of petty fiefdoms, but these dropped out as it threatened to take a revolutionary course under a peasant-soldier alliance. As Talmiz Khaldun (quoted before) put it, "The upper classes (including the "princes") were terrified at the growth of a democratic spirit among the soldiers, became suspicious of the results of the revolt, and lost their enthusiasm after the first flush of the rebellion was over." The "princes," actually, then helped the Raj crush the rebellion that was beginning to respect no class restraints. The lesson was not lost upon the British.

The princes had "rendered signal services by acting as breakwaters to the storm," Khaldun wrote and quoted English historian P. E. Roberts as saying that "to preserve them as a bulwark of the Empire has ever since been a principle of British policy." Queen Victoria's proclamation of 1877, on becoming the Empress of India, read thus: "We hereby announce to the native princes of India that all treaties and engagements made with them by or under the authority of the Honorable East India Company are by us accepted and will be scrupulously maintained and we look for like observance on their part.... We shall respect the rights, dignity and honor of native princes as our own..."

Years later, after Independence, this pledge would haunt Pakistan's establishment. In 1947, chafing at the raw territorial deal (the East and West Wings of Pakistan were thousands of miles apart and had vast Indian territory in between), it eyed Kashmir, a contiguously neighboring state with a clear Muslim majority. Pakistan's rulers saw the Partition as a triumph for the "two-nation theory (that a Hindu nation and a Muslim one coexisted untenably and uncomfortably in undivided India of the pre-

Independence past)" and Kashmir as logically belonging to their country. The entire political class of India, however, was preparing to treat Kashmir as the test case for the secularism of the country's adoption. They argued that a Muslim-majority state could very well be part of a non-theocratic India. The British, meanwhile, appeared to be bound by Queen Victoria's still operative legal commitment to loyal "princes" including Maharaja Hari Singh of Kashmir. And he preferred to take his time over making his political choice. His task was hardly easy not only because he was a Hindu but, even more, because he was not on the best of terms with the Kashmiri contingent of the subcontinent's freedom struggle.

The Pakistan government was not prepared to allow him much time. In October 1947, it dispatched armed tribesmen from the country's North-West Frontier Province (or, according to Pakistan, regular troops in disguise) into the Valley of Kashmir. The looting raiders were not exactly received with open arms by the local population as a whole. But, as the invasion took place, there was a revolt against Hari Singh in the part of Kashmir that adjoined the western part of Pakistan.

Rattled by the raids and the revolt, the Maharaja turned to the Indian government for urgent armed assistance. Understandably, official Indian versions avoid stressing this but, by all other accounts, New Delhi seized the opportunity to demand Kashmir's accession to India as the price of support. (The Kashmiri origins of Jawaharlal Nehru, India's first Prime Minister and a frequent visitor all his life to the Valley he loved, might partially explain the insistence.)

On October 26, 1947, the Maharaja signed the much-debated Instrument of Accession. Soon, Indian soldiers landed in Srinagar, Kashmir's capital, and blocked the advance of the marauding tribesmen. Both India and Pakistan agreed that the accession would be confirmed by a referendum once hostilities had ceased. In May 1948, the regular Pakistani army was called upon to protect Pakistan's borders. Fighting continued throughout the year between Pakistani irregular troops and the Indian army in Kashmir. This first war ended on January 1, 1949, with a cease-fire arranged by the United Nations. The number of battle deaths alone, excluding the killings of civilians, was put at 1,500.

The UN recommended that both India and Pakistan should adhere to their commitment to hold a referendum in the state. A cease-fire line was established where the two sides stopped fighting and a UN peacekeeping force established. The referendum, however, has never been held. Thereby hangs a tale, which will be told in the next chapter.

In 1954, Jammu and Kashmir's accession to India was ratified by the state's constituent assembly. In 1957, it approved its own constitution, modeled along the Indian constitution, but surrendering to New Delhi all powers in relation to defense, communication and foreign affairs.

Since then, India has regarded Jammu and Kashmir under its control as an integral part of the Indian Union. The state includes the Hindu-majority part of Jammu and the Buddhist-majority one of Ladakh. To the west of the cease-fire line, Pakistan controls roughly one third of the state. A small region, which the Pakistanis call Azad (Free) Kashmir, and the Indians call Pakistani-occupied Kashmir (PoK), is semi-autonomous. The larger area, which includes the former kingdoms of Hunza and Nagar, called the northern areas, is directly administered by Pakistan.[1]

In 1962-63, following the Sino-Indian war, India and Pakistan held talks under the auspices of Britain and the U.S. in an attempt to resolve their differences over Kashmir, but without success. The first India-Pakistan war was the smallest in the series, but it was also the most significant, as it created and ensured the endurance of the Kashmir issue.

* * *

THE second India-Pakistan war came after 18 years, during which the issue became familiar to an international audience at the United Nations. General Ayub Khan, in power in Pakistan, had reason to think it a good time for a tactical advance in the disputed territory. India had got the worst of it in the Sino-Indian war, and the debacle had debilitating political consequences for the country. The Rightwing Opposition—always opposed to the long-raised slogan of "Hindi-Chini bhai-bhai (Indians and Chinese are brothers)" and non-alignment, always for an India-US axis—went on the offensive. A depressed and somewhat disgraced Nehru died in 1964, and was succeeded as the nation's leader by low-profile Lal Bahadur Shastri.

In mid-1965, the Pakistani military regime sent guerrilla forces, again, into the Indian part of Kashmir in the hope of stirring up a rebellion that would either oust the Indians or at least force the issue back on to the international agenda. It turned out, however, that the general had made two major miscalculations. He had seriously overestimated the extent of support Pakistani forces would encounter among the Kashmiri population, though India could not be said to have conquered its heart. Besides, he had been grossly and grievously overoptimistic about American backing for the ambitious operation.

The souring of Sino-Indian relations had led to a predictable and very perceptible shift in the India-US paradigm. The Rightwing rhetoric about nurturing relations between the world's "largest" and "greatest" democracies and opting out of the stance of nonalignment had been revived in a loud manner. The sixties witnessed a reverse swing of the US relations in South Asia, though this was to prove a passing phase. Washington's wooing of Pakistan earlier had led to the conclusion of an Agreement of Cooperation in 1959, but the provisions of the pact did not stop the U.S. from making serious (if short-lived) efforts to win over India.

Pakistan's first military ruler, General Mohammed Ayub Khan (1958-69), who had taken the country into the CENTO (the Central Treaty Organization, a US-headed military bloc including the UK, Turkey and Iran) protested, when the U.S. issued a statement declaring its neutrality in the 1965 India-Pakistan conflict and even cut off its military supplies to its erstwhile ally. But, as Washington took care to point out, both sides were using US-supplied equipment. As we shall see, history is being repeated in the region today, with the superpower trying to preserve an alliance with both the South Asian arch-rivals at the same time and raising the specter of another war, one that can turn nuclear this time.

Reverting to the 1965 war, hostilities spread by August and the escalation culminated in a full-scale Indian offensive toward Lahore on September 6. Fighting, frequently very bitter, continued until a UN-sponsored cease-fire took hold on September 23.

The 1965 war was militarily inconclusive; each side held prisoners and some territory belonging to the other. Losses were heavier than in 1947—about 3,800 troops on the Pakistani side and 3,000 on the Indian. Pakistan was also reported to have lost some 20 aircraft and 200 tanks, while corresponding figures for India could not be confirmed.

A notable outcome of the 1965 war for Pakistan was a new security partnership with China. Because of this, the U.S. withdrew its military assistance advisory group in July 1967. In retaliation, Pakistan declined to renew the lease permitting the US use of the Peshawar military facility, and the Americans left in 1969. US-Pakistan relations grew even weaker as the superpower became more deeply involved in Vietnam and its interest in South Asian security matters waned. China, which (along with Iran and Indonesia) had extended political support to Pakistan in 1965, stepped into the breach. It became Pakistan's military supplier, meeting at competitive prices the needs of all its three services, which was especially attractive in view of the wartime losses and the US embargo.

The Ayub army had other sources of supply as well: it acquired submarines and Mirage aircraft from France, for example. But, a notably close security relationship was built in those years with the giant neighbor in the north. Ayub Khan formulated his security concept of a "triangular tightrope"—an attempt at restoring ties with the USA without endangering newfound relations with China and, if possible, the Soviet Union, while support from other developing nations was welcome, too. The Chinese partnership has proved an enduring part of the package. Cold War calculations ensured that Washington did not ever object too strenuously to Pakistan's ties with staunchly anti-Soviet Beijing. The U.S. did not prolong its embargo on arms to Pakistan, relaxed it in phases and then was fully back to business in 1973. The US-Pakistan-China triangle does not represent too tough a tightrope-walking in the post-September 11 scenario, now that Beijing is jumping on to the global "anti-terror" bandwagon with great alacrity.

In 1966, the cease-fire was followed by the Tashkent Declaration signed on January 10, by Ayub Khan and Shastri in the capital of Soviet Uzbekistan. The declaration followed summit-level talks between the two sides under the good offices of Moscow: the Sino-Indian war and the Pakistan-US freeze had given post-Khrushchev Soviet leadership a fresh leverage with both of the South Asian adversaries. Officially, the result was reported to be the restoration of status quo ante. Politically, however, it was also a reverse for Pakistan, all the more so for being seen as such by a sullen population that had earlier been encouraged to expect miracles from the martial law ruler. The war did serve to keep the Kashmir issue alive, but failed to put it on the international agenda, as planned. Without seeming to say much, the Tashkent Declaration had much to say on the issue, and in India's favor:

> The Prime Minister of India and the President of Pakistan agree that both sides will exert all efforts to create good-neighborly relations between India and Pakistan in accordance with the United Nations Charter. They reaffirm their obligation under the Charter not to have recourse to force and to settle their disputes through peaceful means. They considered that the interests of peace in their region and particularly in the Indo-Pakistan subcontinent and indeed, the interests of the peoples of India and Pakistan were not served by the continuance of

tension between the two countries. It was against this
background that Jammu and Kashmir was discussed, and
each of the sides set forth its respective position.

The declaration, thus, talked about the UN Charter and
not any UN resolution. Not a word, notably, was said about
any international attempt at the resolution of the issue;
instead, a beginning of a bilateral discussion was implied.

The war had far-reaching political consequences for
Pakistan, and few for India. Shastri's death soon after the
Tashkent summit paved the way for the Indira Gandhi era
in India. Nehru's daughter rose to national leadership in
the late sixties by raising purely internal issues, though a
successful confrontation with Pakistan was to prove the
culmination of her career. The military debacle, meanwhile, spelt also a major political reverse for Ayub Khan
and his associates.

The late sixties were trying times for the lot. By 1969,
matters had come to such a pass that the Pakistani army
once again felt called on to intervene and "save" the country. On March 25, an aging, ailing and disgraced Ayub
Khan transferred power to army commander in chief
General Agha Mohammad Yahya Khan who, predictably,
declared himself president as well as chief martial law
administrator. He also announced plans for Pakistan's first
national general elections since Independence and a new
constitution. The elections in December 1970 were fair, a
little too fair perhaps: they led to the next subcontinental
war and a break-up of Pakistan.

* * *

THE third war in the series began after Pakistan's first
national elections, which led to a civil war in the country's

East Wing. In East Pakistan, the Awami (People's) League led by Sheikh Mujibur Rehman won an overwhelming majority, which should have sufficed to put him at the nation's helm. In the western part of Pakistan, the Pakistan People's Party of Zulfikar Ali Bhutto won the majority. There were two reasons why the results could not readily be accepted and acted upon by General Yahya Khan and his martial law regime.

In the first place, the Sheikh had won as a symbol of the Bengali-speaking East and its revolt against the Urdu-speaking rest of Pakistan. It was on the crest of a campaign of ethnic-cultural sub-nationalism, for a better official status for Bengali above all, that the Awami League had ridden to its remarkable electoral victory. Secondly, the Pakistani army, under pressure to give the people democracy, was not going to do so at the cost of its own disproportionately Punjabi base located in the west.

Negotiations on power sharing between the two wings of Pakistan broke down by February 1971, after both sides had taken rigid stances. The growing political turmoil in East Pakistan produced increasing demands for regional autonomy, and autonomists became separatists. Bengalis went on strike and stopped paying taxes.

As a result, the Pakistani army began a crackdown on Dhaka (formerly Dacca), the capital of East Pakistan. This sparked off an unprecedented exodus of refugees from East Pakistan into the neighboring Indian state of West Bengal (now Bangla). By the middle of May, the refugee population had climbed to around 10 million.

The undivided Bengal had its share of the pains of the Partition. It is acknowledged, however, that the victims of both the religious communities suffered less of the brutal atrocities visited by the Hindus/Sikhs and Muslims upon each other in Punjab. Bengali cultural traditions ensured that female bodies did not quite become the battlefields for both the communities and the newly created countries they did in Punjab. It was now the turn of this state to go through a comparable trauma.

Reports of massacres, mass burials and gang rapes by Pakistani forces kept pace with the increasing refugee influx into India. According to a conservative estimate, a million of the fugitives might have perished for the 10 million who made it to the Indian side of the border. No reliable estimate of the number of gender crime victims is available.

The tragedy elicited a massive tide of solidarity with the people of East Pakistan in India, especially across the border in West Bengal. The song of pioneering Bengali poet Rabindranath Tagore, "Aamaar sonar Bangla (Our golden Bengal)," adopted as Pakistani Bengal's anthem, was heard from numerous Indian platforms. International outrage was growing, too, and forced the Nixon Administration in the U.S. to halt its attempts to reopen military supply lines to Pakistan.

The demand inside India for a war with Pakistan, in order to "liberate" East Bengal, grew rapidly. Almost the entire political spectrum, from the Right to the Left, was united in this campaign. Within the government, the war gained support as the only way to stem the tide of refugees. Prime Minister Indira Gandhi put together a strategy with twin objectives: return of the refugees and creation of a new state in East Pakistan.

India began providing the resistance movement, known as the "Mukti Bahini (liberation force)," with sanctuaries, training, and weaponry. By November, the Mukti Bahini was attacking military installations in East Pakistan from bases along the Indian border. This forced Pakistan's hand. It declared a war on India along the western frontier on December 3, 1971.

Pakistani forces began hostilities in the west with attacks on Indian airfields. They met with little success. Within 24 hours, India had seized air superiority, launched attacks against West Pakistan, and blockaded the coast. The Indian army also moved quickly into East Pakistan and routed the enemy forces.

Pakistani forces in East Pakistan surrendered to the Indian army on December 16. The next day, both India and Pakistan declared cease-fires. In the face of its comprehensive defeat, Yahya's Pakistan had little choice but to accept the break-up of the country and creation of Bangladesh. India was the first country to recognize the new state. Pakistan had to follow suit three years later in 1974.

It was a shattering blow to Pakistan's military-political complex. The country lost about 9,000 of its soldiers, as against India's loss of about 5,500 (4,000 on the western front and 1,500 on the eastern). A phenomenal 95,000 Pakistani soldiers ended up as prisoners of war (POWs), about 5,000 of them in Bengali hands. The toll among the Mukti Bahini rebels remains unconfirmed.

The war was followed by the signing of the Simla Agreement on July 2, 1972, by Indira Gandhi and Zulfikar Ali Bhutto who had replaced Gen. Yahya Khan. Many hawks in India have, since then, seen a victory for a wily Bhutto, which continues to be cited as the official gospel on all questions of India-Pakistan relations including

Kashmir. They claim, without serious credibility, that India could have then imposed its own Kashmir and other solutions on the region, ignoring the political support for Pakistan from important sections of international opinion.

Two major provisions of the agreement merit note. One of these stated that "the two countries are resolved to settle their differences by peaceful means through bilateral negotiations or by any other peaceful means mutually agreed upon between them." India has maintained the more narrow interpretation that disputes be settled bilaterally, though Pakistan has been unsuccessfully arguing for a looser interpretation—one that did not exclude a multilateral settlement of the Kashmir dispute.

The second provision of proven long-term importance stated: "In Jammu and Kashmir, the Line of Control resulting from the cease-fire of December 17, 1971, shall be respected by both sides without prejudice to the recognized position of either side. Neither side shall seek to alter it unilaterally irrespective of mutual differences and legal interpretations. Both sides further undertake to refrain from the threat or use of force in violation of this line." Pakistan has until this day refrained from questioning the legitimacy thus conferred upon the Line of Control (LoC). This has given rise to the idea of converting the LoC into a permanent international border as a Kashmir solution (of which later).[2]

The Cold War played a conspicuous, though not a conclusive, role in the war that created Bangladesh. Any illusions, which Pakistan may have entertained about achieving essentially military parity with India through international pacts, were demolished. The USA and China tilted demonstratively in Pakistan's favor during the crisis, but without making much of a difference to its course. The Nixon Administration even went to the extent of dispatching a warship (USS *Enterprise*) of the dreaded, nuclear-armed Seventh Fleet to the Bay of Bengal, but in vain. The primacy of India in the region appeared to be assured after the conclusion of the Indo-Soviet Treaty of Peace, Friendship and Cooperation in August 1971, just on the eve of the war. The treaty included a provision that more than hinted at military assistance to each other in times of need. The U.S., as noted before, was too deeply mired in Vietnam then to care to carry the Cold War beyond safe limits or to distracting lengths in South Asia.

This, of course, did not prevent a reckless Cold War campaigner like Henry Kissinger from continuing to play a cloak-and-dagger game in Bangladesh. As Assistant to President Richard Nixon for National Security Affairs in 1971, he had masterminded the much-trumpeted US 'tilt' towards Pakistan. As the U.S. Secretary of State (1973-77), he scripted a bloody sequel to the Bangladesh liberation. Talking of 1971 and the Pakistani army's genocidal rampage in East Pakistan, intrepid US journalist Seymour M. Hersh in his *The Price of Power: Kissinger in the Nixon White House* notes how little the human tragedy mattered to the former Harvard professor with that famous "tilt" to peddle. Hersh writes: "Nixon and Kissinger, refusing to listen to the bureaucracy, which came close to open rebellion on the issue (like the embassy staff that protested against Washington support for the massacre), chose to support Pakistan. They maintained that position, even as the war escalated to a near-showdown with the Soviets, who were supporting India, Pakistan's perennial enemy, in its objection to the terror tactics in Bangladesh. In his memoirs, Nixon quoted Kissinger's observation at a key point in the conflict, as the potential for a Soviet-American clash deepened: 'We don't really have a choice. We can't allow a friend of ours and China's (that is, Pakistan) to get screwed in a conflict with a friend of Russia's (that is, India).'"

Christopher Hitchens in *The Trial of Henry Kissinger* recalls how the ace US diplomat "had attempted the impossible by trying to divide the electorally victorious Awami League, and to dilute its demand for independence by making 'a covert approach' to Khondakar Mustaque, who led the tiny minority (in the party)…willing to compromise on the main principle." Hitchens adds: "As soon as Kissinger became Secretary of State in 1973, he downgraded all those (in the US embassy in Dacca) who had signed the genocide protest in 1971. In the fall of 1974, he inflicted a series of snubs on Mujib, on his first visit to the United States as head of state." The "snubs" included a boycott of Mujib's meeting with President Ford and opposition to the Bangladeshi leader's request for food aid and debt relief.

Worse was to come. Recalling Kissinger's eight-hour stopover in Bangladesh during a brief tour of the region in November 1974, Hitchens adds: "Within a few hours of his departure, as we now know, a faction at the US embassy in Dacca began covertly meeting with a group of Bangladeshi officers who were planning a coup against Mujib. On 14 August 1975, Mujib and forty members of his family were murdered in a military takeover. His closest former political associates were bayoneted to death in their prison cells a few months after that."

All this shows that the end of the Bangladesh war did not mean an immediate end to US interest in the region. It is more important to note, however, that it did not spell any decline of American interest in Pakistan. The interest was always a rider to the deeper US involvement in the oil-rich Middle East. The Bangladesh war and its outcome came as blessings in disguise for the Pakistan-US alliance and the Bhutto regime setting out to rebuild it. The loss of East Pakistan led soon to Pakistan's withdrawal from the SEATO (Southeast Asia Treaty Organization, whose other members at the time were, besides the U.S., the UK, Australia, New Zealand, Thailand and the Philippines). Pakistan had never looked upon itself as part of Southeast Asia, and Bhutto turned with relief to a bigger role in the CENTO and, thus, to the Islamic Middle East.

The development enhanced Pakistan's former status as a friend of the U.S. to one of a "frontline state" in the effort to contain the Soviet Union. The resumption of American military supplies to Pakistan in 1973 signaled recognition that the US relations with the country had a future. What these special ties had in store for the region have been illustrated by the agonies of Afghanistan in the eighties and nineties as well in the post-September 11 period and the accompanying surges in tensions between the subcontinent's arch-rivals.

The Bangladesh war had considerable internal consequences for both the countries. Immediately, of course, victory in the war appeared to mark post-Independence India's highest point and to make Indira Gandhi the most powerful leader of the country and the subcontinent. It did not take too long, however, for India and Indira to discover the political and economic prices that had to be paid for the victory.

Politically, the victory paved the way for a return to the political center-stage of the religious-communal Right, which the voters had contemptuously rejected in a national election months before the war's outbreak. Then Opposition leader Atal Behari Vajpayee hailed Indira as "Durga" (Hindu mother-goddess seen as a demon-slayer) on the floor of Parliament, as she announced Pakistan's surrender. He waited until his second term as the Prime Minister decades later to deny the statement with the least of credibility. The salutation signified a studious effort to make the war serve the cause of an Indian version of fascism, substituting Islam for Semitism and seeking to pit the country's Hindu majority against its Muslim minority.

The Vajpayees of India saw no irony in hailing the war outcome as a defeat for the "two-nation theory" as well as a victory for a Hindu India. Nor in launching campaigns later against a continuing influx of impoverished and illegal Muslim immigrants now renamed "infiltrators" from Bangladesh.

Meanwhile, the economic cost of the victory, running into about Rs (Indian rupees) 4,000 million at that time for the Indian army alone, ensured that the euphoria was even more short-lived than it might otherwise have been. A steep, across-the-board hike in prices, particularly of essential commodities, was inevitable. This was one of the major factors that fuelled an all-Opposition movement against the Indira government, started in 1974.

This was also the year of Pokharan I, the first Indian nuclear test conducted in the Pokharan desert of the state of Rajasthan. Its official description as a "peaceful nuclear explosion (PNE)" did not suffice to allay nervousness in

Pakistan. In yet another irony, almost the only political notable to oppose the testing was then Socialist leader George Fernandes, who was the Defense Minister of India when India declared itself a nuclear-weapon state about a quarter century later.

The anti-Indira movement led to the electoral rout of the Congress Party in 1977 and its replacement in power by the Janata Party. The latter was an umbrella organization of parties including, importantly, that of the religious-communal right—the Bharatiya Jan Sangh, rechristened Bharatiya Janata Party. Despite fluctuating political fortunes, the BJP (with its pro-Bomb and anti-Pakistan belligerence, its anti-minorities agenda, and its big-power ambitions for India) has ever since remained a shrewd and serious player for power at the nation's helm.

In Pakistan, there was a period of readjustment for the civilian politician, Z.A. Bhutto, who replaced the utterly discredited General Yahya Khan. After Bangladesh and the Simla Agreement (which won domestic laurels as well for his diplomatic skills), Bhutto could not easily return to public-rally rhetoric about a "thousand-year war with India." The first elected leader of Pakistan, however, set out seriously to repair the damages suffered by the military and rebuild the armed forces. The country's defense budget and the forces' strength continued to grow, keeping pace with each other. Even more far-reaching in implications for the subcontinent and South Asia was his response to India's nuclear test of 1974—the launch of Pakistan's own nuclear program.

Bhutto was to discover soon, however, that a strengthened army and civilian power could not coexist easily in Pakistan. When his domestic position eroded rap-

idly in the mid-1970 and his charisma waned, he turned to
the army to deal with domestic unrest. He was rebuffed.
Allegations of poll rigging in March 1977 resulted in mass
demonstrations demanding Bhutto's resignation. Army
chief General Mohammad Zia-ul-Haq not only refused to
put the forces at the political leader's disposal, he arrested
Bhutto and his associates on July 5, 1977, and declared
Pakistan's third period of martial law.

* * *

THE first thing to note about the fourth India-
Pakistan war (May 5-July 26, 1999) is that it came within
a year of the nuclear-weapon tests of India and Pakistan. It
came before the subcontinent could forget the statements
by leaders of both the countries that, after the tests, the
danger of even a conventional war between the two had
disappeared. It was the first South Asian war to take place
under a nuclear shadow. This was why, though the short-
est war of the series, this was also the scariest.

The next thing to note about the Kargil war (so
named after its Himalayan theater) is that it followed, and
did not precede, an India-Pakistan dialogue and signing of
a document. In February 1999, three months before the
war, Prime Minister Vajpayee undertook a famous and
feverishly media-hyped bus ride to Lahore, hours across
the western border of Punjab. He was to attend a summit
meeting with his Pakistani counterpart, Nawaz Sharif.

The mission may have appeared a mystery at first. For
one thing, Vajpayee was the leader of an Indian party that
believed any talk of peace between India and Pakistan
sounded like treason. On the Pakistan side of the table,
Sharif represented the Muslim League. It felt the compet-

ing Pakistan People's Party, along with Bhutto and his daughter Benazir Bhutto, were unacceptably pro-Indian. That was despite the fact that it was Bhutto who had declared willingness to fight a "thousand year-war" with India!

It was under Vajpayee and Sharif that India and Pakistan had conducted their Pokharan II and Chagai nuclear weapon tests respectively just nine months before. The governments headed by them had not been on the best of terms. New Delhi had been leveling charges of attacks on the Hindu minority in Kashmir by "Pakistan-sponsored terrorists"; and Islamabad had been responding by reiterating opposition to repression of the Kashmiri "freedom struggle."

Why then the bus ride, with a crowd of BJP and RSS leaders of impeccable anti-Pakistan credentials vying with each other to keep Vajpayee company? How come the BJP's no-nonsense nationalism (which did not, for example, let memories of Buddha and Gandhi mar its nuclear militarism) was tempered with nostalgia for the past left behind in Pakistan? The mystery was soon solved. The main Vajpayee mission, it became clear, was to pursue the theme that nuclear weapons promoted peace between the neighbors.

What was new about the Lahore Declaration signed by the Prime Ministers at the end of a two-day summit (February 20-21) was the part dealing with the nuclear-weapon issues. The Vajpayee mission was part of a post-Pokharan II image-mending exercise. On the morrow of its tests and before Chagai, India might have challenged Pakistan to a trial of strength, but the attempt now was to tell the world that nuclear weapons had invested the two countries with a new sense of responsibility. The declaration pledged that both "shall take immediate steps for reducing the risk of accidental or unauthorized use of nuclear weapons and discuss concepts and doctrines with a view to elaborating measures for confidence-building in the nuclear and conventional fields, aimed at prevention of conflict." The accompanying Memorandum of Understanding detailed steps contemplated in this direction. As we shall see later, not a single one of these measures has been implemented. Just four years later, in 2003, new calls for peace talks and moves toward peace would begin. But, as we will later see, like these discussions that predated a war by a matter of months, they were a complete public relations ploy that had little to do with promoting peace.

The bus ride and the bonhomie in Lahore were soon forgotten amidst cries of 'Betrayal!' by India. An otherwise little known, high-altitude area of Kashmir (in the Ladakh region) was to hit the headlines and become a burial ground for hopes raised among the gullible by the Lahore Declaration. An official Indian army account stated: "The terrain of the Kargil and surrounding regions of the LoC was inhospitable in the best of times. Some of the characteristics of the region are jagged heights of up to 16,000 feet and harsh gusts of wind and temperatures plunging to about –60 degrees Celsius in the winter. There had existed a sort of 'gentleman's agreement' between India and Pakistan that the armies of either side will not occupy posts from the September 15 to April 15 of each year. This had been the case since 1977 but, in 1999, this agreement was cast aside by the Pakistani army in hopes of trying to gain the upper hand in Kashmir and plunging the Indian subcontinent into a brief and limited war and raising the specter of nuclear war."

The unstated charge was that Vajpayee and India had been taken for a ride. The army account added: "The intruders on the heights were an amalgam of professional soldiers and mercenaries. They included the third, fourth, fifth, sixth and 12th battalions of the Northern Light Infantry (Pakistan's NLI) who were out of uniform. Among them were many Mujahiddin (holy warriors)..." Indian estimates of the number of infiltrators varied from 5,000 to 10,000. "The intruders were also well-armed with AK-47 and -56, mortars, artillery, anti aircraft guns, and Stinger missiles." New Delhi, more than once, cited some Western news reports about the infiltrators being a mixture of Pakistanis, Afghans, Kashmiris, and even British Muslims, arguing that this showed the planning and preparation behind the operation.

No comparable official Pakistani version was forthcoming, as Islamabad claimed initially that India was encountering only another campaign by the Kashmiri freedom fighters. It abandoned the claim towards the end of the war, admitting the participation in the campaign across the LoC of an unspecified number of its soldiers. Then army chief General Pervez Musharraf, widely regarded the architect of the war, told the BBC there had been what he called "occasional and aggressive patrolling" by Pakistani troops on the Indian side of the LoC. He said this had been done to "pre-empt any possible Indian attack on Pakistan" and claimed "a great victory."

Looking at the operation from a liberal Pakistani viewpoint, strategic analyst Samina Ahmed (head of the International Crisis Group in Pakistan) wrote: "It is improbable that there were any real hopes of a sustained successful campaign in a remote and desolate area where the inclement weather in the fall would have forced all combatants to withdraw. A more likely Pakistani goal was for a renewed international focus on a long-standing conflict over a disputed territory between two nuclear states. This expectation did bear fruit but with disastrous diplomatic consequences." She added: "...the Sharif administration seemed oblivious to the growing international consensus about Pakistan's culpability. While military and foreign office spokesmen extolled the military advances of the mujahideen in Kargil, the diplomatic war was already lost."

On July 12, 1999, days after Sharif's unannounced dash to Washington, Pakistani withdrawals from Kargil began, which India proclaimed as its victory. The withdrawals were completed in two weeks according to a negotiated time frame. The cost of the operations for India alone was estimated at Rs 100,000 million (about 2,000 million $ U.S.). The war had already, however, done even more serious damage to the prospects of South Asian peace.

The number of battle deaths in Kargil was estimated at 1,300 (according to India) and 1,750 (according to Pakistan). What caused much greater and graver concern, however, was the number of times (no less than 13) nuclear threats were issued by the sides against each other during the conflict. The concern was deepened by the kind of media coverage the war received by and large on both sides, the degree of jingoism promoted in the name of a just cause in both the countries.

The wartime polemics hit a particularly ugly patch

when the two sides entered into a bitter dispute over the return of the bodies of men killed in the fighting. India said that it had the bodies of a number of Pakistani soldiers, but that Islamabad would not take them since this would amount to an admission of regular Pakistani soldiers' deaths inside Indian territory. Pakistan accused India of playing politics with the dead. Lifeless bodies were used again to lacerate a national psyche, when allegedly mutilated bodies of soldiers returned by Pakistan were repeatedly displayed on Indian television channels.

Strangely, not a single major voice was raised in India against such efforts to extend the war by macabre means. The editor-in-chief of a national daily, in fact, admitted at a subsequent New Delhi seminar that he had indeed received a story about mutilation and return of Pakistani bodies as well, but had decided not to run it in the "national interest." The electronic media went berserk whipping up war hysteria. It gave full coverage to the funerals of some soldiers, and the footage was crude propaganda. In one of these stories, the father of a slain soldier was prompted into a promise to send his other sons as well to a similar fate.

Both countries came earlier under fire from Human Rights Watch, an international group, which said the two sides used repression and abuse to keep the conflict alive. The group accused Pakistan-backed militants of massacring Hindu civilians, and Indian security forces of summary executions, rape and torture. The conflict was over, but not without deepening the religious-communal divide in Kashmir, which had once been entirely free from the worst of India's political viruses.

The most notable political consequence of the war

for Pakistan was, predictably, a change of leadership. Gen. Musharraf became the country's fourth military ruler in October 1999, and sent both his civilian challengers, Sharif and Benazir Bhutto, into exile. Predictably, again, the Pakistan-US strains of Kargil's reported creation were not unduly prolonged (as Pakistan then played a role in the U.S. invasion of Afghanistan). For India, the war proved a prelude to the electoral return of Vajpayee and the BJP to power in New Delhi at the head of a National Democratic Alliance (NDA), also in October 1999. The questions raised by the Opposition about the "intelligence failure" that led to the war or the "Kargil cover-up" were a minor embarrassment to his government. But this scandal was more than overcome by the resurgence of militarism that proved rewarding to the religious-communal Right.

CHAPTER 4

POWER GAMES IN PARADISE

No Winners in Kashmir, but Peace a Perennial Loser

> If there is a paradise somewhere on this earth, it is here, it is here, it is here.
> —Moghul emperor Jehangir (1605-1627), on seeing the Kashmir Valley

> They make a desolation and call it peace.
> —Agha Shahid Ali, Country without a Post Office (1997)

> As Calais was written upon the heart of Mary, so is Kashmir upon mine.
> —Jawaharlal Nehru

> Kashmir is in our heart, Kashmir is in our blood.
> —Gen. Pervez Musharraf

Three of the four India-Pakistan wars, waged since the post-colonial creation of the two countries, have been fought over Kashmir. The single exception was the Bangladesh war, which, too, ended in a settlement with important provisions in relation to the Kashmir dispute: both the countries continue to cite the 1972 Simla Agreement whenever the Kashmir issue crops up between them. What makes this Himalayan territory the heart of the first and most formidable problem of South Asian relations? What has made this erstwhile tourist paradise an area of enduring tensions, this playground of princes a victim of power rivalries?

Most Indian and Pakistani answers to the question—clichéd-sounding perhaps but crucial all the same—look upon it all as an India-Pakistan problem, and little more. The answers begin with the achievement of Independence by the two countries and proceed on the assumption that the solution to the problem will consist in completion of the Partition process, one way or the other. Kashmir is seldom seen as primarily, if not purely, a Kashmiri concern, or as a problem with a pre-Independence past as well.

We shall begin, too, at Independence and with the origins of the India-Pakistan issue, but let the trail lead us to the Kashmiri background. And to the problem of a people caught in the crossfire and denied an opportunity to define their own identity and decide their own future.

As recounted in the preceding chapters, Kashmir as a princely state was not covered in the Partition, and spared the horrors of that holocaust. But, it had to pay dearly for the privilege. By all accounts, it was the Pakistani establishment that set in motion the chain of events that was to banish peace from the loved landscape for long years to come. Pakistan's founding President Mohammed Ali Jinnah was quoted once in the initial days of Independence as saying that "Kashmir is the unfinished business of the Partition in India." He meant that it should become part of Pakistan. This was only a mild articulation of the methodically nursed popular grievance about attempts to cheat Pakistan of a region of Muslim majority right next to the truncated territory it had been given. The assumption that the Hindu ruler of Kashmir alone stood between Kashmir and Pakistan added to the resentment.

Maharaja Hari Singh, however, was in no hurry to make up his mind at the time of independence in 1947. It was an open secret in the court circles in Srinagar that he was keeping his options open till the last, and that he was not averse to an accession of the state to Pakistan on terms acceptable to him. He even entered into a temporary agreement with the Pakistan government, but soon felt threatened by the arrangement.

As noted before, when the Pakistani military authorities dispatched tribal raiders into his kingdom, he turned to India for help. His communication to Lord Mountbatten not only makes comi-tragic reading for its desperate attempt to retain royal dignity in a rather unbecoming situation, it also makes clear that the accession he was offering India could not complete the process by itself.

Informing Mountbatten of "a grave emergency" and requesting "immediate assistance," he brought up the subject of accession: "As Your Excellency is aware, the State of Jammu and Kashmir has not acceded to either the Dominion of India or Pakistan. Geographically, my State is contiguous with both of them. Besides, my State has a common boundary with the Union of Soviet Socialist Republics and with China. In their external relations the Dominion of India and Pakistan cannot ignore this fact. I wanted to take time to decide to which Dominion I should accede or whether it is not in the best interests of both the Dominions and of my State to stand independent, of course with friendly and cordial relations with both. I accordingly approached the Dominions of India and

Pakistan to enter into standstill agreement with my State. The Pakistan Government accepted this arrangement. The Dominion of India desired further discussion with representatives of my Government…"

Under the agreement, the Pakistan government was already running the post and telegraph system inside the state. The Maharaja, however, added that, despite the agreement, the neighbor government was allowing "strangulation of supplies like food, salt and petrol to my State."

On the emergency, he wrote: "Afridis (Afghan tribesmen), soldiers in plain clothes, and desperadoes with modern weapons have been allowed to infiltrate into the State, at first in the Poonch area, then from Sia1kot and finally in a mass in the area adjoining Hazara district on the Ramkote side. The result has been that the limited number of troops at the disposal of the State had to be dispersed and thus had to face the enemy at several points simultaneously, so that it has become difficult to stop the wanton destruction of life and property and the looting of the Mahura power house, which supplies electric current to the whole of Srinagar and which has been burnt. The number of women who have been kidnapped and raped makes my heart bleed. The wild forces thus let loose on the State are marching on with the aim of capturing Srinagar, the summer capital of my government, as a first step to overrunning the whole State."

He charged: "The mass infiltration of tribesman drawn from distant areas of the North-West Frontier Province, coming regularly in motor trucks, using the Manwehra-Mazaffarabad road and fully armed with up-to-date weapons, cannot possibly be done without the knowledge of the Provincial Government of the North-West

Frontier Province and the Government of Pakistan. In spite of repeated appeals made by my Government no attempt has been made to check these raiders or to stop them from coming into my State. In fact, both radio and the Press of Pakistan have reported these occurrences. The Pakistan radio even put out the story that a provisional government has been set up in Kashmir."

He claimed: "The people of my State, both Muslims and non-Muslims, generally have taken no part at all." The reports were that the raids were accompanied by an anti-Maharaja revolt in the western areas bordering Pakistan, while the raiders were not received with open arms anywhere else.

It was evident from what followed that Srinagar had already discussed the matter with New Delhi: "…I have no option but to ask for help from the Indian Dominion. Naturally, they cannot send the help asked for by me without my State acceding to the Dominion of India. I have accordingly decided to do so, and I attach the instrument of accession for acceptance by your Government. The other alternative is to leave my state and people to free-booters. On this basis no civilized government can exist or be maintained."

"This alternative," declared the Maharaja, "I will never allow to happen so long as I am the ruler of the State and I have life to defend my country." He then proceeded to relinquish his rule. He informed Mountbatten that he was setting up an interim government with popular polit-ical leader Sheikh Abdullah at its head. Mountbatten's reply to the Maharaja recognized the incompleteness of the accession effected by a prince with a disputable authority to speak for the state's people. Stating his government's decision to accept the state's accession to the Dominion of India, Mountbatten added: "In consistence with their policy that in the case of any State where the issue of accession has been the subject of dispute, the question of accession should be decided in accordance with the wishes of the people of the State, it is my Government's wish that, as soon as law and order have been restored in Kashmir and its soil cleared of the invader, the question of the State's accession should be settled by a reference to the people." (Meaning, in modern parlance, by a popular referendum.)

The representative of the retreating Empire had, with a few strokes of the pen, given birth to the Kashmir problem with its basic ingredients: the princely accession, the promise of a referendum or plebiscite, and the stipulated condition that could never be satisfactorily met or established to have been met.[1] For ever since then, practically, the accession was denied finality: Pakistan would continue to demand a plebiscite, and to press the demand through means including the military; and India would continue to insist that, since the condition about invaders had not been met, it had a right to regard the state as an integral part of the country. Mountbatten's reply noted "satisfaction that Your Highness has decided to invite Sheikh Abdullah to form an interim Government." The choice fell upon the Sheikh probably because a history-minded Nehru saw him as a link to Kashmir's past and people. The link, however, was soon to be lost as power politics prevailed over the past and the people.

The Sheikh's was a past of the anti-monarchy or anti-autocracy struggle in Kashmir, inspired and supported by India's independence movement like its counterparts in the 500-odd princely states of British India. He took a master's degree in chemistry from the Aligarh Muslim University in the United Provinces (now Uttar Pradesh) of India and returned to Srinagar and to a Kashmir in turmoil in 1931. He plunged into the popular uprising against Hari Singh's despotism, and thus began a political career of far-reaching consequences for the subcontinent's fortunes.

Liberal and Leftwing Kashmiris are proud to recall that the uprising was preceded by a strike in Srinagar's silk factory in 1924. The agitating workers raised slogans against Maharaja Pratap Singh. At the time, the future ruler of Kashmir, Hari Singh, was an advisor to the Maharaja. Troops and the police, along with the cavalry, attacked the workers, many of whom were wounded. The episode is recounted to stress the secular origin and character of the anti-autocracy struggle, though it soon took up the demand for increased educational and employment opportunities for the state's Muslim majority that was largely denied these under the Hindu kings of the Dogra dynasty.

The uprising was sparked off by a rally in June in Srinagar, at the end of which a faceless Abdul Qadeer, a domestic helper, pointed to the palace and said, "Destroy its every brick." This was reported to the palace and he was arrested and tried for treason. The trial was transferred to the central jail, following huge demonstrations. On July 13, 1931, thousands thronged the central jail to witness the in-camera trial. When the mob demanded an open trial, the authorities were frightened and guards were ordered to fire into the crowd. Seventeen demonstrators were killed on the spot, and others later died from their injuries.

July 13 from then on became the Martyrs' Day observed every year in Kashmir. And, the Sheikh, who participated in the protest, stayed on to lead it. In 1931, he founded the Muslim Conference, which he converted into the National Conference (NC) in 1939. The change was not merely one of nomenclature. It aimed at broadening the movement to include the state's minorities, particularly Hindus and Sikhs. It also envisaged the entire movement as part of a subcontinent-wide anti-colonial struggle.

The Sheikh's commitment to "Kashmiriyat" or Kashmiri culture, reflected recognition of its rich compositeness and its deep roots. A visitor to the state, especially the Valley, may be surprised to encounter the same recognition among the common people even today. Srinagar's Sankaracharya Hill (where an ancient Hindu philosopher-missionary from Kerala is said to have set up a temple and preached) has never been a terrorist target and this testifies to a place in the popular mind for days when Kashmir was Brahmin country. Buddhism was brought here by the missionaries of Asoka in 274 BC, and is still the dominant religion in Ladakh, a major district.[2] Several Hindu dynasties followed. The last Hindu king, Udiana Deva, was replaced by the first Muslim ruler Shams-ud-Din, in 1346.

* * *

IT was in 1586 that Moghul (Persian for Mongol) emperor Akbar conquered Kashmir and consolidated Muslim influence in the region. In 1752, Afghan chieftain Ahmed Shah Durrani defeated the Moghuls and annexed Kashmir. The Afghans were followed by Sikh warrior-king Ranjit Singh. He conquered Kashmir in 1819, but his disorganized empire fell to the British in 1846 when they took control of Punjab.

Dogras did not conquer Kashmir, but bought it in 1846. The British sold the "paradise" of Jehangir to self-titled Maharajah Gulab Singh of Jammu for 7.5 million rupees under the Treaty of Amritsar. Gulab Singh later also brought Ladakh, Zanskar, Gilgit and Baltistan under his control.

The Moghuls (whom the Kashmiris resented for treating their state only as a playground and a pleasure garden), the Afghans, and the Sikh all encountered pockets of popular resistance. The Kashmiris, however, reserved their most dogged resistance for the rather despised Dogras. A succession of Maharajahs followed, and so did several uprisings of the Kashmiri people, of whom a large proportion was now Muslim. In 1889, Maharajah Pratap Singh lost administrative authority of Kashmir due to worsening management of the frontier region. The British restored full powers to the Dogra rule only in 1921.

The Sheikh's recognition of the Kashmiri struggle as part of a wider freedom movement was natural. The consolidation of Dogra rule in Jammu and Kashmir coincided with the strengthening of the Indian freedom movement under Mahatma Gandhi's leadership. The freedom struggle was soon to find an echo in several princely States and nowhere with more ardor than in Kashmir. The National Conference inevitably found itself drawn towards the Indian National Congress and thus a foundation of friendship was laid between Sheikh Mohammad Abdullah, Jawaharlal Nehru and Mahatma Gandhi.

It was, obviously, under duress that Maharaja Hari Singh agreed to the appointment of the Sheikh as the emergency administrator in the interim government formed in Kashmir after its accession to India. The NC had organized a Quit Kashmir movement just a year before calling upon the Maharaja to leave Kashmir, and the Sheikh had just emerged from jail. He was, soon, however, confirmed in power as the Prime Minister of Jammu and Kashmir.

* * *

THE post-1947 political life of the Sheikh consisted of two distinct phases. In the first, he played a major role in thwarting what he saw as the designs of Pakistan's establishment in Kashmir and assisting in the state's conditional accession to India and its consolidation. The second phase saw him pitted against, and being punished by, India on the issue of unfulfilled condition of the accession. Through both the phases, however, he remained staunch in his preference for the Indian option for Kashmir and in his advocacy of greater autonomy for his state.

Through both, he also remained the most respected political leader of Kashmir. As any politically observant visitor to the state can vouch, he still commands reverence here, even among sections that do not share his pro-India or pro-accession views at all. Jinnah visited Srinagar twice to try and convince the NC and the Sheikh that Pakistan was their better option. But, to no avail. The Kashmiri leader sensed in Pakistan's founder a contempt for the Kashmiris, and recorded this in his autobiography titled "Aatish-e-Chinar" or "Flames of the Chinar" (the chinar tree being a symbol of Kashmir). Not only had Jinnah "dismissed his best bet in the Valley, Maulvi Mirwaiz Yusuf Shah, as a rotten egg." According to the

Sheikh, when an NC activist, Ali Mohammad Tariq, asked Jinnah soon after the Partition whether the future of Kashmir would be decided by the people of Kashmir, he was stunned by Jinnah's riposte: "Let the people go to hell."

On the raids by the Afghan tribesmen, the Sheikh agreed with Margaret Bourke-White's description in *Halfway to Freedom*: "Their buses and trucks, loaded with booty, arrived every other day and took more Pathans to Kashmir. Ostensibly they went to liberate their Kashmiri Muslim brothers, but their primary objective was riot and loot. In this they made no distinction between Hindus, Sikhs and Muslims." She added: "The raiders advanced into Baramulla, the biggest commercial center of the region with a population then of 11,000, until they were only an hour away from Srinagar. For the next three days, they were engaged in massive plunder, rioting and rape. No one was spared. Even members of the St. Joseph's Mission Hospital were brutally massacred."

This tribal invasion was no accident, according to the Sheikh. It was a diversionary tactic created by the newly formed State of Pakistan. "The withdrawal of British forces from the tribal belt had left these people without any livelihood. The ruler of Pakistan feared that these lawless people might proceed to plunder Peshawar and other big cities of Pakistan. They were asked, therefore, to proceed to Kashmir, having been assured of their bounty through plunder of the countryside. Pakistani leaders were hoping to reap a double benefit: getting rid of the tribals and bringing Kashmiris to their knees. When the tribals refused to budge from Baramulla, Abdul Qayyum Khan, an NWFP Pathan leader, sent their religious leader, Pir Manti, to persuade them to advance towards Srinagar," the Sheikh wrote.

According to confirmed reports as described by Sheikh Abdullah in his autobiography, Pakistani agents in Srinagar city decided to destroy all the bridges so that, if the Indian Army was dispatched, its movement could be sabotaged. National Conference volunteers were posted at the bridges and Hindus and Muslims alike were prepared to guard their national honor, having heard about the atrocities inflicted on innocents. The ruler's appeals to Pakistan were of no avail. The raiders caused havoc in different parts of Kashmir. The Kashmir state troops were incapable of offering effective resistance to the raiders. Later, the Sheikh told the Jammu and Kashmir Constituent Assembly: "...from 15 August to 22 October 1947, our state was independent...and our weakness was exploited by our neighbor (Pakistan)...The state was invaded." Recommending continued accession to India, he said: "...it is my considered judgment that the presence of Kashmir in the Union of India has been the major factor in stabilizing relations between the Hindus and Muslims of India."

The post-1947 government had the support of India's central government under Nehru in New Delhi to meet the Kashmiri aspirations for independence half-way and to keep the pro-Pakistan forces at bay. A signal achievement for the Sheikh in this regard was the introduction of Article 370 in the Constitution of India as a "temporary" measure to impart the state a special statutory status entailing greater autonomy in matters excluding defence, foreign affairs and communications.

Article 370, however, proved a red rag to the religious-communal Rightwing bull in India. Political pressures obliged the government of India to distance itself

from the Sheikh and his party on questions about
Kashmir's future. Founder of the Jan Sangh (parent of the
BJP) Shyama Prasad Mukherjee made an issue of the special status by entering the state without the required per-
mit and courting arrest on June 20, 1953. He died in jail
there. The event increased the embarrassment for New
Delhi. The New Delhi-Srinagar relations were also
strained by the unpleasant turn the Kashmir case, which
India had taken to the UN, was acquiring.

From then on, the debate over Kashmir's constitutional status deepened and embittered the differences
between the Sheikh and the Nehru government. The
aggravation of the relations led to the Kashmir leader's
arrest on August 9, 1953.

With him in jail, the Jammu and Kashmir
Constituent Assembly work was completed, and the
state was given a new Constitution of its own in 1957.
Under the new statute, which gave the state a governor
and a chief minister in place of a president and a prime
minister, it was spelt out for the first time that Kashmir's
accession to India was "final and irrevocable" and that
the state was "an integral part" of India. From inside the
jail, Sheikh Abdullah formed a Plebiscite Front and
demanded that the Kashmiri people be given the right
to self-determination in accordance with the UN resolutions.

He was not released until 1975, after spending 22
years in detention. He emerged from the prison with
something like Nelson Mandela's stature, if only inside
Kashmir.

His release in 1975 was immediately followed by an
apparently pre-arranged accord with the then Prime

Minister Indira Gandhi and his installation as the chief minister of the state. In 1977, however, the Congress withdrew support for the NC and the Assembly was dissolved. In the subsequent elections, the NC won and he was re-elected chief minister. Through the final phase of his political life, he surprised many of his Kashmiri followers and admirers by continuing to support the accession. He is reported to have explained to a group of university students who asked him about this that, in his judgment, Kashmir would be better off by being part of a "pluralistic" India, which was also likely to grow faster "economically and technologically."

The students may not have agreed, but he remained a father figure to them as to many, many other Kashmiris. They agreed with Kashmir's poet Allama Iqbal, who had opted for Pakistan but acknowledged that the Sher-e Kashmir (Lion of Kashmir) as the leader was known "had wiped the fear of the tyrant from the hearts of the people of Kashmir."

When Sheikh Abdullah died in 1982, a record one million mourning Kashmiris were reported to have joined his funeral procession in Srinagar's Lal Chowk. With him passed a restraining influence, underestimated by India, on a people whom history was turning rebellious.

Cracks about the "Sheikh dynasty" are common enough in Kashmir. Farooq Abdullah, the Sheikh's son and successor in office who stayed chief minister during the standoff of the summer of 2002, commands no comparable respect. Nor is Farooq's son, Omar Abdullah (a minister until recently in the BJP-headed government in New Delhi and who was anointed as the NC chief on the eve of the latest state elections), likely to prove a reincarnation of the Sheikh.

The internationalization of the Kashmir problem, talked about in Farooq's and Omar's time, especially following the standoff, was something that began in the fifties on the floor of the United Nations. Ironically, it was the result of India's own initiative in taking its complaint to the UN against "Pakistani aggression" in Kashmir in 1947. India's representative at the UN, the colorful and caustic V. K. Krishna Menon, told the Security Council in January 1957 that India had taken the case to the UN on January 1, 1948, against "an act of aggression" by Pakistan. In his speech of 1962 at the Council, he was still insisting that India came originally to the UN over a "situation" and not a "dispute." This did not prevent the stationing of a UN force in the disputed area, where it stays to date. "When the complaint of aggression was bypassed, and the matter turned into a dispute," says former diplomat A. K. Damodaran in an introduction to a selection of those marathon speeches at the UN (some running into hours) titled "*Krishna Menon on Kashmir*," "Pandit Nehru was surprised". Apparently, Menon was not. He expected Britain to be succeeded by the U.S. and allies as promoters of strife in the subcontinent.[3]

At one stage in the debate, addressing the Council on which six members were Pakistan's military-pact allies, Menon said: "I look around the table, and see I have to fight my battles." He brought up, again and again, the question of US arms to a Pakistan which was not helping to bring peace to Kashmir, including the part held by that country. For the first half of 1956, he noted, the aid came to $92 million which, according to an official claim, made up 40 per cent of its defense budget. He warned the U.S.:

"...give a child a knife to play with and he will hurt somebody. He will not ask the permission of the parent to do that."

With the passage of time, the case appeared to become weaker. India's stand that it accepted only the first of the UN resolutions on Kashmir, dated January 17, 1948, did not seem acceptable to a growing section of world opinion. Its repeated statement that a plebiscite could be considered "only after the aggression is vacated" began to sound stale and suggest recalcitrance. Its rejection of the Gunnar Jarring Mission's idea of arbitration of the dispute struck quite a few as unreasonable, considering that there seemed to be barely any possibility of the problem being bilaterally resolved. India was still better off in the international arena in those days. Menon could talk of 62,000 tourists, 9,000 of them foreign, still flocking to Kashmir in the summer of 1956, of Western journalists who reported on the state freely and sometimes even flatteringly, and of films being shot in idyllic outdoor settings. He could speak, without being contradicted, of the Indian armed forces being received as "liberators" at least in parts of Kashmir, and of the local resentment against the "rapine and plunder" by raiding tribesmen from across the border. No such claims can be made with credibility in or about the totally alienated Kashmir today.

The Valley wore a semblance of normalcy and was safe enough for tourists until 1988. Portents of the approaching storm became perceptible in 1986. In that year, the ruling NC entered into an electoral alliance with the Congress governing in New Delhi. Many in Kashmir saw this as a betrayal of Kashmir's autonomy. A new party, the Muslim United Front (MUF), attracted the support of this section of the people, including pro-independence activists, disenchanted Kashmiri youth and the pro-Pakistan Jama'at-e Islami (Islamic Assembly), and appeared poised to do fairly well in state elections in 1987. Blatant rigging, marked by an extremely low voter turnout, assured a comfortable NC victory. Arrests of hundreds of MUF leaders and supporters followed. By all unofficial accounts, this was the signal for the launch of the Kashmiri insurgency, as the country knows it today. Young MUF supporters took to the gun. Militant groups multiplied, and they increasingly crossed over to Pakistan for arms and training.

Soon, the militant formations split into two broad camps—one advocating an independent Kashmir and the other supporting accession to Pakistan. A few years later, a further divide followed between groups that stuck to the gun and those that opted for a peaceful struggle. These broad divisions remain. In the late 1980s, the most prominent pro-Pakistan group was the Hizb-ul Mujahideen (Holy Warriors' Corps) and the largest pro-Independence formation was the Jammu and Kashmir Liberation Front (JKLF).

On the morrow of the fixed elections, all the groups launched campaigns of competitive violence. Select NC leaders were assassinated. Bombs were detonated at government buildings, buses, and the houses of present and former state officials. A statewide boycott of the November 1989 national parliamentary elections was successfully enforced.

One month later came what some consider a turning point in the history of Kashmiri terrorism. JKLF militants abducted Rubaiya Sayeed, a daughter of then Home

Minister Mufti Mohammad Sayeed in the New Delhi government headed by V. P. Singh. They then freed her when the government gave in to demands for the release of five detained militants. The BJP in the Opposition then deplored what it saw as a week-kneed surrender by the government. A popular Rightwing theory is that this incident opened the floodgates of terrorism in the state. The theory is still being touted, though the BJP-led government accepted with even greater alacrity similar demands from the terrorist hijackers of an Indian civilian plane to Kandahar in Afghanistan in December 1999. The fact, however, remains that the episode led to more terrorist strikes and to a massive crackdown on the militants by the central and state forces.

On January 19, 1990, the central government imposed direct rule on the state. From January 26, India's Republic Day, Kashmiris were placed under an almost continuous curfew for eight full months as martial law was imposed. More than half a million Indian troops entered the state. They were followed by reinforcements—big enough to make them, first, look like a menacing occupation force and, then, behave like one in many instances.

The common civilians had to either flee the state or scurry for cover as the armed groups and the security forces collided head-on in a no-holds-barred confrontation. The government's campaign against the militants was marked by widespread human rights violations, including the shooting of unarmed demonstrators, civilian massacres, summary executions of detainees, gang rapes, enforcement of unpaid or underpaid labour, and extortions. The militants' counter-offensive included attacks on and killing of individuals, abductions, assassinations of government officials and suspected informers, bomb blasts as well as other forms of sabotage and, last but not the least, murder and intimidation of Hindu residents by a section of the rebels.

The religious-communal reprisals against the Indian state by the militants, even if only a minority among them as is often insisted, represented a major propaganda reversal for their professed cause. An estimated 70,000 Kashmiri Hindus, or Pandits as they are known, are said to have fled the state over the years. It is widely believed in the Valley that the flight was encouraged, and even engineered in the case of Srinagar, by the BJP's Jagmohan, appointed Governor of the state, placed under New Delhi's direct rule in 1990 after Farooq Abdullah's resignation in protest. The plight of the uprooted Pandits in other parts of the country, regularly reported in the media and repeatedly deplored by the BJP and its camp-followers, is now among the major factors that keep the Kashmir issue agonizingly alive in India.[4]

Jammu and Kashmir limped on to its first post-1989 parliamentary elections in May 1996. The militants called for a boycott, again. To go by the voting figures, they failed this time. It was an open secret, however, that the security forces had forced a number of voters to go to the polls. During the state assembly elections in September of that year as well, residents of Srinagar and other cities complained that they had voted at gunpoint. The elections led to the formation of the first state government since 1990, under the NC and Farooq Abdullah.

* * *

IT was in the nineties that armed struggle ceased to be the sole tactic of the militants. In late 1993, the All-

Parties Hurriyat (Freedom) Conference (APHC), an umbrella organization of the leaders of all the political and militant organizations fighting for independence, was founded to act as the political voice of the independence movement. The APHC has functioned as a front for a peaceful campaign, despite internal rivalries. The JKLF, which spearheaded the movement for an independent Kashmir, declared a cease-fire in 1994.

The militant groups not to abandon the gun included the Hizb-ul Mujahideen and the Lashkar-e Toiba (Soldiers of the Community). The last, along with some other groups, was reported to include a large number of non-Kashmiris. The weapons they have used include AK-47 and AK-56 assault rifles, light machine-guns, revolvers, and landmines. The militants are also reported to have sophisticated night-vision and wireless communication equipment. Officially, the Pakistani government has denied involvement in arming and training Kashmiri militants, but there are no takers for the claim.

On the other side were arrayed the central government forces. These included the Indian Army and India's federal security forces, the Central Reserve Police Force (CRPF), and the Border Security Force (BSF). The army's role in the conflict expanded in 1993 with the introduction of the Rashtriya (National) Rifles, an elite army unit created specifically for counterinsurgency operations in Kashmir. The Rashtriya Rifles have been the main force in charge of counterinsurgency operations in Doda, Rajouri and Poonch. As of June 1999, some 400,000 army troops and other federal security forces were deployed in the Valley, including those positioned along the Line of Control. The number has increased manifold since then.

The local Jammu and Kashmir policemen were generally not involved in counter-insurgency operations, as their sympathies were suspect. In 1995, however, the Special Task Force (STF) and the Special Operations Group (SOG), counter-insurgency divisions of the police made up of non-Muslim, non-Kashmiri recruits, including some former militants, were formed apparently to create the impression that the effort had local support. These police forces often operated jointly with the Rashtriya Rifles.

* * *

CAUGHT in the crossfire between the security forces and the militants, increasingly since then (through the days of the India-Pakistan nuclear tests in 1998 and the intensified hostilities between the two countries leading up to the standoff), have been the common people of Kashmir. Their human rights have been the main casualty in the conflict, though the least of priorities for political forces, leaders and their constituencies in both the countries.

We have already taken note of the human rights abuses by the brutalized security forces and the bloody-minded militants. According to one count, nearly 1,000 civilians, over 2,000 members of the security forces, and 10,000 insurgents have been killed from 1988 to 1999. This is an underestimate of the victims of terrorists, according to another set of figures that put the number of the slain in the oft-hit districts of Doda and Rajouri alone at over a thousand in this period. And, by all accounts, killings are not the only and possibly not even the worst of human rights abuses for Kashmir to have suffered.

The situation, however, is illustrated even better by the human rights violations committed by a third category of participants in the conflict. The "surrendered militants," as they are called, are the common Kashmiri's most dreaded scourge. Since at least early 1995, Indian security forces have armed and trained local auxiliary forces made up of surrendered or captured militants to assist in counter-insurgency. They function outside the structure of the security forces, but are still part of these under international law, for all practical purposes. Some of them are even housed in army compounds. Human rights defenders and journalists have been among their principal victims.

A clinical report by the Human Rights Watch (Asia) brings out best, perhaps, the cruelties and crudities of the system. Says the report: "While reports of some kinds of abuse have decreased since 1994, such as the indiscriminate use of lethal force against unarmed demonstrators, other abuses, notably summary executions and torture, show no sign of abatement, due in part to the activities of the state-sponsored militias. As noted above, these groups operate without any accountability. Wearing no uniforms, their members cannot be easily identified. There is no one to whom civilians may register complaints about the group's behavior. As one Kashmiri doctor told [us]. 'When someone misbehaved, he was wearing a uniform, so he was accountable. We could call his commander. Now, when these renegades misbehave, there is no one to call. No one accepts responsibility for them, though we know the government is sponsoring them.'"

HRW "obtained overwhelming evidence of the fact that these groups are organized, armed and protected by the Indian army and other security forces and operate under their command and protection, despite the Indian government's claims to the contrary. The government uses the groups in a number of ways: as informers who watch and report on the activities of the militants; as spies to infiltrate existing militant organizations; or as members of paramilitary 'renegade' organizations to attack members of Jama'at-e Islami and Hizb-ul Mujahideen and other militant groups. Members of these militias are also used to support Indian government policies. In public statements, Koko Parray (a 'renegade' leader) has indicated his group's support for the elections and intention to field candidates and ensure that people in areas under its control vote despite the militants' boycott."

In January 1996, a taxi driver in Srinagar told HRW that several days earlier he had been approached by two members of a paramilitary group who demanded the use of his taxi. The driver stated that the men told him they wanted to go to a village 10 km outside Srinagar. "The driver took them, but when they got there, one of the men pulled out a grenade, the other a pistol. One of the men showed a card, which the driver could not see, and said they were 'Task Force' and that they needed the car, but they would return it by 3:00 p.m. that afternoon. Then the men said that they would drop the driver off at a bus stop so he could get back to Srinagar. One of the two men drove. As he drove, they passed by an army camp. The soldiers waved the car by without stopping it. The men dropped the driver off. The driver returned to Srinagar and waited at the taxi stand that afternoon, but the taxi was not returned to him until two days later."

This was just petty harassment, compared to what they were really capable of. "Human rights activists have increasingly come under attack in Kashmir. Between April 1995 and April 1996, two human rights monitors were killed and one critically injured. The impact on Kashmir's human rights community has been devastating. Lawyers who had formerly taken up petitions on behalf of victims of abuses no longer do so out of fear of reprisals, particularly from the mercenary groups. Many have left Kashmir. The few human rights activists who have continued to document abuses in Kashmir do so at considerable risk to themselves." The "renegades" were responsible.

One of the many cases: "The body of Jalil Andrabi, a prominent human rights lawyer and pro-independence political activist associated with the JKLF, was found in the Kursuraj Bagh area of Srinagar on the banks of the Jhelum River on the morning of March 27, 1996. According to press reports, the body was in a burlap bag. Andrabi, who was forty-two, had been shot in the head and his eyes had been gouged out. He had apparently been dead for at least one week. According to eyewitnesses, Andrabi was detained at about 6:00 pm on March 8 by a Rashtriya Rifles unit of the army, which intercepted his car a few hundred yards from his home in Srinagar. On March 9, the Jammu and Kashmir Bar Association filed a habeas corpus petition in the Jammu and Kashmir High Court, and the court ordered the army to produce Andrabi. However, the army denied that Andrabi was in custody. Over the next two weeks, the court continued to grant the government extensions for replying to the petition."

The murder sparked off widespread protests in Kashmir and condemnation from civil liberties groups in India and abroad. In Srinagar, a protest march led by JKLF leader Yasin Malik was broken up by police. Reporters' cameras were smashed and the body was seized.

HRW reports: "Andrabi had previously received death threats from government-sponsored so-called 'renegade' forces.... The incident followed several other attacks on human rights activists in Kashmir, and about a week before the incident, Andrabi had told Human Rights Watch, Asia that he had received warnings that he 'would be the next.'"

Another case: "Mian Abdul Qayoom, 46, was until April 1995 the president of the Jammu and Kashmir Bar Association and one of Kashmir's most prominent human rights monitors. Under his direction, the bar association produced voluminous records of human rights violations by Indian security forces in Kashmir. On April 22, 1995, he was shot by two unidentified gunmen (again, 'renegades'). The incident left Qayoom permanently disabled."

HRW requested information from the government of India about the incident. "The National Human Rights Commission (NHRC) stated that the attack on Qayoom 'was a sequel to inter-gang rivalry.' The NHRC provided no other information or evidence.... 'Inter-gang rivalry' is the standard phrase used by the government to downplay abuses by state-sponsored militias."

The report adds: "In 1992-1993, three leading human rights activists were killed in Srinagar. On December 5, 1992, H. N. Wanchoo, a retired civil servant and trade unionist who had documented hundreds of cases of extrajudicial executions, disappearances and torture by the security forces, was shot dead by unidentified gunmen. On February 18, 1993, Dr. Farooq Ahmed Ashai, an orthopedic surgeon who documented cases of torture and indiscriminate assaults on civilians, was shot by Central

Reserve Police Force troops, who fired at his car, which was marked with a red cross, apparently in retaliation for an earlier militant attack. The troops then reportedly delayed his being taken promptly to a hospital for emergency care. He died shortly after finally reaching the hospital. On March 3, Dr. Abdul Ahad Guru, a leading member of the…JKLF, who had documented abuses by Indian security forces, was abducted by unidentified gunmen and shot dead. The government of India has never made public any action it has taken to investigate these killings and prosecute those responsible."

The press was also a favorite and frequent target: "Ikhwan-ul Muslimoon and other state-sponsored armed groups in Kashmir have demonstrated a particular antipathy toward the press. In July 1995, four journalists with the dailies *Greater Kashmir* and *Naida-i Mushraq* were abducted by Ikhwan-ul Muslimoon forces and held for four days. After ordering several newspapers to temporarily cease publication in November 1995, Koko Parray accused all the Kashmir journalists of being militants: 'there is little difference between the editors and the Hizbul Mujahideen. Journalists are writing posters and pamphlets for them.' After several days, the papers were permitted to resume publication."

Yet another "renegade" assault: "On December 8, 1995, Zafar Mehraj, a veteran Kashmiri journalist, was shot and critically injured as he returned from an interview with Koko Parray, the head of the state-sponsored paramilitary group Ikhwan-ul Muslimoon, at Parray's headquarters in Hajan, a small town 50 km from Srinagar. Mehraj, 43, was working for Zee Television, an independent television corporation. He had previously been threatened by both the security forces, who suspected him because of his ties to militant group and his travel in Pakistan, and some militant groups who resented his contacts with Indian officials. Although the identity of the gunmen who shot him may never be known, the evidence strongly suggests the involvement of state-sponsored militia forces."

The description of what followed suggests the ambience of terror in the state: "Three bullets hit Mehraj. One caused a superficial wound; one entered his left upper back and exited the right upper back; one entered his left upper stomach and exited his right upper stomach. Two or three minutes after Mehraj had fallen to the ground, he heard the taxi and minibus leave together. He tried to wave down passing vehicles, but several passed him before a truck finally stopped. The driver told him that he could not risk his life by helping him but, if Mehraj could climb into the back of the truck by himself, the driver would take him to a place where he could get a lift to a hospital. Mehraj climbed into the truck, and the driver drove approximately ten kilometers to a small market town where Mehraj saw a police constable. Mehraj got out of the truck and told the constable that he had been shot. The constable told him to take a motorcycle taxi to the hospital."

The report quotes Mehraj: "I asked two or three drivers to take me to the hospital but they all refused. Finally, I begged a driver on the other side of the road. I said, 'I have old parents and one young child. Please help me.' He told me, 'Don't make any noise. Get inside calmly.' He took me to (a) Srinagar...hospital, not by the main road but by the back road. I walked into the emergency room."

The Home Ministry informed HRW that Mehraj had been returning from an interview with "the chief of a militant outfit," and that while the incident was still under police investigation, it was "believed that [Mehraj] has been the victim of inter-gang rivalry."

In what was perhaps his last interview, APHC leader Abdul Ghani Lone, assassinated on May 21, 2002, told journalist Lawrence Lifschultz of the "racket" involving "renegades": "The war in Kashmir has become a corrupt racket. We know it here. Most people in India are in the dark. Let me give you just one example. If one hundred men go to Pakistan for training, then at least 70 to 80 per cent are being sent by the Indian Armed Forces. Less than 30 per cent are being sent by the Mujahideen groups. The Pakistani officer on the other side knows that 80 per cent of those arriving have been sent by his counterpart from the Indian side. He knows it. But he doesn't care. He too has his incentives."

Lone went on: "And, the Indian officer on this side doesn't care. If the boys come back and surrender as planned, then the Indian officer pockets most of the Rs. 30,000 available to each boy who surrenders. They grab that money. If 80 boys come back and 40 surrender, then 40 rifles given by Pakistan to the militants land up in the hands of the Indian Army. In the course of time, the other 40 young men will be killed and these weapons will also be picked up by the Indian Army. This is the system. Who cares?"

The months-long India-Pakistan military standoff in the summer of 2002, obviously, could not have made a vast and welcome difference to the human rights violations. Little wonder, New Delhi's offer of a post-standoff package to Kashmir did not exactly inspire rejoicing in the streets of Srinagar, which I visited in August 2002. The package consisted of "free and fair" state assembly elections with a broader than usual participation if possible and proxy talks with the Hurriyat leadership through a Kashmir Committee under a Ram Jethmalani of no distinguished political record (having been dismissed as India's Law Minister not long before).

The run-up to the elections had already been marred by Lone's assassination. The Vajpaye government was making a valiant effort to make political capital of the tragedy, but in vain. Few trusted in the sincerity of the Prime Minister's tribute to the slain leader as a man of "peace." Lone himself, in the same interview, had bluntly unkind words for the rulers in New Delhi: "...Vajpayee [had earlier] said that as Prime Minister he would not traverse the same 'beaten path' in Kashmir. We thought something new might be possible. But, he has taken the same 'beaten path' as all the others. They are rogues. You can't expect anything from these people."

There was no love lost between Lone and Pakistan's establishment, either. He was categorical: "They [Pakistan's rulers] have definitely let us down. This is on the record. They have let us down. What moral support have they given us? This was the time to provide us moral support.... If India is not ready to talk with the Kashmiris, then Pakistan should be able to say that we will talk with the Kashmiris and take note of their views."

"But," he added, "Pakistan follows its own national interest. Kashmiris can be sacrificed. Their sentiments can be sacrificed. It is the same case with India. They say there is no need to talk to the Hurriyat or the Kashmiri people.

Alienation is there. Day by day, alienation is piled upon alienation. They only wish that we should be their slaves."

Lone's assassination in Srinagar, wrote Lifschultz, was "a poignant reminder of that phase in Kashmir's 'dirty war,' which reached its peak during the early and mid 1990's. It was then that certain militant groups systematically set out to target and assassinate specific political personalities who refused to accept the notion that they had only 'one option'—accession to Pakistan. During this period individuals that faced Indian repression on a daily basis still remark that they often had to 'watch their backs' as carefully as the dangerous terrain that lay before them. As Lone makes unmistakably clear in the interview, he was a proponent of a 'third option' for Kashmir—the option of independence for Kashmir, or a new form of sovereignty, accepted by both India and Pakistan as being integral to both their national interests."

We do not know how many in Kashmir would have agreed with him, but the New Delhi package had certainly no political taker. Kashmir, I found, spoke with many voices. But there was a common message that they all sought to articulate.

It was not the paradisal summer resort, but a scorching Srinagar where I talked to four political players representing very different sections of a spectrum, besides the local intelligentsia and the Kashmiri in the street. The political temperatures, too, were unusually high this August in what seemed a captive capital. Amidst the dust and heat raised by the announcement of Jammu and Kashmir election and the extra-electoral exercise of the Kashmir Committee, the common message was loud and clear.

The message was that no section of opinion in the Valley looked upon the package of moves including the elections and the talks through the Kashmir Committee the way official India presented it. All sections were tacitly agreed that the package was a product of international, especially American, pressure. Some said so, others said it in other words. Some found in this a source of hope for a solution to the Kashmir problem, and others thought otherwise. None, however, saw in the moves a new and independent initiative by New Delhi.

All sections were also agreed that official India had alienated ordinary Kashmiris. Not only in the immediately obvious sense. Even if there had been no atrocities or excesses by the army and the paramilitary forces (any such denial or even any attempt to equate these with terrorist strikes causes instant anger and revulsion), no local citizen can feel but alienated in a Srinagar where he sees an armed Indian soldier every 100 yards and where he is frisked several times in a day—in the vegetable market, in the electricity office, at the petrol bunk, in the bank, anywhere, everywhere.

The alienation was shared by sections actively opposed to or not associated with separatism or militancy. It was best illustrated, in fact, by the bitterness in sections that had cast their lot with India.

The four leaders were: All-Parties Hurriyat Conference Chairman Professor Abdul Ghani Bhat, Jammu Kashmir Democratic Freedom Party President Shabir Ahmed Shah, People's Democratic Party leader Mehbooba Mufti, and National Conference leader and Speaker of the outgoing Jammu and Kashmir Assembly Abdul Ahad Vakil. The four represented a spectrum of political opinion, ranging from pro-Pakistan to pro-India, with the major shades in between.

Bhat, an effective communicator, made no bones about the Hurriyat's special relations with Pakistan. Reacting to Shabir Shah's strong criticism about the Hurriyat being under Islamabad's thrall, the APHC Chairman was at his remorseless best. Rolling big eyes, waving hands like a magic wand, he exclaimed: "...why should I mince words, Pakistan supports the cause of the people's right to self-determination. It is India which denies this inalienable right of ours." He hastened to add that this did not make him Pakistan's "surrogate" and that "Pakistan is a supporter, not a master."

Interestingly, it was the leader with faith in Pakistan who was also optimistic about what India's package could achieve. This was because he did not regard it as really India's own package, but as a US prescription for India. Asked if he did not think it would all return to square one after the elections and the committee-initiated talks, he said: "Mr. Colin Powell (US Secretary of State) called for a resolution of the Kashmir dispute. And the Election Commission (of India) was quick, actually too quick, to fix the dates of elections in Jammu and Kashmir. India got wind of what was happening globally: there was now recognition that Kashmir was the undercurrent of tensions in South Asia. India had to do something to relieve the global pressure."

"Therefore," he concluded professorially, "we should not feel discouraged by the prospect of the situation returning to square one. Let us hope for the best and pre-pare for the worst."

Shabir Shah had harsh words about Hurriyat's proximity to Pakistan. "*Mulaazim apnaa stand kaise le sakte hain?* (How can those on someone's pay-roll take their own stand?)," he asked. This did not, however, make him a trusting ally of India.

The man who had spent 23 years in "Indian jails" (as his friends and even foes repeatedly recalled) did not view the package very differently from the Hurriyat. His party had not called for a boycott of the elections, but he continued to insist on "a political dialogue before the polls." Like the Hurriyat, he, too, thought that the Indian government had yet to recognize "the ground realities" here. Still, he hoped for an improvement of the package, and pleaded for an "initiative from Atalji (the Prime Minister)" suggesting that he, too, saw an extra-Indian sanction behind the entire exercise.

Shah argued for an extension of the dialogue process to include Pakistan and "the Kashmiri people" because they are all "parties to the dispute." He said that "history won't forgive the stand that the time for India-Pakistan amity efforts was over with Atalji's bus ride to Lahore." The JKDFP leader, in his characteristically breathless manner, pleaded that "the USA should play a role to facilitate the talks" and praised the peace efforts by the European Union.

Mehbooba Mufti, young and English-educated, thought the package had created "confusion." "On one hand, they want talks with elected representatives (of Kashmir) and, on the other, they have already announced the election dates which hang like the Damocles' sword over our heads. These two can't go together…. I wish the elections had not been thrust (upon us)."

The sister of Rubaiya (whose abduction by the militants a decade and a half ago was a turning point in the State's recent history) said, while trying to talk to "a minority that has been anti-India," New Delhi was not addressing the concerns that made "the majority support the minority."

All the three voiced contempt for the ruling National Conference and its claim to represent the State.

Refusing to discuss the response of Chief Minister Farooq Abdullah to the package Bhat told a media conference in Srinagar: "Main naukaron ki baat nahin karta, main maalikon ki baat karta hoon. (I don't talk about servants, I talk about the masters)." Reacting to the NC's demand for the dialogue to include it, Shah said: "We'll put up a (a sweeper) *safai karmachari*—we respect *safai karmacharis*—against Farooq from any seat. And, let the Indian government send its own, not any international, observers. If the Chief Minister wins, the NC can also be included in the talks." Mehbooba said: "The minimum they could have done to restore the confidence of the masses in this election is to give them a new dispensation, persuade the Chief Minister to step aside and have the President's Rule."

It was only a free and fair election that could prove or disprove them. The interesting point, however, was that the package did not strike the NC, either, as a credible New Delhi initiative. Abdul Ahad Vakil was particularly puzzled by the talks with the Hurriyat. "The Prime Minister said in his Independence Day speech that Kashmir was an integral part of India. The Hurriyat want a plebiscite, they're with Pakistan. What meeting ground is there for talks?" Vakil stressed that "we're part of the NDA (National Democratic Alliance) government (in

New Delhi), of the national mainstream and can't be bypassed."

As unpopular with him as the package was the idea of a US role in Kashmir, though he did not connect the two. "To please Pakistan, they talk of a Kashmir dispute. But, what are they (the USA) doing in Palestine? What about self-determination there?" This was before a US delegation met the Hurriyat leadership and tried to talk them into electoral participation.

Alienation was, of course, a recurring theme in all the conversations. Bhat vowed that the Hurriyat would never "forget the destroyed homes and honor." Shah urged the release of prisoners including Yasin Malik (falsely implicated in a financial scam, according to him), Jama'at-e Islami leader Syed Ahmed Geelani, and other leaders besides "countless youths arrested without charges." Mehbooba talked with indignation of a 16-year young girl raped recently by three BSF soldiers as the latest in a long series of such crimes. Vakil was agitated about the "alienation" that would be caused by bringing people from other parts of India to conduct the elections as though "Kashmiris were all dishonest."

* * *

OVERALL, it did not appear as though the package could deliver. More than half a century after the creation of the Kashmir problem, there seemed to be no solution, not even a semblance of it, in sight. At least none can be expected realistically from the political masters and manipulators of Pakistan and India, from the pious hypocrisy of their periodical parleys on the subject. They cannot be expected to strike a common subcontinental

chord and orchestrate moves towards an enduring regional one under the baton of impresarios of a wildly warmongering imperialism.

We must look elsewhere for workable ideas of a
Kashmir solution, even outlines of ideas that obviously
need further elaboration and examination. We may not
look in vain, if we do not confine ourselves to a futile
search for concrete and creative proposals among bureaucrats' files and diplomats' documents in New Delhi and
Islamabad. Here are just a couple of ideas from other, unofficial quarters, which should raise hopes of people-sup-
ported peace initiatives that can influence the powers-
that-be.

The first came from Pakistani intellectual and peace
champion Eqbal Ahmad. His proposal (as quoted in
Confronting Empire: Interviews with David Barsamian) was
"that we seek an agreement which leaves the Pakistani part
under Pakistani control. Jammu and Ladakh, which do not
share the premises of Kashmiri nationalism, should be left
under Indian sovereignty. The Valley should be given independence. But the agreement among the three—Kashmiri
leadership, Pakistan, and India—must envisage uniting
Kashmir with divided sovereignty. Unite the territory, keep
sovereignties divided, which in our time is fairly possible.
Remove the lines of control, remove border patrols, make
trade free among these three, make India, Pakistan, and the
independent Kashmiri government jointly responsible for
the defense of this mountain area…"

"My proposal," Ahmad pleaded, "would create,
instead of a bone of contention, a bridge of peace. Allow
each community maximum autonomy with divided sovereignty. Kashmir would then serve as the starting point of

normalizing relations between India and Pakistan. And if India and Pakistan normalize relations, with free trade, free exchange of professionals, and reduction in our arms spending, in ten years we will start looking like East Asia. We are competing with each other with so little money. Four hundred million people in India out of a population of 950 million are living below the poverty line... this condition has to be removed."

Justin Podur, a South Asia specialist, comments: "Ahmad's words are no less true now than they were three years ago—in this and in much else. They are only a little more difficult to make happen, now that the US is in the region, building bases, destabilizing, and pouring gasoline on the flames. That only makes sensible proposals like Ahmad's more urgent, not less."

The second proposal comes from Admiral L. Ramdas, former Chief of India's Navy and now a leading anti-nuclear activist. The first part of the proposal relates to an immediate need arising from the standoff: "Pakistan has pledged to stop the infiltration into Kashmir permanently. This will require monitoring. India has proposed a joint patrolling of the border. This has not been agreed to by Pakistan.... It is, therefore, proposed that a force drawn from among the members of the South Asian Association for Regional Cooperation (SAARC) under a mutually agreed leadership could provide the necessary compromise for the monitoring to be established."

As for the larger solution, besides urging acceptance of the LoC as a permanent international border between the two countries, he suggests: "To facilitate the emergence of peace in the region as early as possible, the following process as a via media could be considered: First,

Kashmiris on both sides of the border should be given the choice of being the citizens of either India or Pakistan, and, if they want to move from one side to another, be given the opportunity to do so in peace and security. To implement this, both countries should agree to some form of international supervision. This role could be performed by a SAARC monitoring team as proposed earlier. Second, the people displaced from their lands and homes by the current conflict, such as the Kashmiri Pandits, should be allowed to return in peace and security. Third, the border between India and Pakistan in Kashmir should be kept porous to enable Kashmiris on both sides to cross it for personal, family and business reasons without too many hassles."

He adds: "Both countries should reaffirm the pledges to negotiate all outstanding issues between them peacefully and not resort to war, proxy or otherwise. This formulation should meet the concerns of the two countries adequately. This means, first of all, a cease-fire along the LoC. Pakistan should agree to a policy of no-first-use of nuclear weapons, which India has already adopted. This is the equivalent of a nuclear cease-fire."

Both the formulations are, without doubt, debatable. Ahmad's solution may sound to some as unattainably idealistic. Admiral Ramdas' may appear to quite a few like a plea for completion of the Partition process and to underestimate the pain this may involve. Both, however, have exciting new elements that deserve exploration. The need is for more of unconventional ideas to ensure that South Asia is not exposed again to the danger of a nuclear disaster.

CHAPTER 5

THE DESERT AND THE MOUNTAIN

Knocking on the Door of the Nuclear Club

> The sword itself often provokes a man to fight.
> —Attributed to Greek epicist Homer

> What would you think of a man who not only kept an arsenal in his home, but was collecting at enormous financial sacrifice a second arsenal to protect the first one? What would you say if this man so frightened his neighbors that they in turn were collecting weapons to protect themselves from him? What if this man spent ten times as much money on his expensive weapons as he did on the education of his children? What if one of his children criticized his hobby and he called that child a traitor and a bum and disowned him? And he took another child who obeyed him faithfully and armed that child and sent it out into the world to attack neighbors? What would you say about a man who introduces poisons into the water he drinks and the air he breathes?.... Such a man would clearly be a paranoid schizophrenic...with homicidal tendencies.
> —Robert Anton Wilson, *The Illuminatus!*

> We will eat grass, but make the Bomb.
> —Zulfikar Ali Bhutto

We knew the world would not be the same. A few people laughed, a few people cried. Most people were

silent. I remembered the line from the Hindu scripture, the Bhagavad Gita... 'I am become Death, the destroyer of worlds.' I suppose we all felt that, one way or another.
—Robert Oppenheimer, on watching the explosion of the first atom bomb

I heard the earth thundering below our feet and rising ahead of us in terror. It was a beautiful sight.
—A. P. J. Abdul Kalam, scientist and would-be President of India, watching the nuclear weapon tests in Pokharan

South Asia was not ever to be the same after May 11, 1998. On that fateful day, the desert site of Pokharan in Rajasthan, one of the poorest of India's states, shook with three nuclear-weapon test explosions. On May 13, two more tests followed to complete the process and enable the country's emergence as a proudly self-proclaimed "nuclear-weapon state." On May 28 came Pakistan's riposte in the form of five tests on the mountain site of Chagai, followed by a single test at the same site on May 30. Reverberations of the entire subcontinental event are being heard even today.

The militarist jingoism masquerading as media hype, which greeted Pokharan II (Pokharan I referring to blasts of a lesser bellicosity conducted in 1974 at the same site) in India, was remarkable in many ways. Striking, in the first place, was the elation of the extra-loud at what they saw as an exciting surprise sprung upon the country and the world by a new government under the BJP and Atal Behari Vajpayee. Fortnightly journal *India Today*, for example, was histrionic in its reporting of history:

"For the six men who assembled in the sitting room

of the prime minister's official residence at Race Course Road that hot Monday afternoon," the periodical said, "it was a tense wait. As three simultaneous nuclear explosions rocked the scorching sands of the Pokharan test range in the Rajasthan desert at 3.45 p.m., the only sound they heard was the purring of an air-conditioner. The prime minister's principal secretary Brajesh Mishra lifted the receiver hesitantly to hear an excited voice cry 'Done!'...Mishra re-entered the room."

The story continued: "Seeing his expression, Prime Minister Vajpayee, Home Minister L. K. Advani, Defense Minister George Fernandes, Finance Minister Yashwant Sinha and Planning Commission Deputy Chairman Jaswant Singh could barely control their feelings. Advani was seen wiping away his tears. Picking up the receiver, Vajpayee, in an emotion-choked voice, thanked the two scientists—who made it happen—Department of Atomic Energy (DAE) chief R. Chidambaram and head of the Defence Research and Development Organisation (DRDO), Abdul Kalam." The reporter wanted to leave no dry eyes among the readers.

The surprise element was a soul-uplifting experience for the chief editor of national daily *Indian Express*. It was "a cause for reassurance" to him "that even in these cynical times when we tend to believe so easily that any fellow-Indian's loyalties are purchasable for a few dollars, a scholarship or a green card the establishment has managed to keep such a major move a secret despite the snooping that extends from the Capital's cocktail circuit to outer space." The allusion was to the report that the US had not detected the tests. This became a major talking point among all those tireless authors of months-long tributes to

Pokharan II. It was even brandished as proof of the anti-imperialist bona fides of the blasts. It was not long, however, before less flattering explanations were forthcoming.

One of these was that the non-detection was due to the negligible yield of the tests. This, of course, has been hotly contested by India's atomic science establishment, reveling in its pseudo-patriotic halo ever since Pokharan II. Praful Bidwai and Achin Vanaik in *South Asia on a Short Fuse* argue that a "complacency" in the US Administration then under Bill Clinton about the BJP's intentions and a "downgrading" of the level of nuclear monitoring of the region were the real reasons. The "complacency" was conveyed to the authors by a State Department official who asserted: "We don't believe the BJP is about to do anything radical—like nationalize foreign capital, start a war over Kashmir, or conduct a nuclear blast. We expect them to be sensitive to US concerns; we appreciate the fact that the BJP was among the few parties in India which during the Cold War were strongly anti-Soviet and generally supportive of the US." Interestingly, in retrospect, the BJP rulers proved capable of two of the three "radical" things mentioned. There is nothing to suggest that this has strained the special BJP-US relations that the official acknowledges. Quite the contrary, as we shall see.

As for the monitoring, the authors say: "Yes, there was some activity at Pokharan range, but the site had been downgraded in the DIA's (Defense Intelligence Agency's) list of priorities. Other sites, in Bosnia, Afghanistan, Sudan, and in Russia, were far more important. Only a junior officer had been put in charge of looking at the Rajasthan desert in northwestern India, where Pokharan is situated. (The officer was yet to notice the explosions when Vajpayee announced them to the media at 5:30 p.m. Indian Standard Time or 8 a.m. on the East Coast in the U.S.) The intensity of monitoring, too, had been reduced: only casually scanned images rather than high-alert, frequent monitoring recommended for sites…"

Yet another, even more unflattering, explanation has been suggested. We shall reserve this for the end of the chapter. What needs to be noted at this point is that, while the U.S. may have detected the tests late on its own, it was the first to be officially informed about them by India's Prime Minister. On May 11 itself, right after the triple testing, before explaining its rationale to India's Parliament or public, Vajpayee rushed a communication to President Clinton. The message defended the tests by naming threats from both China and Pakistan. It also offered the cooperation of India—as a nuclear-weapon state—to the U.S. in the campaign against nuclear proliferation and for nuclear disarmament. It was a loud and clear knock on the door of the nuclear club.

The precise timing of the tests may have taken most people by surprise. But, few could have been shocked by the blasts taking place in the time of BJP power. The party and its camp followers have never made any secret of their nuclear ambitions for the country and the religious community with which they largely identify it. A craving for the "Hindu Bomb" was part of the very basic platform of the Bharatiya Jan Sangh, the BJP's parent. This is an inheritance the offspring has cherished. When Vajpayee declared after Pokharan II that he had "waited all my life for this," he was not exaggerating.

As an Opposition leader in Parliament, he kept up

the pro-Bomb campaign through the late sixties and seventies. After Pokharan II, his propagandists repeatedly recalled his reported response to China's nuclearization: "The only answer to an atom bomb is an atom bomb." But, outside Parliament, in rallies across the northern states of India, the former rabble-rouser and his flock made it abundantly clear that the Chinese challenge was not the chief provocation for their policy and philosophy of nuclear nationalism. It was inspired by two passions, one related to the future and the other to the past. The Bomb was to be the "Brahmastra," the Weapon of Brahma, which would make India a world power and also serve to settle scores with the "enemy within," within the country and the subcontinent. With Pakistan and India's own Muslims: citizens who were later to be labelled "Babur ki aulad" or Children of Babur (the Tajik founder of the Moghul dynasty). The Jan Sangh had adopted the policy as early as 1951, before either China or Pakistan had one on nuclear weaponization.

The English-language media (with very few honorable exceptions) kept up its campaign in praise of Pokharan II, aimed at the elite and the middle-class intelligentsia. It hailed the tests as a triumph for Indian science and as an expression of a new, no-nonsense nationalism. As a passport to an enhanced international status, as a promise of upward national mobility. Its counterpart in Indian languages, especially Hindi of the BJP's traditional northern bastions, did without the veneer of sophistication. It rejoiced over the event in unabashedly religious-communal terms and reported the tests as a threat to Pakistan. Its response was the same as the "mass" response that the BJP, the RSS and the rest of the Sangh "parivar (family)" organized in the streets, above all, for media consumption.

The electronic media outdid everyone else in projecting drum-beating and dancing in the streets by the party cadre as a patriotic upsurge. "Jai Shri Ram," once the pious chant of the devotees of Hindu deity Ram, became the chauvinist war cry of crowds posing for the camera. (The salutation was also the slogan that greeted the Prime Minister's announcement in Parliament of the success of the tests and the proclamation of India as a nuclear-weapon state.) The "parivar" came out with plans to raise a shrine to Shakti (the Hindu Mother Goddess as an embodiment of energy) at the Pokharan site and, even more dramatically, to carry sacred urns of the desert sands around the country. Better sense prevailed against such recklessness with radioactivity, but attempts continued to whip up a holy hysteria within safer limits.

Anand Patwardhan, film-maker and peace activist from Mumbai, captured in his *Jang Aur Aman* or *War and Peace* scenes of the celebrations that have embarrassed even the Pokharan-proud in power. Official censors continued their outrageous efforts to stop its screening for the common Indian, and Patwardhan had to take the issue to the court and to the people.[1] In one of the scenes, far-Right demonstrators cut their fingers and take bloody pledges of solidarity with Pokharan II; in another, they burn Pakistan's national flag; and every one of the tributes to the tests sounds like a vow of vengeance. All this might have passed muster but for the contrasting scenes of small but significant and courageous protests by peace activists, as well as Patwardhan's cuts to Mahatma Gandhi and his messages of non-violence and inter-religious harmony. These could just not be allowed in a film for unrestricted viewing!

The tests were not only the dictate of the BJP's ideology, but an electoral mandate as well in this instance. The party's manifesto for the parliamentary elections of February 1998 promised that, if elected to power, "the BJP would review India's nuclear policy and exercise the option to induct nuclear weapons." It came to power at the head of a coalition named the National Democratic Alliance (NDA), but the promise stayed. The coalition adopted in March a National Agenda for Governance (NAG), which reiterated the nuclear pledge in identical terms. The all-round surprise over the tests was still warranted, because these should have taken longer even to go by the formulation in the manifesto and the NAG.

Vajpayee himself interpreted the formulation to mean that India would "cross the nuclear threshold" only if it was considered to be "absolutely necessary" after a "strategic review." Defense Minister George Fernandes, on his takeover, denied any commitment to exercise the nuclear option and stressed that the decision would be taken solely on the basis of a policy review and re-evaluation. The review was never undertaken. The concerted and conspiratorial attempt; it would appear in retrospect, was indeed to pre-empt any demand for such a review and to ensure that no public debate prevented or delayed the pre-determined break with an important national policy.

Fernandes himself, it turned out subsequently, was far from privy to the final decision. According to media reports, citing "highly placed sources," orders for the tests had been issued even before the new government won a vote of confidence in the Lok Sabha, the Lower House of India's Parliament, as constitutionally required. The RSS, the extra-constitutional part of the new establishment, on the contrary, was in the picture throughout: the newspapers controlled by it, the *Organiser* in English and *Panchajanya* in Hindi, broke the Pokharan II story as their "exclusive." Another media disclosure around the time was that the previous, pathetically short-lived, minority government of Vajpayee in 1996, too, had tried to conduct the tests. Orders had reportedly been issued for the tests on the 13th day of the government, when it faced its first vote of confidence in the Lok Sabha—and lost.

Vajpayee and the BJP saw no need to consult either the Opposition, including the Congress, or any party of its own coalition prior to Pokharan II. The then Leader of the Opposition, Sharad Power of the Congress, protested ever so mildly against the non-consultation, but the Congress eventually joined in the chorus of approval for the tests along with the non-BJP constituents of the NDA. The Left remained the lone anti-Pokharan II section of the party-political spectrum. Neither the denial of a public debate nor the absence of political consultations, however, stopped the media and other peddlers of Pokharan II from claiming a "national consensus" behind it.

They continued to repeat the claim, despite India's democracy helping to disprove it. As Nobel Prize-winning Indian economist Amartya Sen has pointed out, "the main political party to escalate India's nuclear adventure, namely the BJP, did not get any substantial electoral benefit from the Pokharan blasts. In fact, quite the contrary, as the analyses of local voting since the 1998 blasts tend to show. By the time India went to polls again, in September 1999, the BJP had learned the lesson sufficiently to barely mention the nuclear tests in their campaign with the voters." It may be added that the party lost the election in

Pokharan, where the tests have been followed by out-
breaks of mysterious human and animal diseases, triggering
off a local agitation for the closure of the site.

Sen was making a point about the poor popular support for Pokharan II. The BJP could have never bothered
less. Party strongman and then Home Minister (now
Deputy Prime Minister) Lal Kishan Advani shed pre-
tences of punctilious regard for the coalition partners' sen-
sibilities, and went around making public speeches about
the implementation of an old, old party program. Besides,
in the aftermath of the blasts, the government's and the
Prime Minister's immediate concern was about the international reaction. This, ironically, prompted New Delhi to
pro-actively pave the way for the reactive Pakistani
nuclear tests.

Vajpayee's first post-Pokhran II communication to
the US President named both China and Pakistan, and
the long-suspected clandestine nuclear cooperation
between the two that has worried successive regimes in
Washington. When Pakistan pounced on this as proof of
the tests threatening regional peace, China was projected
as the main challenge. Fernandes took up the case but
overstated his brief when he called China a "serious
threat" in public, alleging attempts by it to build an
unidentified South-East Asian military base close to
India's eastern coast and even a helipad on Indian territory. The furious Chinese reaction forced New Delhi on to
its back-foot. Now it needed Pakistani tests to justify
India's own and set about provoking Islamabad's Nawaz
Sharif regime into them.

Pakistani scholar-activist Eqbal Ahmad described the
modus operandi: "There were too many provocations by

BJP leaders to recount…These included warnings by L. K. Advani…that Pakistan should note a change in South Asia's 'strategic environment'; Prime Minister Vajpayee's statement that his government might forcibly take Kashmiri territory under Pakistan's control; the handing over of the Kashmir affairs portfolio to the hard-line home minister who had so enthusiastically overseen the destruction of the Babri Mosque; and the actual heating up of a limited but live conflict along the Line of Control in Kashmir. Pakistan's chief of army staff returned from the front line with the assessment that we might in fact be witnessing the slow beginning of a conventional war…Delhi did little to reassure Islamabad. These developments greatly reinforced among Pakistani officials a sense of foreboding."

Recounting how "Indian leaders goaded Pakistan," Ahmad regretted that "Pakistan fell for it." As he saw it, "India was the focus of adverse world attention, both governmental and popular, and was likely to remain so for a while…. Rather than take Delhi's burden upon itself, it was time for Islamabad to mount diplomatic initiatives and international campaigns to put pressure on India both within SAARC and worldwide…" He added: "…it would have been better for Islamabad to stay cool and calculating, utilizing the opportunities Delhi had presented. But, reason did not prevail."

It did not, because Islamabad and Sharif could not take an independent decision. Pakistan was hardly without its own enemies of any idea of subcontinental peace. Leading Pakistani peace activist Zia Mian brings alive the post-Pokharan II political ambience in his country: "Reason is easily lost in a darkness populated with fears and secrets. When India tested its nuclear weapons in May 1998, Pakistan lost it. There were 'strident apocalyptic warnings' of the consequences of Pakistan not following India in testing nuclear weapons. Some wanted to take advantage of the opportunity to test, to restore what they called strategic balance, an ugly euphemism for a balanced capacity for murder. Others simply sought advantage, with Benazir Bhutto playing her father's (Zulfikar Ali Bhutto's) role—she famously took off her bangles at a rally in Lahore and flung them at the crowd urging them to take the bangles to Prime Minister Nawaz Sharif since he was not man enough to stand up to India and order nuclear tests. Still others recited the Quran, as if God would want the death of millions."

Sharif gave in. It was the turn of Chagai, in remote Baluchistan, to reverberate with nuclear-weapon test explosions. "The whole mountain turned white," said the official statement by an anonymous Pakistani Oppenheimer. In a televised address, the Prime Minister tried telling the nation what he had been forced to do: "We have jumped into these flames without thinking through our minds and calculating, but going into a decision made by our heart, the decision of courage."

Celebrations, strikingly India-like, followed. Crowds burnt India's national flag, amid cries of "Pakistan Zindabad (Long live Pakistan)!" and "Allah-o-Akbar (God is great)!" Anand Patwardhan's camera captured the scene, which India's film censorship board wanted deleted in defense of the country's dignity. Firecrackers were burst and sweets distributed in the streets. The government joined in with gusto.

Mian recalls: "Cities and towns were decorated with

banners and giant posters carrying pictures of Pakistan's nuclear weapons scientists and Prime Minister Nawaz Sharif against a backdrop of mushroom clouds. The weapons became public monuments as giant replicas of the Ghauri and Shaheen nuclear missiles, a red light glowing from the rocket engine, were put up in central locations in major cities. Even the mountain in Chagai...became a symbol, with enormous white fibre-glass models glowering by roadsides. It is the first public monument on the main road to Islamabad from the airport: nuclear icons to create a proper nuclear state of mind."

We have talked so far only about the immediate backgrounds to Pokharan II and Chagai. The Indian and Pakistani Bombs, however, have a longer history. It is obvious that the tests of 1998 were preceded by years of preparation. They were indeed preceded by Pokharan I, India's first nuclear test, in 1974. A look at the long run-up to the emergence of the two nations as nuclear-weapon-sate neighbors yields important insights—not only into the complex of local factors leading up to the undesirable outcome but into the role the U.S. started and continued playing in the preparations long before the infamous September 11.

Independent India under Prime Minister Jawaharlal Nehru started off as a determined opponent of nuclear weapons everywhere including South Asia and a doughty champion of global nuclear disarmament. He was the architect of India's scientific infrastructure for the now innocent-sounding objective of "development of nuclear energy for peaceful purposes," and founded an Atomic Energy Commission with Homi Bhabha as its first chairman. There is some evidence that Bhabha was not averse to the idea of nuclear weaponization, but Nehru was unreservedly opposed to it.

The first Prime Minister of India declared himself against "any (nuclear) test anywhere." In 1957, he told the lower house of India's parliament, Lok Sabha: "We have declared quite clearly that we are not interested in making atom bombs, even if we have the capacity to do so, and that in no event will we use nuclear energy for destructive purposes." Did he have an uneasy premonition, when he added: "I hope that will be the policy of all future (Indian) governments?" The litmus test for his anti-nuclear-weapon commitment was, however, to come five years later, and he passed it.

The United States:
The Knight Advocating Nuclear Armor

IN 1962 came India's war with China. The country's military debacle marked a turning point in India's political life, giving a massive fillip to the hitherto rather minor force of the Right including its far segment represented by the Jan Sangh. Amidst a flurry of reports about a Chinese nuclear test round the corner, the Prime Minister came under tremendous pressure to opt for an Indian Bomb. He refused to cave in, and stuck to the stand until his death two years later.

The pressure, to which he was subjected, was not purely internal. Much of it was, in fact, proxy pressure, mounted on behalf of the U.S. This should have been no surprise, considering that 1962 was also the year of the Bay of Pigs, of the Cuban missile crisis that marked a nuclear high in the Cold War. The world, however, had to wait for the declassification in 1995 of a top-secret US government document of 1961 to be told about Washington's efforts to goad India into nuclear weaponization, even while talking no end about non-proliferation in international fora. Even today, many in South Asia, including those to whom Pokharan II was sold as a daring defiance of the U.S., have yet to hear the story.

The document, discussing "anticipatory action pending Chinese Communist demonstration of nuclear capability," examined the idea of providing active assistance in transferring nuclear-weapon technology to India and promoting the country as the Asian counterweight to a nuclear China. "While we would like to limit the number of nuclear powers, so long as we lack the capability to do so, we ought to prefer that the first Asian one be India and not China." Then US Ambassador John Kenneth Galbraith did not want to risk his relations with Nehru and his own progressive reputation by suggesting this to the Prime Minister. Alternative methods—including enlistment of Homi Bhabha's support for the cause of nuclear proliferation and, more important, a "covertly mounted informational campaign"—were considered and, in all probability and by all indications, adopted as well.

A pro-Bomb camp and campaign of covert sustenance took shape in India soon enough. Politically, the period saw the birth and growth of an overtly pro-US party, Swatantra, but its Gandhian founder C. Rajagopalachari would not back the Bomb option. It was left to the Jan Sangh and Vajpayee (whose "a bomb for a bomb" plea in a parliamentary debate has been noted before) to carry forward the composite campaign of an indirectly pro-US, explicitly anti-NAM, and effusively pro-Bomb camp. Nothing might have come out of these

US efforts in the early sixties, but at least some sections in India's political spectrum learnt not to expect Washington to stand seriously in the way of their nuclear ambitions for India.

The campaign did not succeed immediately, but the camp was nursed and enlarged over the next two decades. China conducted its first nuclear-weapon test in October 1964 about five months after Nehru's death. Bhabha reacted by claiming in a public speech that India could also do it in 18 months. But India chose not to do so for an entire decade, which witnessed a total of 15 Chinese nuclear tests. Even Pokharan I of 1974 was no response to an external security threat, either from China or Pakistan (still licking its wounds from the Bangladesh war), but to an internal challenge. The war had taken a heavy economic toll as well, and India was hardly equipped to deal with it. An unprecedented price rise led to a major political offensive, backed by an almost all-in Opposition unity, against Indira Gandhi and her government. Pokharan I was perhaps intended to create a major diversion, a moment and a mood that would reduce the relevance of the agitation drastically.

Pokharan I of 1974 elicited almost no internal opposition. Ironically, in retrospect, it was only then Socialist George Fernandes who protested against the testing. The rest of the Left accepted the official claim that it was a peaceful nuclear explosion (PNE).[2] The Jan Sangh and its fraternity were among the first to hail the event, though not in explicitly militarist terms. Pokharan I, too, however, failed to pay political dividends. The Opposition agitation acquired dimensions that drove the Indira government to declare an internal emergency in 1975. Two years later, the Jan Sangh was a junior partner in the first non-Congress coalition under an uncompromisingly anti-nuclear Gandhian, Morarji Desai. Pokharan II had to wait until the BJP, the offspring of the Sangh, became the dominant partner of another non-Congress coalition at the nation's helm.

But, what paved the way for Pokharan II was also the nation's adoption in 1974 of a posture of nuclear ambiguity. A series of official statements since Pokharan I, starting with Bhabha's in 1964, made it clear that the nuclear option was now an open one for India. While it allowed India to pursue traditional role in the international arena for universal nuclear disarmament, it also let preparations continue on ground for the country's next dangerous nuclear stride. Pokharan I, recalls Amartya Sen, was "followed by numerous affirmations of India's rejection of the nuclear path rather than any explicit savoring of the destructive powers of nuclear energy." But it also marked, points out Vanaik, a "descent into the abyss of nuclear-deterrence thinking" and "preparedness to visit mass destruction upon the people of a supposedly adversary state."

With the benefit of hindsight, it is clear that the perils and pitfalls of the policy of ambiguity were underestimated by many now on this side of the barricade. What also went almost unnoticed was the ambiguity of the response of the U.S. and its allies to Pokharan I. The ease with which the Indira government got away internationally with its explosion and explanation remains intriguing. Did the US strategic thinking reflected in the just discussed document of 1961 have anything to do with this? Will the answer have to wait for the declassification of another document in Washington's archives?

Pakistan's Chagai was, as we have seen, an answer to Pokharan II. President Bhutto, whom the Bangladesh war had put in power in 1971, was in no position to react to Pokharan I with a quick nuclear test in Pakistan. But, he had already initiated Pakistan's nuclear program (and prescribed a bovine diet for his people for the Bomb's sake), and the Indian test inspired him to march forward on his mission. Zia Mian records: "As President of West Pakistan, among his first acts was to set his more than willing scientists to work on reinventing the bomb's nearly 30-year-old technology. Newspapers of the day carried the headline, "Pride, Honour at all Costs to be Redeemed." But the bomb couldn't save him from the consequences of his failure to govern. Overthrown by Gen Zia's 1977 coup, Bhutto died claiming the Americans brought him down because he had tried to give Pakistan the bomb. Ever since, some have seen an American hand behind every move towards freeing Pakistan from the clutches of the bomb."

How different the truth was. As Mian explains, "Under Gen Zia (-ul-Haq), the bomb went underground. The military and the scientists worked quietly, while the Americans turned a blind eye. Pakistan's bomb was of lesser concern than the new Cold War and the need for a proxy in the war against the Soviets in Afghanistan. Eventually, with a little help from friends in China, the scientists finished their work and pushed for a nuclear test. But American economic and military aid was flowing fast. For billions of little green reasons, Pakistan's generals left the bomb in the closet."

In colder language, anti-nuclear scholar-activist Carey Sublette recounts the facts of the friendly role played by the U.S. in Pakistan's nuclear program: "In March 1979, US intelligence announced that the Kahuta uranium enrichment plant in Pakistan had been commissioned. On 4 April, the hard-line nature of Zia-ul-Haq's regime was emphasized when former Prime Minister Zulfikar Ali Bhutto was hanged. Finally, on 25 December, the Soviet Union invaded Afghanistan, ensuring that despite its nuclear weapons program Pakistan would be the beneficiary of a massive infusion of US weaponry, as well as US economic and diplomatic support. The possibility that the US would impose meaningful sanctions of any kind on Pakistan due its nuclear program became slim, then nil when the aggressively anti-Soviet Reagan administration came to power a year or so later."

Noting that China, too, "became involved at an early stage with the program," Sublette records: "During the late 70s and early 80s, a number of Pakistani agents were arrested trying to violate export control laws in the west. In November 1980 Albert Goldberg was arrested at a US airport while attempting to ship two tons of zirconium (useful for reactor construction) to Pakistan. Abdul Qadeer Khan (Father of Pakistan's bomb) attempted to order 6,000 maraging steel rotor tubes in 1983. In 1984 three Pakistani nationals (including one Nazir Vaid) were indicted in the US for attempting to smuggle out 50 krytrons (high-speed switches suitable for implosion detonation systems), and in 1987 the purchase of US maraging steel was attempted. Large quantities of materials were successfully purchased without being detected, including a German uranium hexafluoride manufacturing plant.

"Drawn to the limelight, the leader of Pakistan's uranium enrichment program A. Q. Khan held periodic interviews boasting about Pakistan's nuclear prowess. It was in such an interview in February 1984 that he first made the claim that Pakistan had achieved nuclear weapons capability." It was not, however, before two "dramatic changes" four years later that Washington deemed it prudent to display concern over the nuclear development. The first was the Soviet decision of February 1988 to withdraw its forces from Afghanistan, "a move that removed the geopolitical rationale for the US support for the Pakistani military regime, and the reluctance to pressure Pakistan on...its nuclear weapons program." The second change was the death of Zia-ul-Haq on August 17, 1988: he was killed along with 30 others, when the aircraft in which he was traveling crashed.

The military stepped aside and allowed the return of Pakistan to democracy three months later. In November 1988, Benazir Bhutto became the Prime Minister. The nuclear weapons complex remained in the hands of the military, which formed an independent center of power not under the control of the civilian government. Benazir was, according to Sublette, "unaware of the status of the nuclear program, and when Pakistan passed the milestone of manufacturing fissile cores for weapons, she first learned of it from the US Ambassador to Pakistan." The painstaking review leads Sublette to a clear conclusion: "Throughout the eighties, due to its strategic importance the US had been loath to pressure Pakistan on its nuclear weapons program. To avoid invoking sanctions against Pakistan, the Republicans in Congress had passed the Pressler Amendment, which stated that as long as the administration could certify that Pakistan had not acquired nuclear weapons no sanctions would be invoked.

To avoid triggering the Pressler Amendment a series of "red lines" had been drawn for various milestones, such as producing weapon grade uranium, converting it to metal, and fabricating a core." Under the Amendment, passed in 1985, certification that Pakistan did not possess a nuclear device was denied only once, two years after the Soviet withdrawal from Afghanistan.

An Arms Race Between Neighbors

MAY 1998 was a cruel month for the subcontinent. But worse was, inevitably, to follow on the nuclear weaponization front. In August 1999, in the immediate aftermath of the Kargil conflict, the government of India came out with a Draft Nuclear Doctrine (DND). At the time of its release, the government claimed to be presenting it for a public debate. In fact, however, it has not even been ever submitted to the Cabinet. It enjoys the status of a semi-official document. Nothing else brings out so unabashedly well the "big-nuclear-power" ambitions that went into Pokharan II. Nothing else provides a better idea of the nuclear arms race the region is likely to witness if no reversal of the program spelt out in this blueprint of bomb-based "defence" and "deterrence" takes place in time. Let us take a look at the DND, on the basis of its summary and critique by the New Delhi-based Movement in India for Nuclear Disarmament (MIND) and the all-India Coalition for Nuclear Disarmament and Peace (CNDP).

The objective of the DND, to begin with, is not just "minimum nuclear deterrence" but "credible minimum nuclear deterrence" and, as security experts have not failed to note, these are distinctly and vastly different concepts. The DND admits that its deterrence can fail, in which case India promises adequate punitive retaliation.

India's nuclear arsenal, says the DND, must be such that it will always provide the maximum credibility, effectiveness and survivability. Therefore, the size of the arsenal cannot be fixed but its nature must be dynamic and flexible enough to respond to changes in the security environment (such as changes in the weapons postures of perceived rivals), to changing security needs (as defined by state elites), and to technology advances.

The DND lays down that India's nuclear might must deter any state with nuclear weapons. Under it, India will pursue triadic deployment and have multiple redundant systems, that is, more than just a "bare minimum." India will not strike first but will carry out the promptest possible retaliation, which will also be punitive. This is described as retaliation massive enough to be "unacceptably damaging" to the opponent.

The nuclear arsenal will be tightly controlled by the political center, namely the Prime Minister, but will also be of a highly mobile and dispersed nature. The safety and security of the weapons system is of paramount importance, and all precautions will be taken to ensure against sabotage, theft and unauthorized or inadvertent use of nuclear weapons. The DND says nothing on how this is to be achieved or ensured.

The DND declares that India will not accept any restriction whatsoever on its research and development capabilities or activities in regard to nuclear weapons and related areas. India promises No-First-Use against nuclear weapons states and No-Use against non-nuclear weapons states except where the latter are aligned to nuclear weapons states. The DND delivers the punch line that

India will pursue arms control measures and the goal of complete, global disarmament, to which it proclaims the nation's commitment. The first thing noted by the Indian peace movement about the DND is that, contrary to the official claim at the time of its release; it is actually an attempt to do without a public debate on the nuclear weaponization program and policy. It does so by discussing not why India should "go nuclear" but what nuclear weapons it should have. The BJP-led government presented Pokharan II as a fait accompli, and the DND is presenting an Indian nuclear arsenal as one. The attempt also seemed to be one at deceiving the world opinion and claiming a "democratic" mandate for subsequent deployment of nuclear weapons.

Another basic objection is to the DND's statement that building a deterrent force is "consistent with the UN Charter, which sanctions the right of self-defense." This extension of the cover of the Charter to nuclear weapons is illegitimate, says the Movement in India for Nuclear Disarmament (MIND). This is especially so, given the ruling of the International Court of Justice (ICJ) which has rejected any such right in regard to nuclear weapons except in the case of the most "extreme circumstance of self-defense" on which it has given no ruling at all. Nuclear weapons are instruments of revenge or offense, not defense. In fact, in 1995, the Indian government had submitted its own memorandum to the ICJ insisting that the use of nuclear weapons, the threat of their use (deterrence), their development and preparations to build such weapons were immoral, illegal and unacceptable "in all circumstances"! This is a point to which the CNDP Charter had drawn the nation's attention earlier.

Yet another fundamental flaw in the DND, as peace campaigners see it, is the theory of "deterrence" itself. If nuclear weapons are utterly unreliable deterrents anywhere, they are even more so in the subcontinental context, where any India-Pakistan nuclear missile attack cannot take more than a maximum of ten minutes.

Coming to the specifics, the critique notes two statements in the DND—that "Indian nuclear weapons are to deter use and threat of use of nuclear weapons by any State or entity against India" and that "Any adversary must know that India can and will retaliate to inflict destruction that the aggressor will find unacceptable." These amount to assertion of a need for nuclear deterrence against almost anybody, including major nuclear weapons states, requiring a huge weapons system for "credible" second-strike capacity. "These stances effectively commit India to an arms race with the major nuclear weapons states—an economically, politically and socially suicidal policy."

The DND says there will be no use of nuclear weapons against non-nuclear states if they "are not aligned with nuclear weapons powers." The critique points out: "So Japan, for example, may not get an assurance of non-use, only of no-first-use (NFU). This ambiguity not only dilutes India's earlier NFU commitment but is more objectionable than, say, China's NFU commitment which specifically excludes use against any non-nuclear state regardless of whether or not it is allied to a nuclear state." This is clearly at variance with the section in the same document that says, "Having provided negative security assurances, India shall work for internationally binding negative security assurances by nuclear weapons states to non-nuclear weapons states."

The DND talks of "sequential plans," "flexibility and responsiveness," an "integrated operational plan" and "a targeting policy." "These," says the critique, "make sense only in relation to identified, actual opponents." In other words, it is a spurious claim that India's nuclear weapons are "not country-specific." In fact, talk of such plans and policies can only "vitiate India's immediate security environment," and cannot improve India-Pakistan relations.

The document dwells on triadic deployment and "sea-based assets, multiple redundant systems, mobility, dispersion and deception". It also stresses the objective of developing a capability of "maximum credibility, survivability, and effectiveness". The phrases themselves show that what is envisaged is a far from a minimum deterrent.

Triadic deployment by India will be against the trend among the nuclear powers. Britain has moved towards a single system of deployment (sea-based); France is following suit, and NATO in practice has no land-based deployment. The talk of "sea-based" rather than strictly submarine-based nuclear weapons also "leaves open the option of tactical nuclear missiles on surface vessels" and this suggests plans to go beyond defensive deterrence, says the MIND.

If the DND's idea of instant retaliation is to work, the deployed nuclear weapons should be capable of launch-on-warning, or launch-under-attack, or immediate launch-after-attack. In all these cases, the nuclear weapons system will need to be kept at a high level of operational alert and readiness, with regular training exercises for maintenance. Such a practice by itself is likely to prove provocative.

The insistence on continuous and uncontrolled research in nuclear weapons signals acceptance of "the inevitability of an arms race," and commits India to "enthusiastic participation in that doomed exercise," says the critique. It commits Pakistan, too, to participation in an unending race. It may also compel other countries of South Asia to choose sides in a conflict where the region itself may have doubtful chances of survival.

* * *

THE first question that may strike an Indian who is not a nuclear nationalist, or anyone who knows India, is where the money for the DND's dream is to come from. Not how much it will cost. To the common man, it may be common sense that it will cost more than what the impoverished country can afford. Expert estimates do nothing to prove the bomb poor-friendly.

It has always been difficult to estimate the costs of the invariably secrecy-shrouded nuclear weapon programs anywhere. It is particularly so in the case if a DND-based program, which leaves several important details to an Indian imagination fired by Pokharan II patriotism. The size of the arsenal to be built up under the program can only be speculated upon, taking into account the security threats the program is professedly intended to meet.

A realistic cost projection, even while avoiding an overestimate, cannot ignore the open-ended character of the vision. Space is the limit to the program, which rules out no feature of the state-of-art nuclear-weapon systems including satellite-based monitoring and damage prevention facilities. It needs to be remembered that the flip side of the no-first-use coin is a "second-strike capability": this is ensured by an arsenal so large that, if a first strike by an adversary destroys a considerable part of it, will suffice it to inflict retaliatory damage of an unacceptable order and kind.

The estimates must include the costs of delivery systems (including aircraft, missiles, and submarines) and command, control, communication and intelligence (C3I) systems. The delivery systems are generally assumed to account for about 50 per cent of the cost of a nuclear-weapon program, and C3I systems for about 33.33 per cent.

One of the first estimates came from economic journalist C. Rammanohar Reddy. He assumes a nuclear arsenal of 125-150 bombs, each of a 15-20-kilotonne capacity, comparable to the ones that destroyed Hiroshima and Nagasaki. This is based on former Chief of the Army Staff Gen. K. Sundarji's calculation that deterrence would demand the "ability to devastate five cities in Pakistan and ten in China, each with three bombs." The estimate also postulates a delivery system of 126 missiles tipped with nuclear warheads and a C3I system that will cover a wide swathe of the subcontinent.

Reddy's estimate was that, at the 2001 level of prices, "the total financial demands" of India's nuclear weaponization would be close to a minimum of RS. 400 to 500 billion over a 10-year period, or RS 40 to 50 billion a year. (About US $1 billion annually.) "This is no small amount. Going by the current figures, such annual costs will be equivalent to about 0.5 per cent of the GDP (gross domestic product) for 10 years running. They will consume five per cent of the central government's tax revenue every year and increase the total annual defense expenditure by at least 10 per cent."

Amartya Sen comments: "...half a percentage of the gross domestic product per year...might not sound like much but it is large enough if we consider the alternative use of these resources. For example, it has been estimated that the additional costs of providing elementary education for every child with neighborhood schools at every location in the country would roughly cost the same amount of money." He adds: "The proportion of illiteracy in the Indian adult population is still about 40 per cent, and it is about 55 per cent in Pakistan."

Reddy, too, points out: "The cost of each bomb is the same as that of 3,200 houses under the Indira Awas Yojana (Indira Housing Scheme). The cost of one Agni missile can finance the annual operation of 13,000 primary health centers. The cost of an arsenal of 150 bombs is the same as the central government funding of elementary education in 1998-99."

The main assumption behind this estimate, however, may be overoptimistic. A 150-bomb arsenal, it turns out, is too modest an ambition for the authors of the DND. Bharat Karnad, an influential member of the National Security Advisory Board that drafted the document, has in public suggested that a 400-bomb deterrence is envisaged, citing the Chinese arsenal of that size. With the magnitude of the deterrent force thus doubled, a minimum cost of RS 700 billion over a decade, officially indicated, may even be "a hopeless underestimate," as the MIND puts it.

Sen draws attention to the less noticed fact that "there are other costs and losses as well, such as the deflection of India's scientific talents to military-related research away from more productive lines of research, and also from actual economic production." He adds: "The prevalence of secretive military activities also restrains open discussions in Parliament and tends to subvert traditions of democracy and free speech."

An even more terrible loss is threatened by the facilely fascist translation of "cultural nationalism"—the BJP's mantra—into nuclear nationalism. The nuclear militarists have been trying to target and tarnish the memories and messages of two of the titans of Indian culture and nationalism. The code-name of Pokharan II was "Buddha Smiles Again," and that was a cruel joke to the "dalit" or "untouchable" Buddhists in Mumbai. It was the footage on their protest in Anand Patwardhan's film that has, however, been found obscene and objectionable. And, the Mahatma, who fell a martyr to a fascist bullet in 1948, died a second death when K. Subrahmanyam, convener of the National Security Council's advisory board, talked of "non-violent nuclear resistance" in theoretical defense of the most terrorist of weapons known to mankind.

The cost of a DND-triggered nuclear arms race would be even crueler for the people of Pakistan. As Bidwai and Vanaik point out: "Pakistan currently [in 1999 since when the situation has only worsened] spends about five per cent of its GDP [on military projects], more than it does on *all* development programs *put together*." Little wonder if, as Zia Mian notes, "the severity and growing sharpness of Pakistan's crises were enough to bring down the hero of Chagai, Sharif. On October 17, 1999, Gen Pervez Musharraf announced to the nation that the military had to take over to save the country. He said, 'There is despondency and hopelessness surrounding us with no light visible anywhere around.... We have reached a stage where

our economy has crumbled, our credibility is lost...'
Nowhere to be seen now was the nuclear state, once
resplendent in the glow of its greatest achievement."

* * *

THE price of Pokharan II and the sequel to it, as
scripted in the DND, may appear unduly high to the man
in the street. Not so, however, to the elite and the establishment. As they saw it and tried to sell it, it was a price
paid for an eminently purchase-worthy world status. This
was evident even on the morrow of the tests of May 1998,
as I found while reviewing the responses to the blasts in a
section of the English-language press for a publication
titled *The Media Bomb*.

The review ("The Climber's Case") records: "The
theme [of Pokharan II as 'a point of departure'] was
enlarged and embellished by dwelling on the departure in
respect to one particular detail: India vis-à-vis the Third
World. Of the many strands woven into the pro-Pokharan
fabric, none testified more to skill of a cynical kind. It was
a two-phased tactic: First, damn the Third World; second,
damn the anti-nuclear-weapon campaign by identifying it
with the Third World. Opponents of Pokharan thus
became pleaders for perpetuating India's place among the
wretched of the earth writhing under despots and its membership of the club of the world's poor."

"Conversely," the review notes, "Pokharan was projected as a passport to a higher world status. It spelt something like an upward national mobility. Join the nuclear
club, and you will jump straight out of the Third World—
that was the mantra of this media. Never mind about the
state of the nation's economy, especially the majority of its

people. And, who cared about the fate of the erstwhile fraternity of the destitute, with whom we ceased to have anything in common that historic moment of last May?"

There are samples of the pro-Pokharan II press that can still be savored. Here is the editor-in-chief of the *Indian Express* (May 27, 1998) warning New Delhi against seeking support in the Third World: "...only to an inferiorly complexed mind steeped in Nehruvian hypocrisy would a Third World bomb sound like a sexy new idea. Poor nations acquire nukes to find a short cut out of the Third World. At least that's what we have been told over the decades by the pro-bomb lobby. Here we want to use ours to confirm our status as the leader of the world's wretched."

Interestingly, the Comprehensive Test Ban Treaty (CTBT), which the bulk of the world peace movement has been backing, became the cause of the elite section of the Pokharan II camp. New Delhi was advised to sign the treaty without further ado—as no further explosive testing was considered necessary to make India a nuclear-weapon state—and enter the nuclear club. Arguing this, another article in the same paper carried the "Third World"-bashing to a new level of crudity: "...why should the country continue to cry itself hoarse that the CTBT is discriminatory? The treaty certainly does not enable, say Togo, to conduct nuclear experiments, so in that sense it does discriminate against that paragon of non-alignment. But then Togo has not conducted nuclear experiments, and so it does not have the wherewithal to continue the testing programme using supercomputers and micro-nukes. Is that something with which India should be exercised to an order so as to label probably the most comprehensive

international nuclear arrangement as discriminatory?...
On this score, India has always been isolated by this
delightful club of the destitute."

There was little doubt left about enthusiastic official
endorsement of this view. After talks in Tokyo in
November 1999 with then Japanese Prime Minister Keio
Obuchi, for example, then India's Foreign Minister
Jaswant Singh announced that "India's declaration of a
voluntary moratorium on further nuclear testing amount-
ed to a de facto acceptance of the CTBT." Nor was this a
clever attempt to avoid a de jure acceptance of the treaty.
Singh was also reported to have assured Obuchi that New
Delhi was "trying to build a domestic consensus in favour
of the CTBT."

As part of the consensus-building (and on the eve of
Singh's Tokyo visit), leading media campaigner for nuclear
weaponization and strategic analyst Raja Mohan presented a strikingly similar tests-and-treaty perspective:
"Having boldly transformed India into a nuclear-weapon
power, successfully reversed the Pakistani aggression across
the Line of Control, and gained world support for the
restraint in the conduct of the Kargil operations, Mr.
Vajpayee now has a huge opportunity to put the nation on
the path of a confident global engagement.... Immediately
after the nuclear tests, India outlined the broad parameters
of its approach to nuclear weapons. These included a
restrained nuclear posture and a readiness to join global
arms control regimes, including the Comprehensive Test
Ban Treaty."

This was eventually followed by Vajpayee himself
proposing in the United Nations General Assembly a
deadline for the signing of the treaty. All that is history

now, of course, after the advent of George Bush's Presidency in the U.S. and the consignment of the CTBT to virtual oblivion. But, the Pokharan II-CTBT paradigm, sought to be built in those days, made an important point about the international political outlook of the nuclear nationalists. The object of their ardent desire, from the outset, was the status for India as a nuclear-weapon state as well as a satellite. Despite appearances to the contrary, they were confident that Pokharan II would lead to a closer India-US partnership.

That brings us to a curious theory about the US non-detection of the desert tests that we had reserved for the end of the chapter. South Asia specialist Ranjan Goswami, quoted before, raises the question and answers it thus: "One aspect of the tests is striking: the US did not detect India's tests until after they occurred, whereas, in 1994, when Indian Prime Minister (P. V.) Narasimha Rao ordered nuclear testing at the Pokharan test site, US detections of movement at the test site were leaked to the press, forcing India to cancel the tests. Could this be the US tacit sign to New Delhi that the US desires rapprochement with India and that a nuclear-capable India will be condoned for a variety of reasons—one being to counter China? Could it be that India, after having forced Pakistan into detonating its own devices, has given the US a reason to distance itself from the Muslim nation?" Could it also be that such thoughts crossed the mind of the Indian leaders, circa 1998-99? And could it be that they were not unduly wide of the mark?

CHAPTER 6

THE CANKER WITHIN

Fascism Threatens to Light the Nuclear Flame

They take the Christians to be the cause of every disaster to the state, of every misfortune to the people. If the Tiber reaches the wall, if the Nile does not reach the fields, if the sky does not move or if the earth does, if there is a famine, or if there is a plague, the cry is at once, "The Christians to the Lions."

> —Tertullian, Latin polemicist, on a primitive prototype of fascism, third century A.D.

It has been the tragic lesson of the history of many a country that the hostile elements within the country pose a far greater menace to national security than aggressors from outside.

> —"Guru" Golwalkar of the RSS, arguing by implication for a civil war in India, in "A Bunch of Thoughts" (1966)

What Gujarat witnessed [in 2002] was not a riot, but a terrorist attack followed by a systematic, planned massacre, a pogrom. Everyone spoke of the pillage and plunder, being organized like a military operation against an external armed enemy.

> —Harsh Mander Report, "Cry, the beloved country"

Pakistan will not listen just like that. We have a centuries-old debt to settle with this mindset. It is the same demon that has been throwing a challenge at Durga since the time of Mohammed Bin Qasim. Arise, Atal Behari! Who knows if fate has destined you to be the author of the final chapter of this long story. For what have we manufactured bombs? For what have we exercised the nuclear option?

—RSS organ in Hindi, Panchajanya, during
the Kargil conflict, June 29, 1999

"Allah-u-Akbar (Allah is great), Five tests of Islamic Bomb."

—One of the many similar headlines on the
morrow of Chagai in Pakistan's Urdu press,
quoted by journalist Zaffarullah Khan,
"Glorification of Nuclear Nationalism in the
Re-Awakened State!"

It is one factor behind the emergence of the South Asian flashpoint, about which the outside world is truly fuzzy. It is one, in fact, that is not internally recognized, either, for quite the role it has played in bringing the region to the brink of a nuclear end. Neither Pokharan II nor Chagai, nor the standoff of the summer of 2002 would have been possible without the fascism that fuelled it all. The ideology and outlook of religious communalism, which has inspired and influenced so much of sub-continental politics, is not unknown to the region-watchers. Of course, it is something that the constituencies wooed by this communalism are only too familiar with, though the familiarity has not bred contempt enough for its brutalizing politics. Neither within nor without, however, has the phenomenon been seen widely enough for the force it has proved to be.

Fascism has generally been seen, by both outsiders and South Asians including political observers, as foreign to the region. To outsiders, militarism has appeared incompatible with the majoritarian communalism, especially in India, one of the few developing countries not to have fallen to local Fuhrers. It has been difficult to see Hitlers and Mussolinis in dhoti-clad politicians. The politics of promoting religious sectarianism and strife has appeared funny rather than frightening. It has appeared to have more to do with backwardness than with big-power ambitions. Inside the subcontinent, the "it-can't-happen-here" assumption has created for many a comfort zone, which no nuclear shadow crossed even at the height of the standoff.

What many have forgotten is that Western fascism of the thirties and forties, too, found a parliamentary route to power before baring its militarist claws fully. Also forgotten was the fact that the first war of fascism was on the "internal enemy," a national minority projected as the main adversary of the majority, and that its "final solution" consisted in the elimination of this enemy by a combined use of street mobs and state-sponsored storm-troopers, besides concentration camps.

It is no longer, however, merely a theoretical possibility that this can happen in the subcontinent. Not after what happened in India's border-state of Gujarat, the home of Mahatma Gandhi, during the same summer of the standoff. Those were months when there was an organized, ruthless attempt to make an Indian "majority" believe that theirs was a war against an internal "minority" and an external enemy together. Independent India had witnessed several Hindu-Muslim riots before, but this was different. To many, it came as a revelation: of an anti-people, anti-peace force that had been allowed to grow unnoticed in Gujarat, and possibly elsewhere.

It all started in a wayside railway station in Gujarat on February 27, 2002. Violent tragedy struck the Sabarmati Express, which stopped at Godhra on its way from Ayodhya in the State of Uttar Pradesh. The train was carrying quite a few "kar sevaks," free-labor volunteers, of the Ayodhya movement. It was the same movement then spearheaded by present Deputy Prime Minister L. K. Advani that had led to a mob demolition of the Babri Mosque in the town of Ayodhya in 1992. The movement's aim was restoration of a temple of Hindu deity Ram at Ayodhya, His birthplace: first Moghul emperor Babur is alleged (without undue fuss over historical evidence) to have raised the mosque over the ruins of the temple.[1] The movement was revived, again, during the India-Pakistan standoff. The "kar sevaks" on the train were one of the many batches that had carried ritually sanctified bricks for the temple-building to Ayodhya and returning to Gujarat in religious-triumphal fervor.

The instant version of the tragedy, as spread through rumors and unquestioning official reports, was clearly intended to trigger off a response of mob violence. Without waiting for more facts to come out, as is the normal practice, the local media hastened to tell the country that a horrendous minority crime had been committed against the majority. The train was said to have been surrounded by a stone throwing Muslim mob at Godhra railway station with a sizeable Muslim minority population. In a matter of minutes, it was reported, the mob poured cans of kerosene on a compartment carrying "kar sevaks" and set it on fire. About 60 occupants of the compartment, including women and children, were alleged to have been burnt alive.

Crucial parts of this version, evidently intended to inflame religious-communal passions, were to be proved false. The official forensic report, for example, was reported much later to have revealed that the compartment was set on fire from inside, though the original story was that the "kar sevaks" had shut and bolted its doors to bar entry by the mob. The forensic report was not officially released, but was obtained by independent media through other means. A team of independent investigators, for another example, found six months later that many of those reported burnt to death were still alive, that only four of those killed were "kar sevaks," and that the women and children charred to death were among the poor passengers to have packed the compartment as happens on almost every train in India.

In its orchestrated pretense at outrage, the "parivar," the "family" of the far Right with the BJP as its political front, tried to make it appear that Godhra was the first incident of communal violence in the recent phase. The role of the renewed Ayodhya movement in reviving serious Hindu-Muslim tensions and threatening a fresh outbreak of riots was not even mentioned. It, however, is a critical factor in understanding the tensions.

Advani's "rath-yatra," "chariot ride," to Ayodhya, a decade earlier, had left a bloody trail of Hindu-Muslim clashes across the country, with the minority bearing the brunt of it all. The "chariot ride" consisted of a journey to Ayodhya by a bedecked automobile across the country, reminding the Hindus of an alleged wrong and challenging the Muslims to stop the displacement, if not demolition, of the mosque. The resumption of the movement a decade later now was enough to revive those memories and, consequently, grave misgivings in the mind of the people, especially the Muslims. By all accounts, the conduct of the "kar sevaks" as they criss-crossed the country in virtually commandeered trains was not calculated to promote communal amity. Eyewitnesses have talked at length about their provocations to the Muslims on their way—a favorite one consisted in forcing the latter to join in shouting the Hindu religious slogan "Jai Shri Ram." At Godhra itself, they had teased and taunted the Muslims, pulling their beards and, in one case, pulling a woman from the platform into the compartment.

None of this, of course, would have justified the arson. Not one opponent of the Ayodhya movement said it did. The entire far Right and its friends, however, were soon to claim that Godhra justified the massacre that followed all over Gujarat. "Who started it?" was the refrain of the top leaders of the BJP heading the country's ruling coalition. If the party and the "parivar" had been using Gujarat as a "laboratory of 'Hindutva' (Hinduhood)", or a movement of religious chauvinism, chief minister of Gujarat Narendra Modi brushed up his physics to declare: "Every action has an equal and opposite reaction."

Even assuming that there was a minority action, what followed was hardly an equal reaction. For about four months since February 28, the state under the single-party rule of the BJP chief minister was handed over to the self-proclaimed, murderous hordes of "Hindutva" (Hinduhood). These included, besides the RSS, the Vishwa Hindu Parishad or the VHP (the World Hindu Assembly) and the Bajrang Dal (Party of Bajrang, the Monkey God closely associated with Ram). The ensuing massacre claimed an estimated toll of 3,000, mostly Muslims. There is no reliable count of the women victims of unspeakable gender crimes. The crippling economic blow dealt to the minority community is also yet to be quantified.

"Mob violence" may be a misleading description, in an important respect, of the extended tragedy that eclipsed Godhra. The perpetrators of the violence may have constituted a mob in their lawlessness, but not one in the sense of being unorganized. What demands notice, above all, is the kind of organization as well as ideological outlook behind the carnage. Features of classical fascism are writ large all over an internal war of India as reported by sensitive observers.

* * *

THE most anguished as well as agonizing account of the fratricidal fury was forthcoming from a conscientious officer of the Indian Administrative Service (IAS), who resigned in protest against the abuse of the state apparatus as an instrument of majoritarian oppression. Harsh Mander's report, titled "Cry, the beloved country" (taking its title from the famous novel by Alan Paton set in South Africa in the forties), the first to bring out the fascist essence of the violence unleashed in Gujarat, deserves to be quoted extensively.

"Numbed with disgust and horror," wrote Mander, "I return from Gujarat ten days after the terror and massacre that convulsed the state. My heart is sickened, my soul wearied, my shoulders aching with the burdens of guilt and shame. As you walk through the camps of riot survivors in Ahmedabad, in which an estimated 53,000 women, men, and children are bundled in 29 temporary settlements, displays of overt grief are unusual. People clutch small bundles of relief materials, all that they now own in the world, with dry and glassy eyes. Some talk in low voices, others busy themselves with the tasks of everyday living in these most basic of shelters, looking for food and milk for children, tending the wounds of the injured. But once you sit anywhere in these camps, people begin to speak and their words are like masses of pus released by slitting large festering wounds. The horrors that they speak of are so macabre, that my pen falters in the writing. The pitiless brutality against women and small children by organized bands of armed young men is more savage than anything witnessed in the riots that have shamed this nation from time to time during the past century."

Samples of the savagery: "What can you say about a woman eight months pregnant who begged to be spared? Her assailants instead slit open her stomach, pulled out her fetus and slaughtered it before her eyes. What can you say about a family of nineteen being killed by flooding their house with water and then electrocuting them with high-tension electricity?"

Mander added: "What can you say? A small boy of six in Juhapara camp described how his mother and six brothers and sisters were battered to death before his eyes. He survived only because he fell unconscious, and was taken for dead. A family escaping from Naroda-Patiya, one of the worst-hit settlements in Ahmedabad, spoke of losing a young woman and her three month old son, because a police constable directed her to 'safety' and she found herself instead surrounded by a mob which doused her with kerosene and set her and her baby on fire."

Talking of the gender crimes, Mander said: "I have

never known a riot which has used the sexual subjugation of women so widely as an instrument of violence in the recent mass barbarity in Gujarat. There are reports everywhere of gang rape, of young girls and women, often in the presence of members of their families, followed by their murder by burning alive, or by bludgeoning with a hammer and in one case with a screwdriver. Women in the Aman Chowk shelter told appalling stories about how armed men disrobed themselves in front of a group of terrified women to cower them down further."

The report went on to make an important point and to illustrate it: "In Ahmedabad, most people I met—social workers, journalists, survivors—agree that what Gujarat witnessed was not a riot, but a terrorist attack followed by a systematic, planned massacre, a pogrom. Everyone spoke of the pillage and plunder, being organized like a military operation against an external armed enemy. An initial truck would arrive broadcasting inflammatory slogans, soon followed by more trucks which disgorged young men, mostly in khaki shorts and saffron sashes, they were armed with sophisticated explosive materials, country weapons, daggers and *trishuls* (tridents), they also carried water bottled to sustain them in their exertions. The leaders were seen communicating on mobile telephones from the riot venues, receiving instructions from and reporting back to a coordinating center. Some were seen with documents and computer sheets listing Muslim families and their properties. They had detailed precise knowledge about buildings and businesses held by members of the minority community, such as who were partners say in a restaurant business, or which Muslim homes had Hindu spouses who should be spared in the violence..."

The report added: "The trucks carried quantities of (liquefied petroleum) gas (or cooking gas) cylinders. Rich Muslim homes and business establishments were first systematically looted, stripped down of all their valuables, then cooking gas was released from cylinders into the buildings for several minutes. A trained member of the group then lit the flame, which efficiently engulfed the building. In some cases, acetylene gas, which is used for welding steel, was employed to explode large concrete buildings."

"Mosque and 'dargahs' (Muslim shrines) were razed, and were replaced by statues of Hanuman (Monkey God) and saffron flags. Some 'dargahs' at the Ahmedabad city crossings have overnight been demolished and their sites covered with road-building material, and bulldozed so efficiently that these spots are indistinguishable from the rest of the road. Traffic now plies over these former 'dargahs', as though they never existed."

The officer knew what he was talking about, when he wrote: "The unconscionable failures and active connivance of the state police and administrative machinery is also now widely acknowledged. The police are known to have misguided people straight into the hands of rioting mobs. They provided protective shields to crowds bent on pillage, arson, rape and murder, and were deaf to the pleas of the desperate Muslim victims, many of them women and children. There have been many reports of police firing directly mostly at the minority community, which was the target of most of the mob violence. The large majority of arrests are also from the same community which was the main victim of the pogrom."

The report noted that "the camps for the Muslim riot

victims in Ahmedabad are being run almost exclusively by Muslim organizations. It is as though the monumental pain, loss, betrayal and injustice suffered by the Muslim people were the concern only of other Muslim people, and the rest of us have no share in the responsibility to assuage, to heal and rebuild. The state, which bears the primary responsibility to extend both protection and relief to its vulnerable citizens, was nowhere in evidence in any of the camps, to mange, organize the security, or even to provide the resources that are required to feed the tens of thousands of defenseless women, men and children huddled in these camps for safety."

"There are no voices like Gandhi's that we hear today," mourned Mander. "Only discourses on Newtonian physics, to justify vengeance on innocents." The allusion was, of course, to Modi who remained unfazed and went on to make things worse, as we shall see.

Several other non-official investigations have added to evidence that the massacre was a cold-bloodedly planned pogrom. It has been noted, for instance, that Godhra was not immediately and spontaneously followed by the statewide bloodbath. There was a lapse of about 24 hours, during which the VHP held at least two meetings. One of these decided on an Ahmedabad "bandh" (shutdown) on February 28, which served as a green signal for the grisly riots. The second, on the morning of February 28, according to an unabashed VHP itself, prepared the lists that Mander and others saw the "Hindutva" storm troopers using on their missions of selective pillage and murder. The "riots" then broke out all over the state as though at a cue or a command.

These lists Mander describes came from a database

containing the names of tens of thousands of Muslim properties and residences. The important point that their existence proves is that they could not have been created in just one foul morning of fascist plotting. Nor could the logistics of the operation—carried out by cadre armed with thousands of cooking gas cylinders (then in acutely short supply in Ahmedabad) in hundreds of three-wheel "autos" and vans—have been put in place without planning and preparations of weeks.

The preparations for the pogrom had been, in fact, much longer. For at least five years before the grisliest riots of Gujarat, the fascist program of pitting the people against one another and vilifying a vulnerable community had been under way. The program had been carried to the point of an unofficial Partition inside Ahmedabad and other cities: boards saying "Welcome to Hindu Rashtra (Hindu Nation)" had started appearing in different part of the cities and, more menacingly, barbed-wire "borders" of India around Muslim residential areas. Driving these "foreigners" out of the "Hindu Rashtra" was being talked about as the "final solution."

An idea of the hate campaign and what it meant to the minority is provided by an "economic boycott" of the Muslims which the VHP had called for, and even been able to enforce in many places. A leaflet, widely distributed all over the state, captures the fascist flavor of the campaign in its language (originally Gujarati):

> "Save the country! Save the religion!
> "Economic boycott is the only solution! The anti-national elements use the money earned from the Hindus to destroy us! They buy arms! They molest our sisters and daughters! The way to break the backbone of these ele-

ments is: An economic non-cooperation movement. Let us resolve—From now on:

"i I will not buy anything from a Muslim shopkeeper!

"ii I will not sell anything from my shop to such elements!

"iii Neither shall I use the hotels of these anti-nationals, nor their garages!

"iv I shall give my vehicles only to Hindu garages! From a needle to gold, I shall not buy anything made by Muslims, neither shall we sell them things made by us!

"v Boycott wholeheartedly films in which Muslim hero-heroines act! Throw out films produced by these anti-nationals!

"vi Never work in offices of Muslims! Do not hire them!

"vii Do not let them buy offices in our business premises, nor sell or hire out houses to them in our housing societies, colonies or communities.

"viii I shall certainly vote, only for him who will protect the Hindu nation.

"ix I shall be alert to ensure that our sisters-daughters do not fall into the 'love-trap' of Muslim boys at school-college- workplace.

"x I shall not receive any education or training from a Muslim teacher.

"Such a strict economic boycott will throttle these elements! It will break their backbones! Then it will be difficult for them to live in any corner of this country. Friends, begin this economic boycott from today! Then no Muslim will raise his head before us! ..."[2]

The boycott was not to be merely economic, and fascism recognizes no personal freedom. Says another leaflet: "....With the intention of deceiving and defrauding Hindu girls studying in schools and colleges, they (Muslims) adopt Hindu names such as Raju, Pintu, Rajan,

Montu, and Chintu. This is a sinister design, which is well planned and well organized. It is happening in every village and city.... Hindus, wake up! If you want to save your sisters and daughters and if you want to save Gujarat and the rest of India from becoming Kashmir then, from today onwards, keep a watch on your girls and see that they don't keep any sort of relationship with Muslims. The Hindu boys studying in the college could save the Hindu girls from the clutches of the Muslim toughs either by themselves or with the help of a Hindu organization."

This sounds like a joke, but did not sound like one to Hindu girls and Muslim boys punished (through public humiliation, social ostracism and so on) by "people's" courts in the towns of Gujarat. When newspaper stories of this kind came out a couple of years ago, they occasioned laughter at what was widely seen as the lunatic fringe of the BJP camp. Few saw the fringe coming to occupy the center-stage, few anticipated the shattering socio-political consequences of the "cultural nationalism" that the entire Sangh camp swore by.

The state machinery of Gujarat was a participant in the riots, but the central government was not a disapproving onlooker. It could not remain one when the top BJP leadership stood by Modi, as he stood by the rioters. The sympathies of his regime were made clear in several ways: all the arrests in Godhra after the train-burning incident were made under a post-September law against terrorism, and none under it in connection with the wider Gujarat conflagration; the victims of Godhra were given twice the governmental compensation as those of the state-wide sequel; all the police officers caught acting in protection of the minority community were promptly served penal transfer orders. The party leaders parroted Modi's version that Godhra was a plot, whereas the Gujarat disturbances were a "spontaneous" eruption of Hindu wrath. Putting it in other words, Advani said that what happened in Godhra was "terrorism" and that what Gujarat witnessed was only "communalism."

Right in the middle of the riots, it was revealed that Modi and the BJP in Gujarat were planning to advance the state-level Assembly elections, due over a year later, to reap and rake in a rich harvest of communal-Hindu votes. The implication of the success of such a strategy was truly frightening. If adopted as a vote-getting method everywhere, it could make riots before every election in any state a predictable far-Right refrain. The attempt elicited fierce opposition, even from the Muslim minority group inside the BJP, but the party leadership again stood four square by its favorite chief minister. Advani declared in Parliament that, since the Opposition had questioned Modi's moral right to stay in power, the latter was going to the "people"—who, obviously, did not include the minority.

Little doubt was left that Modi's was not just "fascism in one state" after he received two more testimonials. The first of these came from the RSS, the BJP guru and the power behind the thrones in New Delhi as well as Ahmedabad. In a statement, the RSS condemned Godhra, regretted the Gujarat riots as an inevitable reaction, and told the minority: "The Muslims should realize that their safety lies in the goodwill of the majority." The terrified Muslims of Gujarat could not have missed the threat in the message.

The second testimonial to Modi came from the country's highest executive office. Prime Minister Vajpayee is painted by the media as a "moderate" in the party and "parivar" ("family") of minority-bashers. But regardless of his image, he seized the occasion of a high-level BJP meeting to harangue not the perpetrators of the violence but the helpless victims of Gujarat. "They (the Muslims) don't want to live in friendship with their neighbors", he was reported as complaining, and the corollary was clear that the victims had asked for the riots. Those who had seen Vajpayee only in his prime ministerial avatar may have been surprised, but not others who had known him as a rabble-rouser and even when he was a politer parliamentarian of the Jan Sangh (the BJP's parent) decades ago. Gujarat had emboldened the otherwise heavily circumscribed and handicapped coalition head in New Delhi to go back to his "Hindutva" roots for once.

Political commentator Rajdeep Sardesai picked a parallel performance from the Prime Minister's long past in Parliament. It was 1970, and then Opposition leader Vajpayee was speaking on the Hindu-Muslim riots that had just rocked Bhiwandi in Maharashtra. "Whatever the reason," he said, "our Muslim brethren are getting more and more communal, and as a reaction Hindus are getting more and more aggressive. Nobody made the Hindus aggressive. If you want to give the credit for this to us, we are willing to take it. But Hindus will no more take a beating in this country. Hindus will not start, Hindus will not initiate. If you promote Muslim communalism, the other feeling will run high…" Modi could have spoken these lines about Godhra and Gujarat.

Vajpayee of 1970 went on with his shocking analysis: "The question is, why are riots started?…. Some Muslims start the riot—knowing they may lose life and property. One reason could be that our Muslim brethren have concluded that now there is no place for them to live in India, no guardian for them, so it is better to die fighting than to live. Another reason may be that some Muslims are connected with Pakistan and indulge in rioting at Pakistan's behest. Pakistan wants to tarnish our image. Hindus are being driven out of Pakistan. If atrocities are committed on Muslims in India, Pakistan would get the opportunity of making propaganda against India. The third and most important reason seems to be that some Muslim leaders do not want Muslims to merge with the national mainstream." The link with Vajpayee of 2002 is clear in that last line.

He went ahead to ask the question that he and his flock never fail to ask on such occasions: "I agree the feeling of revenge is not good. We cannot allow any individual to take the law in his hands. But will this rule apply only to Hindus? Will it not apply to Muslims?" Comments Sardesai: "This argument of discriminatory politics has always been the crux of the Hindutva secular, pseudo-secular divide and the basis of the sangh parivar's propaganda. It didn't start with L. K. Advani and his rath-yatra, although the home minister has come to represent the ideological heart of Hindutva. Vajpayee, too, has always been a torchbearer of the same legacy. The difference is that whereas in 1970 he was an articulate opposition Jan Sangh MP who could wear his Hindutva badge on his waistcoat, today he is the prime minister of a rag-tag coalition which has to pay lip-service to the constitution."

The "Hindutva laboratory" of Gujarat had witnessed experiments earlier on the Christian minority as well— and with similar support from the party in power in the state and at the centre and the Prime Minister. There was another parallel, too. The country was shocked by the

eruption of anti-Christian violence in same Gujarat's trib-
al belt of Dangs on Christmas day, December 25, in 1998.
It later turned out, however, that the campaign (by the
VHP and the Bajrang Dal and a newly formed Hindu
Jagran Manch or Hindu Awakening Forum) against
Christian missionaries, mostly from the southern state of
Kerala, and converted tribesmen had been growing since
November 1997.

An independent investigation team led by former
Bombay High Court judge S. Suresh found that the
Christmas attacks on a large number of churches and missionary institutions, many of which were burnt down, bore
all the marks of meticulous planning. The "Hindutva"
activists allegedly descended in hordes on several villages
around the same time—between 7 and 8 p.m.—to indulge
in similar acts of vandalism.

Assaults had been made on priests and nuns for over
a year. These were accompanied by a vicious propaganda
through leaflets, portraying the missionaries as traitors and
thieves. The leaflets also urged Christian tribesmen to
"purify yourself through 'yagna' (ritual sacrifice) and
become a Hindu." They were warned of dire consequences, if they paid no heed to the "Hindutva" counsel.

In the towns and cities, meanwhile, a mendacious
campaign was launched against education imparted by
Christian missionaries. A widely distributed pamphlet said:
"Friends, we Hindus keep awake day and night and earn
our living through our hard work. But do we ever think
about the education of our children? With the intention of
giving them the best educations you get them admitted in
schools such as St. Xavier's and St. Anne's and consider it
prestigious. In fact, this is the biggest mistake of your life."

The reasoning was stark: "In order to make the Hindus forget their religion, the Christian schools inject the tenets of Christian religion into the tender minds of the students right from their childhood. On account of your irresponsibility and the Christian education influenced by the Christian tradition, when your child becomes a youth, he or she is already a half-Christian." This is a lie that tens of thousands of non-Christians educated in these institutions can nail. But the campaign, which combines xenophobia with communalism, has continued.

So has the "Ghar Vapsi" (Homecoming) program of the "parivar" outfits in a wide tribal belt, extending far beyond Gujarat. According to Christian organizations, the program aimed at re-conversion of tribal Christians to Hinduism is violent and coercive. There is no need to doubt their word. That is how a "Hindutva" propagandist, Nagendra Rao, himself describes the program in one of his Internet declamations:

"If Muslims and Christians use perfidy and force in conversion, as they frequently do," says Rao, "[we have to meet it] with merciless ferocity and militant determination…. Collateral damage in such cases is regrettable and cannot be condoned. However, let not the Hindus continue to beat their breasts until the end of Kali Yuga (the current epoch in Hindu cosmology) about it. If necessary, let us face Armageddon keeping in mind the more militant verses of the Bhagavad Gita of Sri Krishna. It is the duty of the Khatrey (one of the warrior caste) to be merciless in avenging injustice, even to the point of slaughtering one's uncles, grandfathers, cousins… (as happens in the fratricidal war of epic *Mahabharata*)."

Adds Rao: "A time comes when Hindu Rashtra needs

to stand up and be ready for the final answer. 'Vijaya prapti na tu virgati'—victory or martyrdom. We Hindus have been turned into eunuchs or lambs for the slaughter because of the totally misguided 'ahimsa' (non-violence) bleatings of Gandhi, and the secularism rantings of Nehru. ...Gandhi's and Nehru's heritage has to be washed away...before real Hindu Dharma (religion) rises again like the phoenix from the flames. Honor, duty, tolerance, ecumenism which characterize Sanatana Dharma (Ancient Religion) are all in danger of being swept away.... We have to deliver the only message that militant Islam and jingoistic Christianity understand—ruthless, unwavering force..."

The Vajpayee response to the black Christmas in Dangs was true to type. He told the media in New Delhi that it was all "shameful." He announced his plan for an on-the-spot assessment of the situation. One visit to the laboratory of combustible hate, and he was not abashed any more. Now, he had a different line for the media: "There is need for a national debate on conversions." Many saw in that statement a green signal for further and more ferocious attacks on Christians, a crucial extra bit of encouragement for the killers of Graham Staines. In January 1999, this Baptist missionary (serving lepers in the eastern state of Orissa) was killed along with his sons Philip (10) and Timothy (6), burnt alive in a jeep while sleeping in it.[3]

A very similar message was sent out by the unconcealed support from the BJP's national leadership and the party-led central government for the pogrom against Muslims. On September 3, 2002, VHP leader Ashok Singhal termed Gujarat a "successful experiment"—and warned that it would be "repeated all over India." He was reported as saying: "Godhra happened on February 27 and the next day, 50 lakh (five million) Hindus were on the streets. We were successful in our experiment of raising Hindu consciousness, which will be repeated all over the country now."

Singhal also spoke glowingly of how whole villages had been "emptied of Islam," and how whole communities of Muslims had been dispatched to refugee camps. This was a victory for Hindu society, he added, a first for the religion. "People say I praise Gujarat. Yes, I do."

The end of the riots was only a new beginning in Gujarat for politics of a no-holds-barred "Hindutva." Modi became, if not a Mahatma, at least a Chhote Sardar (Little Sardar), after Sardar Vallabhbhai Patel, Deputy Prime Minister under Nehru. Patel, the "Iron Man" of Gujarat, was considered less soft on Pakistan than Gandhi and Nehru.[4] Modi took out a "gaurav yatra" or "a pilgrimage of pride," during which he made a series of speeches aimed at keeping communal tensions alive and the Muslims in terror. It was clear that Gujarat was past the point of easy or early return to normal relations between the two communities. Even more noteworthy, however, was the fact that the Gujarat riots marked a new political low for the nation, with state-aided fascism gaining some legitimacy.

* * *

ALL this was a development that had taken place over a decade or so. Until the end of the eighties, the camp of "Hindutva" appeared a curious self-contradiction. It claimed to speak for the country's majority, but actually seemed to represent anything but the political mainstream: so poor was its representation in Parliament and state legislatures. It talked more of India's tradition than any other party, but it set itself against the most conspicuous tenets of what, till its advance to the threshold of power, was seen widely as a "national consensus." The country's heartland was considered its natural habitat, but it remained peripheral politics all the same. How exactly did the transformation take place?

The question was asked in a startled world of scholarship as well. Thomas Blom Hansen, a keen student of contemporary India, poses the question thus: "....Is Hindu nationalism really revealing the dark side of the middle class culture and social world of the 'educated sections' who have dominated Indian public culture and the Indian state for so long—the authoritarian longings, the complacency, and the fear of the 'underdog', the 'masses', and the Muslims?" He does not call the phenomenon under study "fascist," but the description obviously fits.

He concludes: "...it was the desire for recognition within an increasingly global horizon, and the simultaneous anxieties of being encroached upon by the Muslims, the plebians, and the poor that over the last decade (nineties) have prompted millions of Hindus to respond to the call of Hindutva at the polls and in the streets, and to embrace Hindu-nationalist promises of order, discipline and collective strength." To Muslims as the bugbear have now been added Christians. But, the Pakistan-centered politics and the fear of Western responses to church-breaking keeps the focus on India's largest minority.

The alleged threat from unplanned Muslim families (the threat of the minority population swelling enough to swamp the majority) was used earlier to give the majority a minority-in-the making complex. The complex was later sought to be compounded by the phobia over Christian conversions. The fear of "plebianization" was made feverish by the politics of reservations in education and employment or affirmative action; and the fear led to electoral mandates that forced even low-caste political parties into "Hindutva"-headed power alliances.

Hansen sees where the "Hindutva" nationalism is headed. Recalling the formation of a fragile coalition by the BJP in March 1998, he says: "Less than two months later,…in Pokharan…five nuclear bombs were tested. This instantaneously put India on the global map as a nuclear power and initiated a new phase in the…arms race between India and Pakistan…the BJP could now appear on the domestic scene in its much-desired role as the most resolute defender of India's national pride and…national interest. When a local RSS organizer in Gujarat told a journalist, 'After the nuclear tests, many other nations have realized that India is not merely a developing nation, but a superpower', he was not merely articulating a 'Hindu-nationalist sentiment.'" This was a nationalism that was getting translated and transformed into nuclear militarism.

Indian Fascism and the Italian Model

NOT many realize how natural an evolution this was. Very few know of the very real links of the original fascism with the Indian variant since its inception even as an idea. Italian researcher Marzia Casolari has recorded her findings about these links. These deserve notice in some detail from anyone trying to understand the mind behind the nuclear militarism or the method behind the nuclear madness that threatens South Asia today.

Casolari recalls: "In the 1930s, Hindu nationalism borrowed from European fascism to transform 'different' people into "enemies." Leaders of militant Hinduism repeatedly expressed their admiration for authoritarian leaders such as Mussolini and Hitler and for the fascist model of society." But there was much more to it than mere admiration. "The existence of direct contacts between the representatives of the (Italian) fascist regime, including Mussolini, and Hindu nationalists demonstrates that Hindu nationalism had much more than an abstract interest in the ideology and practice of fascism. The interest of Indian Hindu nationalists in fascism and Mussolini must not be considered as dictated by an occasional curiosity, confined to a few individuals; rather, it should be considered as the culminating result of the attention that Hindu nationalists, especially in Maharashtra, focussed on Italian dictatorship and its leader."

Recounting the support from the "Hindutva" press of those days for fascism, Casolari notes: "[the press backed] in particular the substitution of the election of the members of Parliament with their nomination and the replacement of parliament itself with the Great Council of Fascism. Mussolini's idea was the opposite of that of democracy and it was expressed by the dictator's principle, according to which "one man's government is more useful and more binding" for the nation than the democratic institutions. Is all this not reminiscent of the principle of "obedience to one leader" (*"ek chalak anuvartitva"*) followed by the RSS (Rashtriya Swayamsevak Sangh or the National Volunteers Corps)?"

The research led Casolari to the "first Hindu nationalist who came in contact with the fascist regime and its dictator," B. S Moonje, "a politician strictly related to the RSS." Moonje was the "mentor" of K. B. Hedgewar, who had founded the RSS in 1925. "Between February and March 1931, on his return from the Round Table Conference, Moonje made a tour to Europe, which included a long stopover in Italy. There he visited some important military schools and educational institutions. The highlight of the visit was the meeting with Mussolini." Casolari draws upon a 13-page account of the trip and the meeting in Moonje's diary.

"The Indian leader was in Rome during March 15-24, 1931. On March 19, in Rome, he visited, among others, the Military College, the Central Military School of Physical Education, the Fascist Academy of Physical Education, and, most important, the Balilla and Avanguardisti organizations. These two organizations, which he describes in more than two pages of his diary, were the keystone of the fascist system of indoctrination—rather than education—of the youths. Their structure is strikingly similar to that of the RSS. They recruited boys from the age of six, up to 18: the youth had to attend weekly meetings, where they practiced physical exercise, received paramilitary training and performed drills and parades."

Writes Casolari: "...Moonje played a crucial role in moulding the RSS along Italian (fascist) lines. The deep impression left on Moonje by the vision of the fascist organizations is confirmed by his diary. 'The Balilla institutions and the conception of the whole organization have appealed to me most, though there is still not discipline and organization of high order. The whole idea is conceived by Mussolini for the military regeneration of Italy.

Italians, by nature, appear ease-loving and non-martial, like the Indians generally. They have cultivated, like Indians, the work of peace and neglected the cultivation of the art of war. Mussolini saw the essential weakness of his country and conceived the idea of the Balilla organization...Nothing better could have been conceived for the military organization of Italy... "

Then, she comes to the report of the "more meaningful...meeting with Mussolini." The meeting took place at 3 p.m. on March 19, 1931, in Palazzo Venzia, the headquarters of the fascist government. The diary records: "I shook hands with him saying that I am Dr Moonje. He knew everything about me and appeared to be closely following the events of the Indian struggle for freedom...

"Signor Mussolini asked me if I have visited the University. I said I am interested in the military training of boys and have been visiting the Military Schools of England, France and Germany. I have now come to Italy for the same purpose and I am very grateful to say that the Foreign Office and the War Office have made good arrangements for my visiting these schools. I just saw this morning and afternoon the Balilla and the Fascist Organizations and I was much impressed. Italy needs them for her development and prosperity. I do not see anything objectionable though I have been frequently reading in the newspapers not very friendly criticisms about them and about your Excellency also.

"Signor Mussolini: What is your opinion about them?

"Dr Moonje: Your Excellency, I am much impressed. Every aspiring and growing Nation needs such organizations.

"Signor Mussolini—who appeared very pleased—

said: Thanks but yours is an uphill task. However, I wish you every success in return."

Casolari narrates: "Once Moonje was back in India, he kept the promise made in his diary and started immediately to work for the foundation of his military school and for the militant reorganization of Hindu society in Maharashtra. He really did not waste time, for, as soon as he reached Pune, he gave an interview to *The Mahratta* (newspaper). Regarding the military reorganization of the Hindu community, he stressed the necessity to 'Indianize' the army and expressed the hope that conscription would become compulsory...."

He added: "...leaders should imitate the youth movements of Germany and the Balilla and Fascist organizations of Italy. I think they are eminently suited for introduction in India, adapting them to suit the special conditions (here)...." "In 1934," Casalori goes on, "Moonje started to work for the foundation of his own institution, the Bhonsla Military School. For this purpose, in the same year he began to work at the foundation of the Central Hindu Military Education Society, whose aim was to educate them in 'Sanatan Dharma' (Ancient Religion, a name for Hinduism), and to train them 'in the science and art of personal and national defense."

Moonje's "Preface to the Scheme of the Central Hindu Military Society and its Military School" said at the outset: "This training is meant for qualifying and fitting our boys for the game of killing masses of men with the ambition of winning victory with the best possible causalities [sic] of dead and wounded while causing the utmost possible to the adversary."

Comments Casolari: "Moonje does not give any

clear-cut indication regarding this 'adversary,' whether it was the external enemy, the British, or the 'historical' internal enemy, the Muslims. (The 'Hindutva' camp was to dissociate itself from the freedom struggle soon). The document continues with a long dissertation on the relation between violence and non-violence. In it are drawn many examples from Indian history and Hindu holy books, all in favor of organized violence, in the form of militarism. On the contrary, non-violence is considered a form of renunciation and cowardice."

"Moonje's views corresponded almost perfectly with Mussolini's opinions. The same thought is repeated though in a more forceful and direct language by Signor Mussolini, the maker of modern Italy, when he says: 'Our desire for peace and collaboration with Europe is based on millions of steel bayonets.' Again from Mussolini's Doctrine of Fascism: 'I absolutely disbelieve in perpetual peace which is detrimental and negative to the fundamental virtues of man, which only by struggle reveal themselves in the light of the sun.' Or, 'War alone brings up to its highest tension all human energy and puts the stamp of nobility upon the peoples who have the courage to meet it.' And: 'Fascism believes neither in the possibility nor the utility of perpetual peace. It thus repudiates the doctrine of pacifism, which is born of renunciation of the struggle and an act of cowardice in the face of sacrifice.'"

As for Nazi Germany, Moonje quoted from a booklet titled *Wehrwisssenschaft* (Military Science) by Ewald Banse, a professor at the Brunswick Technical High School: "The starting point of the book is that war is inevitable and certain and that it is imperative to know as much about it and to be as efficient as possible...the mind of the nation, from childhood on, must be impregnated and familiarized with the idea of war," because, the Professor says: "The dying warrior dies more easily when he knows that his blood is ebbing for his national god." Says Casolari: "The spirit of the last sentence is surprisingly coincident with the essence of the Hindu nationalism."

The story continues: "After Moonje's trip to Italy there was no further direct contact between exponents of the main Hindu organizations and the Italian government. However, by the end of the 1930s Italian representatives in India established some connections with the extremist fringes of Hindu nationalism. The Italian consulate in Bombay was very active in seeking contacts with the local political milieu. The Italian diplomatic mission in Bombay was part of a network linking consulates in Bombay and Calcutta with the radical movements of Maharashtra and Bengal."

In the late thirties, "Veer" (Hero) Savarkar, still an idol of the Sangh "parivar," became the president of the Hindu Mahasabha (Conference) and contributed significantly to the 'Hindutva' campaign.

"Two of the main topics of the speeches Savarkar gave at the gatherings organized in his honor and at any other public function of his party were the international situation and Hindu-Muslim relations," Casolari notes and gives an example of how the two themes were combined. At a public meeting in Pune on August 1, 1938, he said: "...India's foreign policy must not depend on 'isms.' Germany has every right to resort to Nazism and Italy to Fascism and events have justified that those isms and forms of governments were imperative and beneficial to them under the conditions that obtained there.

Bolshevism might have suited Russia and Democracy as it is obtained in Briton [sic] to the British people." Starting a controversy with Nehru, who had taken an anti-fascist stand, Savarkar openly defended the authoritarian powers of the day, particularly Italy and, even more so, Germany: "Who are we to dictate to Germany, Japan or Russia or Italy to choose a particular form of policy of government simply because we woo it out of academic attraction? Surely, Hitler knows better than Pandit Nehru does what suits Germany best. The very fact that Germany or Italy has so wonderfully recovered and grown so powerful as never before at the touch of the Nazi or Fascist magical wand is enough to prove that those political 'isms' were the most congenial tonics their health demanded."

Savarkar asserted at another public meeting in Pune on October 11, 1938, "[that] if a plebiscite had taken place in India, Muslims would have chosen to unite with Muslims and Hindus with Hindus." This was a consequence of the principle according to which it was not enough living together for a few centuries to form a nation, as "the common desire to form a nation was essential for the formation of a nation."

"During Savarkar's presidentship (of the Hindu Mahasabha)," Casalori finds, "the anti-Muslim rhetoric became more and more radical, and distinctly unpleasant. It was a rhetoric that made continuous reference to the way Germany was managing the Jewish question. Indeed, in speech after speech, Savarkar supported Hitler's anti-Jewish policy, and on October 14, 1938, he suggested the following solution for the Muslim problem in India: 'A nation is formed by a majority living therein. What did the Jews do in Germany? They being in minority were driven out from Germany.'" Modi would have agreed. After the Indian National Congress under Mahatma Gandhi and Nehru had passed a resolution against German Nazism, Savarkar stated that, "in Germany the movement of the Germans is the national movement but that of the Jews is a communal one." On July 29, 1939, in Pune, he said: "Nationality did not depend so much on a common geographical area as on unity of thought, religion, language and culture. For this reason the Germans and the Jews could not be regarded as a nation." By this logic, Casolari points out, Muslims and Hindus could also not be regarded as belonging to the same nation. Indian Muslims should rather resign themselves to be considered a minority, the recognition of whose rights should depend on the magnanimity of the majority.

Finally, at the end of 1939, when the Second World War broke out and on the occasion of the 21st session of the Hindu Mahasabha, Savarkar made one of the most explicit comparisons between the Muslim question in India and the Jewish problem in Germany: "...the Indian Muslims are on the whole more inclined to identify themselves and their interests with Muslims outside India than Hindus who live next door, like Jews in Germany."

Referring to the Muslims in a book titled "Hindutva: Who is Hindu?", Savarkar asserted: "Their holy land is far off in Arabia or Palestine. Their mythology and godmen, ideas and heroes are not children of this soil. Consequently their names and their outlook smack of foreign origin."

As mentioned previously, all this admiration for the Nazis and fascists did not stop the "Hindutva" camp from offering "responsive cooperation" to the British. In return,

the Hindu Mahasabha requested the government to
increase the local production of modern armaments so
that India could equip its army, without depending on
imports from other nations. Soon after this resolution, the
Hindu Mahasabha started to work for the creation of a
national militia. "Naturally enough," says Casolari,
"Moonje became the person in charge".

In his invitation to the Mahasabha members to a pre-
liminary meeting for the foundation of the militia in Pune,
Moonje said: "I have the pleasure in bringing to your
notice a resolution of the Hindu Mahasabha for the organization of the Hindu Militia in the country for the purpose
of taking part in the defense of India both from external
and internal aggression whenever an occasion of emergency may arise during the course of the Anglo-German
War." "...I believe that it will be quite in the fitness of
things, in view of the historic All-India Military leadership of the Maharashtra, that a beginning should be made
in the Maharashtra; so that the lead may be taken up by
the whole of India afterwards." "Who could be the internal aggressors if not the Muslims?" asks Casolari, and adds:
"The answer seems to be contained in a letter from
Moonje to Khaparde (a comrade) of October 18: '...the
Moslems are making themselves a nuisance. The Congress
government will not stand up but will yield to them. We
cannot expect any consideration at the hands of the
Congress government. We shall have to fight both the
government and the Moslems....'"

Casolari says: "When, in the 1940s, the totalitarian
regimes had already revealed their true colors, the attitude
of the organizations of militant Hinduism towards fascism
and Nazism was still benevolent. In spite of the already,

even if only partially, known atrocities committed by Hitler and Mussolini, the main organizations of Hindu nationalism still praised the dictators and their regimes. This position could be justified, had it been part of a coherent and strong anti-British policy. However, as I have tried to demonstrate, the forces of Hindu nationalism seem to have concentrated their efforts more against the so-called internal enemies—Muslims and the Congress—rather than the foreign invaders."

The same ultra-nationalist forces have today allied with a world-hegemonist superpower in order to settle scores with "internal enemies" of India and South Asia.

The fascist-militarist roots of the RSS and the rest of the "Hindutva" camp are thus very real, and these were nourished further by a post-Independence ideologue of fratricidal nationalism. Madhav Sadashiv Golwalkar, the Guru to the Sangh "parivar," who headed the RSS from 1940 to 1973, harped on the "internal enemies" theme all through his hate-purveying career. After making the statement quoted at the head of this chapter about "hostile elements within the country" posing a greater threat than "aggressors from outside," he asked: "Have all the pro-Pakistan elements gone away to Pakistan?"

A Bunch of Thoughts, a post-Independence collection of sayings and speeches by the Guru, ends with a chapter on "Internal Threats." The three threats listed and expatiated upon are: Muslims, Christians and Communists. It is not just the familiar hit-list that betrays the fascism of the Guru's message. More than once, he also made it clear that the outcome of the Second World War made no difference to the "Hindutva"; admiration for Hitlerism and fascism, though attempts were made later to deny the RSS applause for anti-Semitism.

The Guru's first book, *We or Our Nationhood Defined*, published in 1938, had to be withdrawn from circulation for his embarrassing praise of Hitler and his theories of racial superiority: "German race pride has now become the topic of the day. To keep up the purity of the race and its culture, Germany shocked the world by her purging the country of the Semitic races—the Jews. Race pride at its highest has been manifested here. Germany has also shown how well-nigh impossible it is for races and cultures, having differences going to the root, to be assimilated into one united whole—a good lesson for us in Hindusthan (Hindu land or India) to learn and profit by."

The Guru was, however, to repeat the lesson: "...the non-Hindu peoples in Hindusthan must either adopt the Hindu culture and language, must learn to respect and hold in reverence the Hindu religion, must entertain no idea but the glorification of the Hindu race and culture, i.e. they must not only give up their attitude of intolerance and ungratefulness towards this land and its age-old traditions, but must also cultivate the positive attitude of love and devotion instead; in one word, they must cease to be foreigners or may stay in the country wholly subordinated to the Hindu nation claiming nothing, deserving no privileges, far less any preferential treatment, not even citizen's rights." The point was to be made with grisly force in Gujarat decades later.

The Guru's torch has been carried forward by others. The RSS and the rest of the "Hindutva" camp have lit religious-communal fires repeatedly through campaigns for diverse demands—ranging from a ban on cow slaughter and demolition of the Babri Mosque to deportation of

Bangladeshi immigrants, darkly alluded to as "infiltrators," and revanchist history-rewriting. What runs through all these campaign as a common thread is a fascist militarism that has been updated into a nuclear nationalism.

* * *

THE "Hindutva" fascism has inspired, without doubt, a Muslim-minority backlash within India. It is Pakistan, however, that provides the Islamic counterpart to the Sangh "parivar" and its perversely religious nationalism.

Within the mainland India, the Muslim fundamentalism, on which the majoritarianism feeds and keeps growing further, has taken many forms. It has played the role of a street censor: India, to its everlasting discredit, was the first country in the world to ban Salman Rushdie's *Satanic Verses* in 1989, a year after its publication, in the face of mullah-led protests, though it was not love of literature that prompted the "Hindutva" opposition to the ban. It has donned the male-chauvinist mantle: when the court was hearing the famous Shah Bano case in the mid-eighties, the community itself was made to appear hostile to the idea of a decent alimony for a divorced woman; and Shahi Imam of Jama Masjid (Mosque), Syed Ahmed Bukhari, made Indian television history by calling progressive film actress Shabana Azmi a "singing and dancing girl" and worse in a talk show. It has presented itself as an enemy of social reform: Bohra Muslim intellectual Asghar Ali Engineer has been repeatedly set upon by thugs for his attempts to modernize the community even while combating "Hindutva" communalism.

But it is Kashmir that provides the periodic excesses of the Islamic insurgency that "Hindutva" feeds and fattens most avidly on. The flight of the Kashmiri Pandits from the Valley and their sufferings elsewhere as refugees have been grist to the fascist mill. As we have seen earlier, however, the insurgency is far from entirely indigenous. The fundamentalism here has to be seen also as part of a problem that has proved a Frankenstein's monster to Pakistan's establishment.

Jessica Stern, a well-informed South Asia-watcher, says in a paper of September 2002 (Pakistan's Jihad Culture): "What began as an indigenous, secular movement for independence has become an increasingly Islamist crusade to bring all of Kashmir under Pakistani control. Pakistan-based Islamist groups (along with Hizb-ul Mujahideen, a Kashmir-based group created by Jamaat-e Islami and partly funded by Pakistan) are now significantly more important than the secular Kashmir-based ones...."

She adds: "Whatever their exact numbers, these Pakistani militant groups-among them, Lashkar-e-Toiba and Harkat-ul Mujahideen pose a long-term danger to international security, regional stability, and especially to Pakistan itself. Although their current agenda is limited to 'liberating' Kashmir, which they believe was annexed by India illegally, their next objective is to turn Pakistan into a truly Islamic state. Islamabad supports these volunteers as a cheap way to keep India off balance. In the process, however, it is creating a monster that threatens to devour Pakistani society."

Their power to destroy Pakistan does not come from the barrels of their guns alone. Even more does it come from a system of education designed to promote sectarianism and strife in South Asia and inside Pakistan. Stern talks about "madrasaas" (religious schools) and their unholy mission: "In the 1980s, Pakistani dictator General Mohammad Zia-ul-Haq promoted the madrasaas as a way to garner the religious parties' support for his rule and to recruit troops for the anti-Soviet war in Afghanistan. At the time, many madrasaas were financed by the zakat (the Islamic tithe collected by the state), giving the government at least a modicum of control. But now, more and more religious schools are funded privately, by wealthy Pakistani industrialists at home or abroad, by private and government-funded nongovernmental organizations in the Persian Gulf states and Saudi Arabia, and by Iran. Without state supervision, these madrasaas are free to preach a narrow and violent version of Islam."

Most madrasaas offer only religious instruction, ignoring all secular subjects. And quite a few extremist madrasaas preach "jihad" (holy war), equating it with guerrilla warfare. "These schools encourage their graduates, who often cannot find work because of their lack of practical education, to fulfill their 'spiritual obligations' by fighting against Hindus in Kashmir or against Muslims of other sects in Pakistan."

"Pakistan's interior minister Moinuddin Haider, for one, recognizes these problems," she says. "The brand of Islam they are teaching is not good for Pakistan," he told Stern. "Some, in the garb of religious training, are busy fanning sectarian violence, poisoning people's minds." Haider had announced a reform plan that would require all madrasaas to register with the government, expand their curricula, disclose their financial resources, seek permission for admitting foreign students, and stop sending students to militant training camps. The "reforms so far seem to have failed, whether because of the regime's negligence or the madrasaas' refusal to be regulated, or both."

Stern recalls the U.S.'s role in funding and fuelling this fundamentalism. "The United States and Saudi Arabia funneled some $3.5 billion into Afghanistan and Pakistan during the Afghan war, according to Milt Bearden, CIA station chief in Pakistan from 1986 to 1989. "Jihad," along with guns and drugs, became the most important business in the region." The business of "jihad"—what the late scholar Eqbal Ahmad dubbed "Jihad International, Inc."—continues to attract foreign investors, mostly wealthy Arabs in the Persian Gulf region and members of the Pakistani diaspora. (As World Bank economist Paul Collier observes, diaspora populations often prolong ethnic and religious conflicts by contributing not only capital but also extremist rhetoric, since the fervor of the locals is undoubtedly held in check by the prospect of losing their own sons.)"

The fundamentalists of Pakistan swear no less by Hitlerism than the "Hindutva" fascists. "Many of the militant groups associated with radical madrasaas regularly proclaim their plans to bring 'jihad' to India proper as well as to the West, which they believe is run by Jews. Lashkar-e Toiba has announced its plans to "plant Islamic flags in Delhi, Tel Aviv, and Washington." One of Lashkar's websites includes a list of purported Jews working for the Clinton Administration, including director of presidential personnel Robert Nash (an African-American from Arkansas) and CIA director George Tenet (a Greek American). The group also accuses Israel of assisting India in Kashmir. Asked for a list of his favorite books, a leader of Harkat recommended the history of Hitler, who he said understood that 'Jews and peace are incompatible.'"

"The 'jihad' against the West may be rhetorical (at least for now), but the ten-year-old sectarian war between Pakistan's Shi'a and Sunni is real and deadly," says Stern. Shades of the "internal enemies" of the RSS. "Sectarian clashes have killed or injured thousands of Pakistanis since 1990. As the American scholar Vali Nasr explains, the largely theological differences between Shi'a and Sunni Muslims have been transformed into full-fledged political conflict, with broad ramifications for law and order, social cohesion, and government authority. The impotent Pakistani government has essentially allowed Sunni Saudi Arabia and Shi'a Iran to fight a proxy war on Pakistani soil, with devastating consequences for the Pakistani people."

As a concerned American observer, Stern says: "The United States has asked Pakistan to crack down on the militant groups and to close certain madrasaas, but America must do more than just scold. After all, the United States, along with Saudi Arabia, helped create the first international 'jihad' to fight the Soviet Union during the Afghan war. 'Does America expect us to send in the troops and shut the madrasaas down?' one official asks. 'Jihad is a mindset. It developed over many years during the Afghan war. You can't change a mindset in 24 hours.'"

The "most important contribution" from the U.S., according to her, will be "to help strengthen Pakistan's secular education system." How realistic is it to expect American help for the cause? Not very, to go by a report about what the U.S. had done to schooling in Afghanistan. According to a story in the *Washington Post* of March 23, 2002, the US government had shipped—and continued to ship until lately—millions of Taliban-friendly, fundamentalist textbooks into Afghanistan. The paper's investigation revealed that the US had over 20 years spent millions of dollars producing fanatical schoolbooks, which were then distributed in Afghanistan.

"The primers, which were filled with talk of jihad and featured drawings of guns, bullets, soldiers and mines, have served since then [i.e., since the violent destruction of the Afghan secular government in the early 1990s] as the Afghan school system's core curriculum. Even the Taliban used the American-produced books, though the radical movement scratched out human faces in keeping with its strict fundamentalist code," the paper said.

It reported: "On Feb. 4, [Chris Brown, head of book revision for USAID's Central Asia Task Force] arrived in Peshawar, the Pakistani border town in which the text-books were to be printed, to oversee hasty revisions to the printing plates. Ten Afghan educators labored night and day, scrambling to replace rough drawings of weapons with sketches of pomegranates and oranges, Brown said." The change was that some violent pictures were removed from the printing plates and some fruit added to the academic diet. The paper also reported the reaction of a non-fundamentalist Afghan educator. 'The pictures [in the old schoolbooks] are horrendous...but the texts are even much worse,' said Ahmad Fahim Hakim, a program coordinator for Cooperation for Peace and Unity (a Pakistan-based non-governmental organization)."

That is yet another lesson for those who expect an alliance with the U.S. to restrain the ideology-driven foes of peace in South Asia.

CHAPTER 7

THE POST-911 PARADOX

Will the 'War on Terrorism' Go Nuclear?

> ...no region is a greater source of terrorism than our neighborhood. Indeed, in our neighborhood—in this, the 21st century—religious war has not just been fashioned into, it has been proclaimed to be, an instrument of state policy. Distance offers no insulation. It should not cause complacence...such evil cannot succeed. But even in failing it could inflict untold suffering. That is why the United States and India have begun to deepen their cooperation for combating terrorism. We must redouble these efforts.
>
> —Atal Behari Vajpayee, quoting from an earlier speech to U.S. Congress, in his address to the nation, September 14, 2001

> Following the September 11 attack on the USA, we took a decision in the best national interest which was motivated by the concerns of security of Pakistan and its core interests. Pakistan's solidarity and integrity are most important. We have saved our core interests, the nuclear assets and the Kashmir cause.
>
> —Pakistan's President Gen. Pervez Musharraf, November 20, 2001

If we hope to understand anything about the foreign policy of any state, it is a good idea to begin by investigating the domestic social structure: Who sets foreign policy? What interests do these people represent? What is the domestic source of their power? It is a reasonable surmise that the policy that evolves will reflect the special interests of those who design it. An honest study of history will reveal that this natural expectation is quite generally fulfilled. The evidence is overwhelming, in my opinion, that the United States is no exception to the general rule…

—Noam Chomsky, 'Human Rights' and
American Foreign Policy (1978)

You cannot simultaneously prevent and prepare for war.

—Albert Einstein

From the point of view of the economy, the sale of weapons is indistinguishable from the sale of food. When a building collapses or a plane crashes, it's rather inconvenient from the point of view of those inside, but it's altogether convenient for the growth of the gross national product, which sometimes ought to be called the 'gross criminal product.'

—Eduardo Galeano, Upside Down: A Primer
for the Looking-Glass World (2000)

If a country develops an economic system that is based on how to pay for the war, and if the amounts of fixed capital investment that are apparent are tied up in armaments, and if that country is a major exporter of arms, and its industrial fabric is dependent on them, then it would be in that country's interests to ensure that it always had a market. It is not an exaggeration to say that it is clearly in the interests of the world's leading arms exporters to make sure that there is always a war going on somewhere.

—Marilyn Waring, documentary "Who's
Counting," based on her book Counting for
Nothing (1996)

September 11 pushed America's military into high gear, as Afghanistan and Iraq were invaded, and North Korea was identified as part of the "Axis of Evil." Flashpoints were suddenly everywhere. But few Americans, and others in the West and the rest of the world, were worried about the only region that transformed into a nuclear flashpoint just six months after the Twin Towers tragedy. If one went by official appearances alone, the India-Pakistan standoff escalated out of nowhere, and seemed among the least likely consequences of the war on terrorism. For those watching closely, however, it was a predictable result.

As the preceding chapters show, the subcontinent had been brewing an explosive mix for decades. But why was 9/11 and the subsequent war on terrorism the trigger that brought us closer to nuclear war than anything since the Cuban missile crisis?

The "war on terrorism" led to the creation of the U.S.-headed "multinational coalition against global terror," and India and Pakistan became important members. President George W. Bush set the stage with his famous those-not-with-us-are-against-us threat. But those with him were not necessarily with each other. By coexisting as allies in the coalition, India and Pakistan actually become more implacable adversaries than ever before, with each hoping to turn the situation to a decisive advantage for itself. The standoff was a sequel to September 11.

On September 11, in his first address to the American people after the tragedy, Bush was brief about his plans: "The search is underway for those who are behind these evil acts. I have directed the full resources of our intelligence and law enforcement communities to find those responsible and to bring them to justice. We will make no distinction between the terrorists who committed these acts and those who harbor them."

It was only on September 20, 2001, that the President fully and formally spelt out the target of the proposed anti-terror offensive in his State-of-the-Union address to the US Congress: "Americans have many questions tonight. Americans are asking, 'Who attacked our country?' The evidence we have gathered all points to a collection of loosely affiliated terrorist organizations known as al-Qaida. They are some of the murderers indicted for bombing American embassies in Tanzania and Kenya and responsible for bombing the USS *Cole*. Al-Qaida is to terror what the Mafia is to crime.... This group and its leader, ...Osama bin Laden, are linked to many other organizations in different countries, including the Egyptian Islamic Jihad, the Islamic Movement of Uzbekistan. There are thousands of these terrorists in more than 60 countries."

Bush went on to name Afghanistan: "They are recruited from their own nations and neighborhoods and brought to camps in places like Afghanistan, where they are trained in the tactics of terror. They are sent back to their homes or sent to hide in countries around the world to plot evil and destruction. The leadership of al-Qaida has great influence in Afghanistan and supports the Taliban regime in controlling most of that country. In Afghanistan we see al-Qaida's vision for the world." The President then virtually declared a war on Afghanistan by presenting it with a set of non-negotiable demands.

That brought the war to the subcontinent's doorstep, and presented Pakistan's Musharraf with a choice. India's rulers had not even waited for the State-of-the-Union address to see an opportunity and try to seize it. Six days before that, Prime Minister Vajpayee suggested a special India-US alliance in his televised address to the nation. He had only a single sentence from the Bush statement of September 11—"We will make no distinction between the terrorists who committed these acts and those who harbor them"—to draw upon, and he did. It was a window of opportunity that India has endeavored to keep open ever since.

He wanted Bush to make no distinction between terrorists and Pakistan's rulers, either. To his government, the Prime Minister made it clear, the war on terror was, above all, a war on Pakistan. The "global war on terror," for New Delhi, was only a continuation by other, wider and more effective means of India's war against its neighbor. Vajpayee spelt out the stand in his address of September 14, 2001, and the multinational coalition has made no difference to it ever since.

He started by taking a clash-of-civilizations view of the calamity of days before and the conflict ahead: "…terrorists have struck yet another blow—at the United States of America, at humanity, at the civilized way of life. But I have not the slightest doubt about the eventual outcome. Democracies, open, free and plural societies shall prevail." He quickly proceeded to the theme of India as the worst victim of terrorism in the world: "… at least 53,000 families in India know exactly the pain they are going through at the moment: for terrorists have mowed down and blown up that number here in India over the last two decades." It has never been officially explained how the number was arrived at.

He did not talk explicitly of an India-US alliance

against Islamic terror, but recalled New Delhi's past calls
for such a response to such a threat: "For years we in India
have been alerting others to the fact that terrorism is a
scourge for all of humanity, that what happens in Mumbai
one day is bound to happen elsewhere tomorrow, that the
poison that propels mercenaries and terrorists to kill and
maim in Jammu and Kashmir will impel the same sort to
blow up people elsewhere." He went on to quote from his
own address to the US Congress a warning about the
world's greatest "source of terrorism" in "our neighborhood" where "religious war" or jihad had become "an
instrument of state policy" and calling for India-US cooperation in combating terrorism so clearly identified with
Pakistan.

He declared: "Those who wreak evil have their net-
works across the world. Those who will thwart them must
be united, too. We must strike at the roots of the system
that breeds terrorism. We must stamp out the infrastructure that imparts the perverse ideological poison by which
the terrorist is fired up. We must hold governments wholly accountable for the terrorism that originates from their
countries."

He reiterated: "...to get at the terrorists, the world
community must get at their organizations, at those who
condition, finance, train, equip and protect them. To get
at the organizations, it must isolate, and thus compel the
states that nurture and support them, to desist from doing
so.... The terrorists and those who give him [sic] a safe
haven are enemies of every human being, they have set
themselves against the world. The world must join hands:
to overwhelm them militarily, to neutralize their poison."

Stating that the "fiendish destruction in the US has

immediate consequences for us, it has direct lessons for us", Vajpayee stressed: "As this region has become the hub of terrorism, much of the response to the destruction that the terrorists caused on 11th September, could take place in our vicinity."

The refrain was to be taken up by others. Then External Affairs Minister Jaswant Singh put it even more strongly in a media conference on October 11, 2001: "… it is not as if India has joined the battle of the United States of America. Post-September 11, it is the United States of America that has joined India's battle. It is a battle against terrorism. There is a resolve on the part of the United States of America to fight it until it is rooted out. I do not think one needs to make statements on every policy intent that we want to pursue." There was indeed no need to specify the pro-India and anti-Pakistan course the government wanted the global warriors of the U.S. to pursue in this region. There was no mistaking the confidence, either, that Washington could be convinced of the wisdom of the course.

This theme was also pursued in the United Nations General Assembly by India's Ambassador Kamlesh Sharma. According to a news agency report, Sharma said, "the United States should look beyond Osama bin Laden in its fight against global terrorism." Speaking on October 3, the third day of a debate on terrorism in the context of September 11, he said: "The fact that terrorism is an international problem and can only be tackled collectively is something that countries who have suffered most from it know in their bones."

"The attacks had brought home to a world that probably did not realize this until then, how much of an international phenomenon terrorism truly is," Sharma told the

Assembly. "We therefore hope that the solidarity, which has been manifest over the last two weeks, will continue and that it will not be confined to a hunt for an individual or a group, or to dealing with the symptoms alone."

He noted that only hours before the UN debate began on October 1, a suicide bomber and two accomplices attacked the legislative assembly in the Indian Jammu and Kashmir state, killing 35 people. The group, which admitted the attack, Jaish-e Mohammed, was linked to the Taliban regime in Afghanistan, which Bush has accused of sheltering bin Laden, Sharma said. The charge is yet to be substantiated through a full-fledged inquiry. "Over the last decade, terrorists have killed tens of thousands in almost daily attacks in India," he said.

The argument was extended over the subsequent months into one for India doing an Afghanistan in Pakistan-occupied Kashmir (PoK) or Azad (Free) Kashmir, as Pakistan called it. India's support for the logic of the US strike deep inside Afghanistan—targeted as the sanctuary of the terrorists of September 11—was presumed to warrant Bush backing for Indian raids on the camps of "cross-border terrorism" inside PoK. A "swift, surgical operation" of the Afghanistan kind was being talked about, as we saw before, right through the months of the standoff.

The top government leaders, to be sure, did not talk in public about any such operation. Vajpayee, Advani and Jaswant Singh, in fact, denied plans for the operation, even in the different name of a "hot pursuit." But they let others close to the establishment talk. A high probability of the operation was informally indicated to the media. Strategic analysts, a tribe proliferating since Pokharan II, talked about the "pre-emptive strike," as though only its timing remained uncertain.

The operation was indeed made to appear imminent in the immediate aftermath of the still inadequately investigated terrorist attack on the Indian Parliament on December 13, 2001.[1] The attack served as a signal trigger for the massive deployment of India's troops along the border with Pakistan, the starting point for the standoff. On December 24, an officially sourced news report said: "The Government has directed the Army and the Research and Analysis Wing (RAW) to prepare a blueprint of 'risks and challenges' the country could encounter in the event of a strike on terrorist training camps in Pakistan-occupied Kashmir across the Line of Control. Though Army deployment along the international border and the LoC has been increased substantially, there is no proposal yet to take on terrorist camps in PoK. Official sources said the move to gear up the Army and make intelligence agencies proactive, especially in picking up intelligence across the border, is based on a proposal by External Affairs Minister Jaswant Singh. It is learnt that Prime Minister Atal Behari Vajpayee maintained a studied silence at Saturday's informal consultations of the "Cabinet Committee on Security." Despite the silence, the message was loud and clear. (For the uninitiated, the RAW is the foreign intelligence and covert operations agency, India's own CIA.)

The talk continued and was not abandoned even after the worst of the standoff was over. Strategist peddlers of the proposal insisted that the raids would have been possible and profitable, had the government not dragged its feet and not waited until the Pakistani regime had become part of the coalition. Bharat Karnad, a hawk among hawks and a former member of the National

Security Board, lamented that Muaharraf had been "too agile" in his moves. The threat might have terrified the sane world opinion that feared that such an operation could have a nightmarishly nuclear outcome. This, however, barely made a difference to the India-US bonhomie during the standoff.

Six months after September 11, in March 2002, US Ambassador to India Robert Blackwill told a meeting of New Delhi's policy-makers about the new India-USA relations: "No longer do US officials encounter Indian counterparts who instinctively assume a studied stance of moral superiority. No longer do Indian government representatives face Americans who believe constant public criticism, incessant private nagging and a one-issue agenda should dominate American diplomacy toward India." By then, over 50 American policy-makers at the assistant secretary level and above had visited India since 2001 and there had been an equal number of visits by Indian officials to the U.S., including by the Prime Minister, the home and defense ministers, besides senior members of the national security team.

Noting the change, an MSNBC report said on March 14, 2002: "Traditionally, India's policy establishment has bristled at prospects of having the United States in its backyard. But today, many among India's security affairs fraternity say that although New Delhi does not like Washington lionizing Musharraf and showering him with no-strings-attached economic aid, it should use the United States' current leverage with Pakistan to its advantage."

"India's biggest strategic objective is to get Pakistan cleaned up of extremism. If the U.S. can really get

Musharraf to stop sending terrorists across the border into our territory, good for us," retired Maj. Gen. Ashok Mehta, now a commentator on Indian security affairs, told the channel. "Stability in this region is as much in the United States' interest as ours and critical to removing terror root and branch."

The new India-U.S. relations were really not quite so new. They actually predated 9/11. The first major indication of an attempt at a strategic relationship between the sole, surviving superpower and the would-be regional power came with New Delhi's warm welcome to the missile defense programs of the Bush Administration. Fittingly, it came on the third anniversary of Pokharan II, falling on May 11, 2001.

A Reuters report of that date from New Delhi recalled that "New Delhi raised eyebrows at home and abroad last week by coming out in support of the Bush plan." But this was, obviously, different. Vajpayee "lauded President Bush's vision of nuclear disarmament" and no less as the two nations began talks on Washington's plans to introduce an anti-missile shield. US Deputy Secretary of State Richard Armitage was meeting Vajpayee and Jaswant Singh.

"We welcome every move toward lightening the shadow of the nuclear terror under which we live today," Vajpayee said after giving awards to the country's defense scientists, including those involved in building nuclear-capable missiles. "It is in this context that we have welcomed President Bush's suggestions for steep reductions in nuclear arsenals and a move away from further development of offensive nuclear technologies," he said, according to the report.

"Analysts saw in India's unexpectedly warm response—which implied support for an anti-missile shield—a desire to add a strategic dimension to its new friendship with Washington," said the report.

Armitage, too, played to the Indian gallery. Stating that the planned defense system was aimed at "a handful of rogue states," he "named Iraq, Iran, Libya and North Korea as rogue states and, pressed further, said there was also concern about Pakistan."

Vajpayee, for his part, seized the occasion to sell Pokharan II to the U.S. He said "the world now had a better appreciation of the security imperatives" that led him to order the underground tests and reiterated the need for a nuclear arsenal. "We do believe that a credible minimum nuclear deterrent is a basic security umbrella which we owe to our people."

Days before, the report noted, India had conducted a major military exercise (which included responses to nuclear attacks) along the border with Pakistan, adding to tensions running high over Kashmir. Newspapers quoted scientific adviser to Vajpayee A. P. J. Abdul Kalam, who was to become the President of India, as saying the war games were "aimed at seeing how to use a nuclear weapon in a combat situation." Armitage refrained from even an indirect reaction to the statement of either Vajpayee or Kalam.

The strategic analysts were ecstatic. One of them, C. Raja Mohan, an influential media commentator, said: "The quick and unambiguous support extended by India to certain elements of Mr. Bush's proposals has generated a bit of political heat here. But it also fueled speculation that Indo-US relations might be on the verge of a great leap forward."

Another prominent member of the politically trusted security think-tank, Brahma Chellaney, wrote in the *International Herald Tribune* of the same May 11: "The cycle of action and reaction triggered by missile defenses is bound to drive India closer to the United States. The first evidence of that is from India itself. It is one of the few countries to have extended immediate support to President George W. Bush's national missile defense plan."

His counsel to India was clear: "As a vulnerable state living in a dangerous neighborhood, India has to look at missile defenses strictly through the prism of national interest. One of its top priorities should be to build a strategic partnership with the United States on mutually beneficial and level terms. If New Delhi does not forge close ties with the Bush administration, it may be many years before a fresh opportunity presents itself." The opportunity was not lost.

He argued: "US missile defenses will not threaten India's security. They could even yield strategic benefits if New Delhi handles the issue deftly. It must exploit its missile defense support by pushing the Bush team to take a fresh look at the decades-old technology and military sanctions against India."

He had corresponding counsel for the U.S. as well: "If Washington were to interpret its export-control laws more broadly, it would throw open for sale to India many high-tech commercial items. It also makes no strategic sense for the United States to continue to keep India out of its arms market. Further, there is no reason why Washington should still keep India as a key target of the punitive restrictions of the Nuclear Suppliers' Group." This was essentially a request to fuel an arms race between already bellicose nuclear neighbors—or rather, he hoped, just the Indian side of it. None of his suggestion went unheeded.

Little wonder that the Bush Administration came subsequently to adopt a stand of virtual approval of India's nuclear weaponization. Senior Adviser in the US embassy in New Delhi, Ashley J. Tellis, described as a nuclear policy expert, was unstinted in praise for "India's emerging nuclear posture." Calling India "a reluctant nuclearizer," he testified that "India had avoided and delayed the process and developed it only when forced." No Indian diplomat could have put it more favorably to India.

Chellaney shared the government's ambition to give India the security and status of an American satellite: "Missile defenses are likely to help strengthen and expand US-led security arrangements in Asia and other parts of the world. In future, the US could extend a 'missile umbrella' to its allies, in the way it presently holds out a nuclear umbrella. An India strategically aligned with America could take advantage of certain missile defense benefits to reduce its own security burden."

No one was, thus, really surprised when, on September 23, 2001, President Bush announced a waiver of sanctions against India and Pakistan, introduced when the two countries conducted nuclear tests in 1998. In a White House memorandum, he said that the sanctions were "not in the national security interests of the United States." Washington followed this up with "defense cooperation" deals with both India and Pakistan. None of this signaled a strong disapproval of the standoff that threatened South Asia, or even a concern over where the passions might lead that America was stoking.

Pakistan's Conflicting Responses:
Musharraf, Media and Masses

PAKISTAN'S immediate reaction to the 9/11 outrage was strikingly different from India's. In New Delhi, there was obscene and unconcealed glee at the new opportunity seen in the apocalypse in New York. The silence emanating from Islamabad seemed to betray a sullen unease. The media assumption was that the military regime of Gen. Musharraf was wary of the domestic mass reaction if it gave in easily to the US demands—for permission to use Pakistan's airspace and its logistical and intelligence support in the war on Afghanistan. The President of Pakistan, playing a lone hand, was to prove this assessment wrong and, in the process, upset the calculations of Vajpayee and company.

In a report from Islamabad on September 15, 2001, B. Muralidhar Reddy of Indian newspaper *The Hindu* said: "The English press in Pakistan has been known to be the column of reason and the Urdu press the abode of passion. But the new American focus on Pakistan as the first fallout of the September 11 tragedy has elicited sharp reactions from the liberal 'angrezi' (English) press here as well. Imagining all possible scenarios, all major newspapers today warned of a strong anti-American wave in the country."

The samples included: "If we refuse to go all the way down the road with the Americans, the mood in Washington is to punish us, whether we deserve it or not.... If Pakistan agrees to what the Americans want... that would swell into a massive surge of anti-Americanism within the country with all the armed and trained jihadi elements turning their guns inwards...." (editorial in *The News*). "Appalling as the loss of innocent lives is, the question has to be asked as to why the U.S. is so totally oblivious of the strong hatred it excites in so many despairing corners of the globe..." (Article headlined 'The fury of despair', *The Dawn*). "The injustice and discrimination and disparity, which has been the policy of the main world power towards the third world, especially the Muslim world, could be identified as the main causes of tragedy the Americans are experiencing..." (editorial 'U.S. needs to react wisely', *The Pakistan Times*).

The lead article 'Cruelty of a crushed people' by Robert Fisk in the Peshawar daily *Statesman* said: "And there will be, inevitably, and quite immorally, an attempt to obscure the historical wrongs and the injustice that lie behind Tuesday's firestorms. We will be told about 'mindless terrorism', the 'mindless' bit being essential if we are not to realize how hated America has become in the land of the birth of three great religions."

"But the mood in Washington is not introspective. It is angry and it is looking for quick villains. Even if hard evidence is yet to come by, fingers are already pointing at Osama bin Laden. This has direct implications as the road to Laden passes through Pakistan. Or so at least our American friends insist on thinking," Ayaz Amir, columnist, wrote.

There were warnings to the U.S. "The atmosphere in Islamabad has become both tense and rife with rumors of all kinds," *The Nation* said in an editorial 'Pressure on Islamabad,' adding, "Even a military government cannot totally ignore popular feelings, and the US must not make the mistake of making impossible or over-difficult demands." *The Pakistan Observer* said, "There are reports that US officials are giving veiled threats of retaliation against Islamabad if it did not cooperate. This is quite in line with the typical American behavior of arrogance and haughtiness in dealing with other states."

Musharraf treated all this as unduly alarmist. As acknowledged in retrospect by most observers, including the hawks of India, the general stole a march over the non-uniformed militarists of New Delhi by acceding within days to all the American demands without ado and restoring Pakistan's status as a strategically important frontline state for the U.S. The militant Islamic protests anticipated by the media did materialize, but these actually served Musharraf's purpose: the Pakistani regime could now increasingly claim to be a target of terrorists, about whose cross-border crimes New Delhi kept complaining. The general, therefore, grew increasingly confident and explicit about Pakistan's role as a coalition partner.

The confidence, in turn, did not help to cool India-Pakistan temperatures. India's military response to the December 13 attack on Parliament did not yield the anticipated result. Bharat Karnad was to bemoan that New Delhi had "mightily goofed up" by ordering an all-out military mobilization in the hope of intimidating Islamabad, which had regained a special relationship with the U.S. and, consequently, confidence. Musharraf, certainly, was free with offers of anti-terrorist cooperation with the coalition, but adopted a distinctly different tone about Kashmir. Confronted with the question, he continued to stress that Kashmir's was a "freedom struggle," suggesting that a bit of terrorism was all right in such a struggle.

In Kashmir, the openly pro-Pakistan All-Parties

Hurriyat Conference of Kashmir went further. APHC chairman Abdul Ghani Bhat, in an interview to me in August 2002 (quoted earlier), did not try to duck the question about "cross-border terrorism." Instead, he compared these acts to other efforts now widely accepted as legitimate. Were not the Americans and Europeans, he asked, fighting the Soviet forces on the Afghan soil in the eighties and nineties, "cross-border terrorists." Was not Subhash Chandra Bose of India's own freedom struggle, the man who formed an Indian National Army to march on New Delhi with the Japanese during the Second World, a "cross-border terrorist," Bhat demanded.

Pakistan's rulers also flaunted scorn for world public opinion in insisting upon their right to exercise the nuclear first-strike option, and repeating this insistence, through the standoff. As we have seen before, the threat was one to go for even "a first strike, a second strike, a third strike." Despite much-advertised US diplomatic efforts to defuse India-Pakistan tensions through the period, no official word of condemnation of the talk of nuclear derring-do was heard from Washington.

On September 13, 2001, two days after the New York tragedy, Musharraf reportedly offered "full cooperation" of an unspecified character to the U.S. after a meeting with the U.S. ambassador to discuss terrorism in the region. Ambassador Wendy Chamberlain said the 45-minute talks had been "frank and forthright," suggesting that it had not been all smiles. Pakistan was one of only three countries at the time that recognized the Taliban regime of Afghanistan. The U.S. claimed to have made its displeasure clear over Pakistan's relationship with the regime, which was an American creation.

On October 16, 2001, Musharraf announced that Pakistan's support for US military action in Afghanistan would continue for as long as the campaign lasted, after talks in Islamabad with Colin Powell. Musharraf also said his government had made a decision of principle to support the coalition against terrorism and to allow the use of its airspace and provide intelligence and logistical support for US action against the Taliban regime.

He said Pakistan believed the campaign should be "short and targeted." Soon, Bush was to clarify that the campaign would be nothing of that sort, and indeed to threaten a "war without end." What sections in the media saw as a snub to the Pakistani leader, however, hardly soured the Washington-Islamabad relations, again to the disappointment and dismay of New Delhi.

On November 20, 2001, Musharraf said: "Following the September 11 attack on USA, we took a decision in the best national interest which was motivated by the concerns of security of Pakistan and its core interests... We have saved our core interests, the nuclear assets and the Kashmir cause." About Pakistan's economic gains, the President claimed that its decision to join international coalition was not motivated by economics, but added, "Yet we have gained in economic terms."

In less than two months came a major Musharraf initiative to consolidate Pakistan's place in the coalition. On January 12, 2002, in a televised address to the nation, he took on the Islamic-fundamentalist opposition with surprising directness. Announcing a ban on two militant organizations, named by New Delhi in connection with December 13 (Jaish-e Mohammed and Lashkar-e Toiba) attacks, he also spelt out measures to tackle fundamentalism at its source—the madrasaa or madaari (the religious school).[2]

He seemed to have an audience in mind that was wider than Pakistan, when he said: "Sectarian terrorism has been going on for years. Every one of us is fed up with it. It is becoming unbearable. Our peace-loving people are keen to get rid of the Kalashinkov and weapon culture. Every one is sick of it… The day of reckoning has come. Do we want Pakistan to become a theocratic state? Do we believe that religious education alone is enough for governance or do we want Pakistan to emerge as a progressive and dynamic Islamic welfare state? The verdict of the masses is in favor of a progressive Islamic state." He went on to prescribe new rules, regulations and syllabi for the madrasaas, to bring in secular subjects and keep out unwanted foreign students.

The address did not avoid the subject of Kashmir. Musharraf was more explicit than Islamabad had ever been in asking for American intervention in the dispute. He said, "I would also like to address the international community, particularly the United States on this occasion. As I said before on a number of occasions, Pakistan rejects and condemns terrorism in all its forms and manifestation. Pakistan will not allow its territory to be used for any terrorist activity anywhere in the world. Now you must play an active role in solving the Kashmir dispute for the sake of lasting peace and harmony in the region. We should be under no illusion that the legitimate demand of the people of Kashmir can ever be suppressed without its resolution. Kashmiris also expect that you ask India to bring an end to state terrorism and human rights violations. Let human rights organizations, Amnesty International, the international media and UN peacekeepers be allowed to monitor activities of the Indian occupation forces."

Even India's Foreign Affairs Minister Jaswant Singh was obliged to welcome the reforms proposed by Musharraf. Singh refrained from strongly stressing India's demand, spurned by the President, for extradition of "terrorists" from Pakistan. The minister denounced the Islamabad stand on Kashmir but was unconvincing in his rejection of any "third party intervention," given New Delhi's attempts to secure US support on the issue.

Bush, in his immediate reaction to the address, said: "Reaffirming Pakistan's role as a frontline state in the coalition against global terrorism, President Musharraf unequivocally rejected terrorism, pledging to take action against any Pakistani organization, group or individual involved in terrorism within or outside Pakistan. He clearly stated that the solution to Kashmir lies in peaceful means and dialogue."

Colin Powell chimed in: "This speech reconfirms Pakistan's role as a front-line state in the war against global terrorism. In light of the speech and the strong actions that President Musharraf has taken so far and the new actions to which he has committed his country, the United States believes the basis exists for the resolution of tensions between India and Pakistan through diplomatic and peaceful means."

In his next major televised address to the nation on May 27, 2002, Musharraf was more belligerent towards India and asked again for international intervention, and not only in Kashmir: "I urge the world community to ask India to move towards normalization of relations, which really implies de-escalation, and reduction of tension on the borders, which is of mutual benefit to both countries, initiation of process of dialogue, cessation of atrocities being perpetuated on the people of Kashmir, allowing international media and Human Rights organizations to enter Kashmir and see the realities on ground. I also urge the world that they must take note of the atrocities being committed by the Hindu extremists and terrorists in Kashmir, in Gujarat and elsewhere in India and against Muslims, Christians, Sikhs and also their own Scheduled Castes (Untouchables)."

On Kashmir, in particular, he referred to the assassination of Hurriyat leader Abdul Ghani Lone and the disappearance of the killers despite the crowd at the crime venue and the Indian security deployment: "Have they (the assassins) vanished into thin air?" He ended with an assurance to the "brothers and sisters" of Kashmir: "Kashmir lives in the heart of every Pakistani. Pakistan will always fulfill its duty of providing moral, political and diplomatic support to the cause of Kashmir. Pakistan will always support the Kashmiri struggle for liberation." It was clear that the creation of the coalition against "global terror," with both India and Pakistan as its constituents, was not going to usher in South Asian peace.

The hope that September11 was going to make a serious difference to Pakistan's role in relation to regional peace was belied. An interesting question, to have been raised without receiving due notice, is: was the hope well-founded? A cluster of reports in November 2001 suggested that the U.S. had decided upon a war on Afghanistan, and secured Pakistan's support for the plan, months before the tragedy of the Twin Towers. The announcement on February 8, 2002, of an agreement between Afghan

President Hamid Karzai and Musharraf on reviving the plan for a trans-Afghan gas pipeline from Turkmenistan to Pakistan seemed to reinforce the theory.

A consortium led by US-based company Unocal had originally aimed to build the $1.9 billion, 1,400-km (875-mile) pipeline to run from gas-rich Turkmenistan via northern Afghanistan. In August 1998, however, Unocal halted development of the project after US forces fired missiles at guerrilla camps in Afghanistan in the wake of bomb attacks on US embassies in two African countries, Kenya and Tanzania. Under the original plan, a 740-km (460-mile) stretch of the pipeline would run across northern Afghanistan.

An analytical article by anti-war American journalist Patrick Martin on November 20, 2001, summed up the reports: "Insider accounts published in the British, French and Indian media have revealed that US officials threatened war against Afghanistan during the summer of 2001. These reports include the prediction, made in July, that 'if the military action went ahead, it would take place before the snows started falling in Afghanistan, by the middle of October at the latest'. The Bush Administration began its bombing strikes on the hapless, poverty-stricken country October 7, and ground attacks by US Special Forces began October 19."

Coming to the oil connection, the article recalled: "The United States ruling elite has been contemplating war in Central Asia for at least a decade. As long ago as 1991, following the defeat of Iraq in the Persian Gulf War, *Newsweek* magazine...reported that the US military was preparing an operation in Kazakhstan.... American oil companies have acquired rights to as much as 75 per cent of the output of these new fields, and US government officials have hailed the Caspian and Central Asia as a potential alternative to dependence on oil from the unstable Persian Gulf region. American troops have followed in the wake of these contracts."

The major problem in exploiting the energy resources of Central Asia was how to get the oil and gas from the landlocked region to the world market. The option of using the Russian pipeline system had been rejected and the easiest available land route, across Iran to the Persian Gulf, was not considered safe. Instead, the Afghanistan pipeline route was pushed by Unocal. The talks with the Taliban regime were disrupted by the bombing in Kenya and Tanzania, for which Osama bin Laden was held responsible. Washington soon came up with the demand that Osama be handed over to the U.S. "The pipeline talks languished," Martin recalled.

According to the reports, several covert US adventures in Afghanistan followed. A story in the *Washington Post* (October 3, 2001) said the Clinton Administration and Nawaz Sharif, then prime minister of Pakistan, agreed on a joint covert operation to kill Osama in 1999. "The US would supply satellite intelligence, air support and financing, while Pakistan supplied the Pushtun-speaking operatives who would penetrate southern Afghanistan and carry out the actual killing." The attempt was aborted on October 12, 1999, when Sharif was overthrown in a military coup by Musharraf, who halted the proposed covert operation, according to the story.

The *Wall Street Journal* of November 2, 2001 carried an article by Robert McFarlane, former National Security Adviser in the Reagan Administration. McFarlane said he was hired by two wealthy Chicago commodity speculators, Joseph and James Ritchie, to assist them in recruiting and organizing anti-Taliban guerrillas among Afghan refugees in Pakistan. Their principal Afghan contact was Abdul Haq, the former mujahideen leader later executed by the Taliban.

McFarlane held meetings with Abdul Haq and other former mujahideen in the course of the fall and winter of 2000. After the Bush Administration took office, McFarlane used his Republican connections to arrange a series of meetings with State Department, Pentagon and even White House officials. All of them were for an anti-Taliban military campaign.

According to McFarlane, Haq "decided in mid-August to go ahead and launch operations in Afghanistan. He returned to Peshawar, Pakistan, to make final preparations." McFarlane blamed the CIA for "betraying" Haq, failing to back his operations in Afghanistan, and leaving him to die at the hands of the Taliban. The CIA was conducting its own secret war in the same southern Afghanistan. The *Washington Post* of November 18, 2001, carried a story by Bob Woodward saying that the CIA had been mounting paramilitary operations in southern Afghanistan since 1997.

"With the installation of George Bush in the White House," Martin points out, "the focus of American policy in Afghanistan shifted from a limited incursion to kill or capture bin Laden to preparing a more robust military intervention directed at the Taliban regime as a whole." Martin quotes the UK-based *Jane's International Security* of March 15, 2001, as reporting that the new American administration was working with India, Iran and Russia "in a concerted front against Afghanistan's Taliban regime." India was supplying the Northern Alliance with military equipment, advisers and helicopter technicians, the magazine said, and both India and Russia were using bases in Tajikistan and Uzbekistan for their operations.

Then, there was this interesting report by the BBC's George Arney a week after September 11. According to Arney, US officials had told former Pakistani Foreign Secretary Niaz Naik in mid-July of plans for military action against the Taliban regime:

"Mr. Naik said US officials told him of the plan at a UN-sponsored international contact group on Afghanistan which took place in Berlin.

"Mr. Naik told the BBC that, at the meeting the US representatives told him that unless bin Laden was handed over swiftly America would take military action to kill or capture both bin Laden and the Taliban leader, Mullah Omar.

"The wider objective, according to Mr. Naik, would be to topple the Taliban regime and install a transitional government of moderate Afghans in its place—possibly under the leadership of the former Afghan King Zahir Shah.

"Mr. Naik was told that Washington would launch its operation from bases in Tajikistan, where American advisers were already in place.

"He was told that Uzbekistan would also participate in the operation and that 17,000 Russian troops were on standby.

"Mr. Naik was told that if the military action went ahead it would take place before the snows started falling in Afghanistan, by the middle of October at the latest."

The story was confirmed by the *Guardian* on September 22: The warnings to Afghanistan came out of a four-day meeting of senior US, Russian, Iranian and Pakistani officials at a hotel in Berlin in mid-July, the third in a series of back-channel conferences dubbed "brainstorming on Afghanistan." The participants included three Pakistani generals, besides Naik and officials from Iran, the Northern Alliance of Afghanistan, Russia and the U.S.

Martin concludes: "This is not to say that the American government deliberately planned every detail of the terrorist attacks or anticipated that nearly 5,000 people would be killed. But the least likely explanation of September 11 is the official one: that dozens of Islamic fundamentalists, many with known ties to Osama bin Laden, were able to carry out a wide-ranging conspiracy on three continents, targeting the most prominent symbols of American power, without any US intelligence agency having the slightest idea of what they were doing."

Or (more pertinently for our purposes), without the Pakistani intelligence agency, the Inter-Services Intelligence (ISI), described within the country as "a state within a state," having not only a clear idea of the goings-on but even being closely associated with them. If the reports are correct, Pakistan was a frontline state for the US when both were promoting and propping up Taliban, is one when both are anti-Taliban, and has been one, too, during the transition. If that is so, September 11 could have made no positive difference to peace prospects in South Asia. Quite the contrary indeed has been the case, as the India-Pakistan standoff showed.

It is a triangle of nuclear terror for the entire region

that the US-India-Pakistan segment of the coalition has created. Among those to recognize this is Salman Rushdie, who cannot be accused of cheap anti-Americanism (something that he has, in fact, deplored). In an article titled "Double standards make enemies" in the *Washington Post* of August 28, 2002, he talks of the role of the Bush Administration in bringing South Asia to the brink months before: "In the year's major crisis zones, the Bushies have been getting things badly wrong. According to a Security Council source, the reason for the United Nations' lamentable inaction during the recent Kashmir crisis was that the United States (with Russian backing) blocked all attempts by member-states to mandate the United Nations to act. But if the United Nations is not to be allowed to intervene in a bitter dispute between two member-states, both nuclear powers of growing political volatility, in an attempt to defuse the danger of nuclear war, then what on Earth is it for? Many observers of the problems of the region will also be wondering how long Pakistani-backed terrorism in Kashmir will be winked at by America because of Pakistan's support for the "war against terror" on its other frontier. Many Kashmiris will be angry that their long-standing desire for an autonomous state is being ignored for the sake of US realpolitik. And as the Pakistani dictator Pervez Musharraf seizes more and more power and does more and more damage to his country's constitution, the US government's decision to go on hailing him as a champion of democracy does more damage to America's already shredded regional credibility."

India-born Rushdie is acutely aware also of the other way the Bushies have stoked the subcontinental fires—by benignly ignoring the factor of internal fascism. Says he:

"Kashmir is not the only South Asian grievance. The mas-sacres in the Indian state of Gujarat, mostly of Indian Muslims by fundamentalist Hindu mobs, have been shown to be the result of planned attacks led by Hindu political organizations. But in spite of testimony presented to a con-gressional commission, the US administration has done nothing to investigate US-based organizations that are funding these groups, such as the World Hindu Council. Just as American-Irish fundraisers once bankrolled the ter-rorists of the Provisional IRA, so, now, shadowy bodies across America are helping to pay for mass murder in India, while the U.S. government turns a blind eye. Once again, the supposedly high-principled rhetoric of the 'war against terror' is being made to look like a smokescreen for a highly selective pursuit of American vendettas."

India would like to use the war as a smokescreen for its own vendetta. If the U.S. makes the South Asian situ-ation worse by winking at Pakistan's support for terrorism in Kashmir, as Rushdie says, it does so also by not discour-aging the hawks of its newfound ally, India. Bharat Karnad, quoted before, has no qualms about recommend-ing "cross-border terrorism" by India which he does not expect the Bush regime to baulk at. As he puts it, "It has been almost seven years since RAW (the foreign intelli-gence section of the External Affairs Ministry) activities in Karachi and elsewhere were terminated by a misguided directive… The constraints on the Indian external intelli-gence and other agencies have to be lifted, old intelligence assets dusted off and new ones nursed on a war-footing. At the same time, a policy of renewing contacts with sub-nationalist and ethnic movements in Sindh, Baluchistan and Baltistan has to be set in motion. The long-standing

request of the Mohajir Quami Movement leader Altaf
Hussain to visit New Delhi and to confer with the Indian
leadership should be met as a prelude to stoking the fires
of civil war in Karachi and elsewhere, sending a signal to
Islamabad that while two can play this game, Pakistan, the
far more brittle nation-state, will succumb to the centrifu-
gal forces in very little time."

Karnad also advocates an escalation of the nuclear
threat in the name of calling "Pakistan's nuclear bluff." His
counsel: "The Indian government should publicly declare
that military reprisals for terrorist acts will be restricted
exclusively to PoK, and the responsibility for escalating
the conflict to a full-fledged war, across the recognized
international border, leave alone to the nuclear level, will
be solely Islamabad's. Because the jihadi support is sourced
to PoK, hitting out at terrorist installations there will be
accepted worldwide as a justified response. This will
instantly and permanently skew Pakistan's operational cal-
culus, because while the near-parity in conventional forces
may lead to an impasse, as in earlier wars, which will gain
it nothing, crossing the nuclear weapons-use threshold
will invite sure and certain annihilation of that country
vis-à-vis India's suffering grievous harm."

The hawks have not given up the hope for "surgical"
and "pre-emptive strikes" inside with the backing of the
Bush regime. The hope was renewed for them, in fact, by
the USA's plans for a war on Iraq. In an article in *The
Hindu* of September 12, 2002, Raja Mohan argues for
strong New Delhi support for Washington's case, followed
by the demand for a quid pro quo. "Having been the
biggest victim of international terrorism, India should
have little difficulty in appreciating the case for a preven-

tive war," he says, claiming that India started preparing for precisely such a war after the December 13 attack on its Parliament.

"An [sic] Indian support to the idea of a preventive war will reverberate more loudly in the portals of the UN than all the whining against Pakistan and the dossiers on Islamabad's support to cross-border terrorism that Mr. Vajpayee keeps handing out in Washington and New York," Raja Mohan asserts. "In fact, every single argument that the Bush Administration marshals on a pre-emptive war against Iraq applies with even greater clarity to Pakistan. Mr. Vajpayee does not have to do much except affirm the same right for India and a commitment to exercise that right judiciously."

Eminent Indian intellectual Rajni Kothari sees it all coming in an essay written before September 11 (India's Nuclear Nemesis, contributed to *Out of the Nuclear Shadow*): "As for the American approach in this whole affair, there seems to be a clear effort at becoming a both overt and covert participant-cum-mediator, forcing India to move out of its traditional bilateral posture vis-à-vis Pakistan and moving towards what a leading Indian commentator, V. Sudarshan, has called the growth of an 'India-Pak-US dialogue'. This is very much in keeping with the American global strategy of at once incorporating emerging regional powers and engaging in fostering a variety of 'peace accords' round the world, somehow hoping that the more dangerous the world becomes, the greater will be the dominant position of the United States in it."

Kothari adds: "It may be the end of the Cold War in a manner of speaking but it is certainly not the advent of peace. Indeed, if anything, it heralds even greater dangers

to the survival capacities of peoples, nations and civiliza-
tions." This has found a striking demonstration in the
development of the nuclear flashpoint in South Asia.

* * *

IT was not only by their political and diplomatic role
that the U.S. and its Western allies pushed the region to
the brink of a nuclear disaster in the summer of 2002. Not
only by emboldening both India and Pakistan to take
extreme stances and endanger the entire region. Not only
by allowing both of them utterly unrestrained nuclear conduct. Not only by not allowing any United Nations initiative or intervention in the explosive situation. Bush and
his loyal band led by Tony Blair did so also by directly arming the rivals locked in a deadly standoff. They peddled
arms to the combatant sides in the guise of peacemakers,
in blatant breach of their own domestic laws and mandates. The masks of the leaders of the "multinational
coalition against global terror" slipped off to reveal greasy
faces—of the glorified sales representatives of military-
industrial complexes.

Published reports of the arms trade deals of this kind
should suffice to reveal the pious hypocrisy of the alliance.
In February, Gen. Richard B. Myers, chairman of the US
Joint Chiefs of Staff, visited New Delhi. Shortly thereafter,
US arms maker Raytheon closed a $146-million deal to
sell the Indians counter-artillery radar. The U.S. approved
20 other defense agreements, including a contract for
General Electric to build engines for India's multimillion-
dollar Light Combat Aircraft project.

American analyst Conn Hallinan wrote at the time:
"US technology is also slipping through the back door via

weapons agreements between Israel and India. New Delhi is buying the $1-billion Phalcon airborne radar, which is based on the US AWAC surveillance system, and is negotiating to buy the Arrow anti-missile system jointly developed by the United States and Israel. Boeing makes 52 per cent of the Arrow's components."

Hallinan pointed out: "India is one of the biggest weapons markets in the world, with an annual budget of $14 billion. The United States is the world's No. 1 weapons dealer, with $18.6 billion in arms sales last year." The anti-terrorist allies could provide a textbook model of arms trade partnership. Washington, however, would not want it at the cost of its friendship with frontline state Pakistan.

On July 17, 2002, the US government announced its plan for a sizable military sale to Pakistan. The Pentagon deal would involve six cargo planes in the first major military sale since sanctions against Pakistan were lifted for its cooperation in the war against the al-Qaida network and Taliban. The proposed sale of six C-130 cargo planes and related equipment and services was valued at up to $75 million.

"This...sale will contribute to the foreign policy and national security of the United States by helping to improve the security of a friendly country," the Pentagon's Defense Security Cooperation Agency said. Pakistan needed the planes to improve airlift capabilities both for the needs of its own air force and "as it seeks to support the US government with Operation Enduring Freedom" the agency said in a statement, using the code name for the drive to oust al-Qaida from Afghanistan. Among other rewards for Musharraf's cooperation was the rescheduling of $379 million in Pakistani debt. This was, doubtless, intended to help in the growth of the arms trade, too.

The British contributed much more than their bit to the trade, and in a much more brazen manner as well. On July 19, 2002, lawmakers of Britain criticized Foreign Secretary Jack Straw in a report published Friday for failing to block arms sales to nuclear rivals India and Pakistan during their armed standoff over Kashmir. A joint report by four House of Commons committees—foreign affairs, defense, trade and industry and international development—said Straw failed to apply government guidelines banning weapons exports where there was a risk they could be used for external aggression. They were "surprised" that Straw did not personally examine export license applications to the region during the period of heightened tension over the disputed territory in May and June.

In a letter to the committee, Straw said that 148 licenses had been issued to India during the period and another 18 to Pakistan, but that he had not personally been involved. The lawmakers said the standoff over Kashmir should have triggered criterion 4 of the government's guidelines, which forbids arms exports where there is a clear risk they could be used "aggressively against another country."

"We conclude that if the situation in India and Pakistan in the spring of this year did not fully engage criterion 4, it is difficult to conceive of circumstances short of all-out war which would do so," the committee report said. "The standoff over Kashmir should in our view have led to its application with very great vigor." The disapproval would sound disingenuous indeed, given that the nexus between the government and the military-industrial complex, especially the BAE (British Aerospace) Systems, was no closely guarded secret.

After a visit to New Delhi and to a Defexpo, the Land and Naval Systems Exhibition, there, *Independent's* Will Self wrote on August 1, 2002: "The Brits at Defexpo were altogether more circumspect [than the Israelis] about what they were selling. I even had Stephen Taylor, the Marketing Director of the Defense Manufacturers Association…tell me that most of what his members were in India to sell was 'humanitarian' equipment. Nevertheless, it was disconcerting to see serving British soldiers demonstrating this 'humanitarian' equipment to Indian military top brass (such as humanitarian night scopes that enable a soldier to pinpoint a target with accuracy, presumably so he can stick a plaster on in the dark)." There was nothing humanitarian, either, about the hypocrisy of an anti-war amendment to the export control law that the Labor government in London was taking credit for.

Wrote Self: "The Bill may well say that 'an adverse effect on peace, security or stability in any region of the world or within any country' is a prima facie reason to refuse an export, but that didn't stop Jack Straw and Tony Blair traveling to India this year for a quiet chat about the 17-year hold-up in India's purchase of 60 Hawk jet trainers; a sale—worth millions to BAE Systems—of an aircraft which Squadron Leader Bakshi (Indian Air Force, retired) told me, when I was in Delhi in February, was 'ideal' for ground offensive operations in Kashmiri terrain."

More disturbing news was to follow. An Indian news agency report from London on August 25, 2002, said:

"Britain has stepped up its surveillance of Pakistani activities in the country following reports that Islamabad has been secretly buying from here equipment for making nuclear weapons. Special high-grade metals have been smuggled out of the country and are believed to have reached an uranium enrichment plant in Kahuta, near Islamabad, a media report said...The discovery has infuriated the British Foreign office, which had assurances from Pakistan that it was not shopping in Britain for weapons of mass destruction or related equipment. The British Security agency MI5 is said to have already stepped up its surveillance of Pakistani activities in UK, including diplomats in London involved in the procurement of military equipment."

The report added: "At least one consignment of 47 tons of high-strength aluminum worth 150,000 pounds was sent to Pakistan from a British firm. The material, made to a standard known as 6061 T6, is used to make centrifuges for converting uranium ore to bomb-grade uranium."

"This is not the kind of aluminum you use for soft drink cans, it has a very limited number of applications," the *Sunday Times* quoted a source. Customs and excise officers discovered that the aluminum had been secretly shipped to the Khan Research Laboratories in Pakistan, which manufactures nuclear weapons. The MI5 visited the Blackburn-based company that sold the material and warned that Pakistan and other states may try to circumvent an export ban. There has been no follow-up on the story.

It was not only the U.S. and the UK making a killing on the arms deals. In an article on "Lack of strategic procurement plans" in the *Friday Times* of Pakistan on August 15, Ayesha Siddiqui-Agha wrote: "Some information indicates that potential sellers are cozying up to Pakistan's military establishment selling equipment. The statement by the British naval attaché regarding Pakistan Navy's interest in the Type-22 frigates is one instance of that. There is also news about France's interest in selling its frigates to Pakistan. The Indonesians have also sold limited units of their CASA-transport aircraft (Spanish origin) to the PAF. This is in addition to the American deal of a few C-130s and the Russian transport helicopters."

Non-US, non-UK players were active in India as well. A detailed report by Rahul Bedi in the fortnightly *Frontline* of August 3, 2002, said: "Three howitzer manufacturers from Israel, South Africa and Sweden are currently competing in trials in the Pokharan desert (the site of nuclear tests) to sell India their weapon systems in a contract worth RS.10,000 crore (Rs 1,000 billion) to RS.12,000 crore (RS. 1,200 billion). Soltam of Israel, Denel Ordnance of South Africa and Bofors Defense (now owned by United Defense LP of the United States) of Sweden are putting their 155mm/52 caliber howitzers through rigorous testing. The Army plans to buy initially 200 pieces and eventually build an inventory of around 3,000-4,000 guns through licensed indigenous production in order to equip around 200 artillery regiments over the next two decades."

The report talked of a menacing proposal which "aims at upgrading the artillery's firepower to augment armored and mechanized formations in order to neutralize strategic targets in what planners predict will be a limited engagement influenced by the region's nuclear and missile capabilities."

"The guns will also be subjected to high-altitude test-ing either in Jammu & Kashmir, where many of the guns will eventually be deployed, or in Sikkim before a final assessment is made," the report said. The implication of these plans is ominous: a recurrence of the standoff is a real possibility as preparations are made to continue the con-flict for the long term. Kashmir is no mere border skirmish that can be easily ironed out.

India's post-September-11 relations with Israel have attracted special attention. Says the report: "Entrenched in India, Soltam is involved in upgrading 180 130 M 46 field guns to 155/39 caliber and 155mm/45 caliber under a contract worth around $4.07 million." The report claimed that senior artillery officers "admitted privately" that Soltam's upgrade program was "flawed" and "overambi-tious." But the Army was under heavy pressure not to withdraw from the upgrade deal signed in March 2000. The Ministry of Defense was under intense diplomatic and political pressure from Tel Aviv not to withdraw from the upgrade program, the report quoted sources as saying.

"Israel also exercises considerable influence in Indian defense circles, having become the country's second largest supplier of military equipment after Russia, only a decade since Tel Aviv and New Delhi established formal diplomatic ties in 1992. And, once the Bharatiya Janata Party-led coalition assumed office in 1998, they developed stronger intelligence, security and, reportedly, even nuclear links."

The claim will receive wide credence, given the long-standing ideological commitment of the BJP's political camp to the Israeli and anti-Palestine cause. After all these arms deals, however, there can be little credibility for any claim that the anti-"terror" US-India-Pakistan alliance augurs well for South Asian peace.

CHAPTER 8

SAVING A SUBCONTINENT

People Are the Only Hope for Peace

In this lies our only security and our only hope—we believe an informed citizenry will act for life and not for death

—Albert Einstein, January 22, 1947

Before the terrifying prospects now available to humanity, we see even more clearly that peace is the only goal worth struggling for. This is no longer a prayer but a demand to be made by all peoples to their governments— a demand to choose definitively between hell and reason.

—Albert Camus, on the bombing of Hiroshima, in the Resistance newspaper *Combat*, August 8, 1945

...the atomic bomb has deadened the finest feelings that have sustained mankind for ages. There used to be so-called laws of war that made it tolerable. Now we understand the naked truth.

—Mahatma Gandhi, in his periodical *Harijan*, July 7, 1946

...pseudo-scientific patterns of discourse, much cultivated by the social and behavioral sciences, provide a new and useful ideological device for those who hope to mask force and coercion in technical terminology of problem-solving that may delude people who have no idea what science is all about. That most of this is drivel does

not, unfortunately, limit its effectiveness.
                    —Noam Chomsky, Radical Priorities (1984)

Why, of course, the people don't want war... But,
after all, it is the leaders of the country who determine the
policy, and it is always a simple matter to drag the people
along, whether it is a democracy, or a fascist dictatorship,
or a parliament, or a communist dictatorship... Voice or
no voice, the people can always be brought to the bidding
of the leaders. That is easy. All you have to do is to tell
them they are being attacked, and denounce the pacifists
for lack of patriotism and exposing the country to danger.
                    —Hermann Goering at Nuremberg Trials
                                                   (1946)

If protesting against having a nuclear bomb implant-
ed in my brain is anti-Hindu and anti-national, then I
secede.
                    —Arundhati Roy, The End of Imagination,
                                              August 1, 1998

Let me snatch and break the dagger from the tyrant's
hand,
        let me break the glittering stone in his crown.
        Whether anyone else breaks it or not,
        let me go ahead and break it.
                        —Firaq Gorakhpuri, India's Urdu poet
                                              (1896-1982)

A lost subcontinent—that is what South Asia could
have been today. One and a half billion people—one sixth
of humanity—live on the subcontinent. It is the first and
only region to have survived a war and close stand off
between two nations armed with nuclear weapons. At this
writing, in October of 2003, India and Pakistan have

retreated a few inches from the brink of annihilation. Not to safety, but to the point where the headlines about the situation fade, and in the U.S. disappear completely. Is there hope for this part of the planet? For a convincingly affirmative answer, one must turn away from the official triangle "against terror."

For, the triangle is now the problem, not the solution. After that spine-chilling summer, no one can claim that the multinational alliance has had or can ever have a peace spin-off for the region. Yes, the world did hear much then about how Washington, like a good boxing referee, single-handedly and single-mindedly kept separating the combatants and called off the bout before it could become a calamity. We have heard, however, even more subsequently about the role Bush and his band refrained, and restrained the United Nations, from playing during those agonizing months, even as "peace" emissaries doubled as brokers of arms deals. Nor can the leaders of New Delhi and Islamabad be said to have learnt any lesson from the experience of those days. Even the terms of the bellicosity have changed little: India's hawks now prefer to talk of a "pre-emptive" rather than a "surgical" strike. The generals of Pakistan, meanwhile, continue to defend their fundamental right to a "first strike."

The only hope, in this bleak scenario, springs from a source that is beneath the sight of security experts and strategic analysts: the small but significant peace movement in the subcontinent, especially in India. The hope is the greater, in fact, for the would-be Machiavellis' studied semblance of a haughty disdain for the movement. For, their affectation is a tribute to the movement's truth, a testimony to their fear that it can become a force.

The movement is a fall-out of the nuclear-weapon tests of May 1998, one that the militarists did not anticipate. There was an apology for a peace movement before then, concerning itself in a formal manner with foreign affairs issues, reacting to world events with widely unread statements and occasional actions for the consumption of select and special audiences alone. There was also a committed anti-nuclear camp that, in the prevailing political ambience, could not convert itself into a movement. It took Pokharan II and Chagai to transform the ritual peace campaign and the severely restricted anti-nuclear activism into a real movement.

Activism directed against India's own nuclear establishment as well as against world nuclear powers was as old as Pokharan I of 1974. It was a national policy and phase of "nuclear ambiguity," as its critics put it, of keeping the country's nuclear options open that was left largely unchallenged and made Pokharan II possible. Many now in the movement did not see the dangers of the "peaceful nuclear explosion" (PNE) of over two decades ago, and they are reminded of the fact and rebuked now and then. I am among those who would gladly plead guilty. What needs to be noted even more, however, is that Pokharan II came as a qualitatively different and more dangerous package and was seen so by the anti-PNE sections.[1]

Pokharan II came as a shocking reminder of the kind of politics that had captured power in New Delhi. The accompanying declaration of India as a nuclear-weapon state startled many into a realization of the enormous distance the nation had traveled from the desert site and from its proudly traditional policy of working for world peace and nuclear disarmament. An unmistakable message of fascist militarism was sent out by the obscene and organized celebrations that followed. The leadership of the BJP took particular pride in implementing a major program of its own agenda, even when perched in precarious power at the head of a minority government in the parliamentary system. They had done it despite the fact that they had no parliamentary majority and, therefore, might have been too diffident to go for a new, strident nuclear policy. The point of Pokharan II, as a blasting of hopes for South Asian peace, was to be made again and again through the bombing threats freely bandied about through the Kargil war and the more frightening face-off of 2002.

The mood at the birth of the movement in India was captured by Praful Bidwai in a paper on "The Struggle for Nuclear Disarmament": "The principled, non-jingoistic response of a cross-section of society to India's nuclear tests indicates the beginnings of a powerful nuclear disarmament movement by citizens… The tide has turned. The manufactured 'consensus' over the…decision to cross the nuclear threshold now stands exposed for what it was: flimsy, uninformed, reluctant acceptance of the fait accompli that a particular political party with a unique nuclear obsession had inflicted upon us all without the fig leaf of a security rationale or strategic review."

Similarly, the spirit of the first Pakistan Peace Conference in Karachi in February 1999 found eloquent expression in anti-nuclear activist I. A. Rehman's presentation at the conference. Talking of the response to the nuclear-weapon tests in both the countries, he said: "…there is a huge mass of people in our countries who have not yet come under the spell of the tiny minority that occupies commanding heights in politics and economy. If we are not prepared to mobilize them into a powerful mass movement for peace, ...we may go home to rest our heels. But, if we are true to the sentiment that has brought us here, there is a promise of glorious fight and of rewards history will thank us for."

These expectations about the growth of the movement may have proved a bit exaggerated, but those who hoped to make the movement disappear by simply and steadily disregarding it must be disappointed. In Pakistan, creation of a powerful mass movement for peace will have to wait for creation of enough democratic conditions to enable people's intervention in the domain of "national security." In India, it turns out, the policy and phase of "nuclear ambiguity" has taken a heavy political toll. A sad post-Pokharan II discovery for many is that the nuclear hawks have no political deterrence against their programs to worry about. The main opposition Congress Party has made it easy for nuclear militarism in Parliament and elsewhere by playing only the friendliest of matches with the government on Pokharan II and related issues.

The Congress—the party of India's freedom struggle, of the uncompromisingly anti-Bomb Mahatma Gandhi and of Nehru who said "no" to an Indian response to China's testing—had apparently little of its peace legacy left after the cynical seventies. One of its more articulate members of Parliament and a newspaper columnist, Mani Shankar Aiyar, did speak and write about Pokharan II undoing a "national consensus," but was soon to stop raising the issue: he did not deem it realistic to expect any regime in New Delhi to undo the tests and reverse the nuclear-weapon program. The party's only official criticism of Pokharan II was that it was not consulted and taken into confidence. No such chip on the shoulder stopped any of the other, smaller centrist parties from hailing the tests as a fitting response to the challenge of the times.

On the party-political front, it was only the Left that took a principled and firm stand against Pokharan II. The main protest, however, came from mass organizations, Left-linked as well as independent, representing different sections of the people, ranging from writers, artists, scientists, journalists, workers and employees to women, youth and students. These remain the mainstay of the movement. The composition and character of the movement are nothing to complain about. The Left is a lesser force than either the BJP or the Congress, but its catalytic role has influenced the course of politics on several past occasions. And the mass organizations, more than anything else, can help to make peace a people's issue.

* * *

ALREADY a people's issue was the price they had paid for the nation's advance to nuclear militarism in places one hardly saw outside very occasional media headlines. Write Smitu Kothari and Zia Mian in an introduction to their compilation on nuclear weaponization in India and Pakistan: "There is a not so visible history of opposition to the nuclear future in South Asia. Far removed from the centers of political authority, at the sites where nuclear facilities have been and are being built, be it in uranium mines or nuclear power plants, local communities are engaged in remarkable struggles. Their movements and mobilizations are often not couched in the language of big ideas of social change and protest, but in the small traditions of defending livelihoods, community rights, public health, the right to information. They have marched, fasted, blockaded, occupied, gone to court, they have protested to survive and highlight their concerns."

The first of these places is Pokharan itself. Or, more precisely, Khetaloi village, hardly 2.5 km from the infamous nuclear test site. The village population of about 2,000 remembers May 11 and 13, 1998, the days of the tests, only too well. Army personnel visited them around 11 a.m. on both days and asked them to come out of their houses and stand in the scorching May sun till the evening. Everything nuclear had to be shrouded in secrecy, and the villagers were not told on May 11 why they were being given this order. They were later assured that it was for their own good—their houses might have collapsed on them because of the blasts.

The tests were conducted without the minimum safety precautions for the people of the area, and the consequences have been terrible, say social activists. The Sustainable Economic and Educational Development (SEEDS) India, a student activist body that has worked on the impact of nuclear programs in India, claims that villager Ramkaran Vaishnoi was "the first victim of nuclear testing in India." He died in January 1999 of thyroid cancer, a disease caused by exposure to radiation in many recorded cases. The agency's survey has reportedly revealed that a big proportion of villagers are suffering from throat cancer and complaining of nose bleeding, skin discoloration and itching.

The majority of the villagers are Vaishnois, traditionally lovers of trees and animals (especially the local black bucks). They are vegetarians and depend much on milk and milk products, which are easily contaminated by the radioactive fall-out of nuclear tests. Their cattle are also suffering from mysterious radiation diseases, for which no veterinary treatment is available in the area. The quantity of milk produced per cow has decreased from five liters per milking to one litre. Even the hardy camels of the desert region are said to be suffering from skin diseases.

But how can an underground nuclear test expose someone above ground to radiation? A report by Kalpana Sharma in *The Hindu* daily of November 13, 1998, exactly six months after the tests, said a "study of the health impact of the tests is being planned.... The government is worried that the rain might have led to some contamination of the underground aquifers around the...site. As a result, discussions are under way to set up a secret study of the area to test whether radioactivity can be detected in the soil, water, grass or animal milk." The study has been so secret that the country has not still been told of the findings. There is no official explanation of the release of radiation in underground tests, which has not been denied.

The villagers only grew more resentful at the Prime Minister's reported response on being told of their suffering: "Some people have to make sacrifices." According to Sharma's report, they were also upset that Vajpayee, when he visited the test site, refused to visit the village, too. "Later, when some of them tried to go to Pokharan for his public meeting, the (railway) level crossing on the road to Pokharan was shut and thorns were placed before it so that they could not go across."

They have been trying to get across to the powers-that-be ever since, with similar results. They, however, have not given up. A growing demand of the countrywide peace movement, meanwhile, is the permanent closure of the Pokharan test site. If and when the demand is won, it will be more than a symbolic victory for a tribal village in the Jaisalmer district of the picturesque northern state of Rajasthan.

A victim of Pokharan, too, is another tribal population in another backward state. The uranium mines of Jaduguda in the Chhotanagpur district of the tribal state of Jharkhand (formerly part of Bihar), that provide much of the fuel for India's nuclear research, have created a hell of radiation sickness, genetic mutation and slow deaths, according to many independent accounts.

On September 4, 2000, the Supreme Court of India admitted a petition seeking direction to the Centre and the Uranium Corporation Limited (UCIL) to take stringent measures at the mines in the wake of alarming reports that villagers were affected by the radiation from mines. On August 30, 1999, the court issued notice to the Union government and the UCIL among others on a public interest petition seeking a direction to take immediate steps to insulate people living in the vicinity of the mines from the hazards of untreated effluents. It took a long and arduous struggle for the victims to secure national recognition of the problem, which the nuclear dispensation had continued to dismiss as the creation of anti-national activism.

A month after Pokharan II, in June 1998, Jaduguda witnessed demonstrations by thousands of tribesmen against rising radiation sickness in and around the mines, the lifeline of India's nuclear program. Local press reports warned that the protests might snowball into a national embarrassment close on the heels of the tests.

Activists from a group that was unheard of until the mining began, Jaduguda Organization Against Radiation (JOAR), identified hundreds of adults and 160 children living in four villages in the shadow of the mines as the victims of radiation. JOAR demanded free medical treatment and monetary compensation from the UCIL. After examining 712 people suffering from blood cancer, thalassemia, tuberculosis, congenital deformities, impotency and infertility, the UCIL then grudgingly admitted that 31 tribesmen were suffering from the "possible effects" of radiation.

JOAR convener Ghanshyam Biruli, commented: "When we first raised our voice against ecological and health hazards, we were branded agents of Pakistan's Inter-Services Intelligence to turn ordinary workers against us." Other activists were quoted in the press as saying that the indigenous people had been reduced to "pawns on India's nuclear chessboard."

The worst affected, according to them, were daily laborers working in the subterranean maze of shafts and galleries risking direct exposure. Children crawling on all fours because their ankles were deformed since birth, said the report, were also a common sight in villages around the mines. Hundreds of children had reportedly died due to radiation-related diseases.

On December 27, 1998, a report of the environment committee of the Bihar Legislative Council testified that people living near the mines had been severely affected by uranium radioactivity. The report found truth in JOAR's charge that the UCIL had been dumping "tailings" or waste products in a nearby pond and that this had led to sickness of the tribal people using the pond's radioactive water. The report noted that a medical team sent by the state government had also reached a similar conclusion. Under the committee's pressure, as many as 46 tribal families were moved from the area by the government.

The official reaction was typical. The magistrate of the Singhbhum district, where Jaduguda is located, blamed the media, particularly the BBC, for highlighting the issue and said that it should not have been made public since uranium-related activities fell under the category of "national security." It is in the face of this persistent attitude, legitimized by media-promoted militarist patriotism, that the struggle has continued for such a minimal demand as safe uranium mining.

With a string of nuclear power breeder reactors besides uranium processing and heavy water production units on both the eastern and western coasts of the South Indian peninsula, another section of the people to come into conflict with the nuclear establishment of India is the fishing community. An illustration is provided by the cluster of complaints about the growing problems of the community around Kalpakkam, the site of two nuclear power units and a proposed fast breeder reactor, in the outskirts of the southern city of Chennai on the eastern coast. At a public hearing on the fast breeder reactor project held on July 27, 2002, the proposal elicited strong opposition from the community.

Its representatives said that the discharge of coolant water into the sea from the power plant had caused a sharp decline in the population of popular varieties of fish. There have been reports, too, never convincingly denied, of heavy water leaks at Kalpakkam; and there have been no methodical studies about the extent of marine life that many residents of the area believe to have been affected. Voluntary agencies working in and around Kalpakkam consider the community's fears to be well founded.

The Coastal Action Network has reportedly found an increase in the number of a temperature-resistant variety of jellyfish in the affected area of the Bay of Bengal. This endorses the catamaran-plying fishermen's empirical observations about a significant warming of the waters with hazardous consequences for their and their community's health. According to the Doctors for Safer Environment, which claims to have surveyed some villages close to Kalpakkam, the residents have developed several deformities over the recent years. The groundwater in the whole area is said to have suffered a serious depletion as well as pollution of a dangerous level.

The complaints have all been treated with an official contempt they certainly did not deserve in a democracy. The Department of Atomic Energy (DAE), presiding over the entire nuclear establishment, has disdained to conceal its impatience with the idea of public accountability, particularly in matters of safety. Today, India is a nuclear-weapon state without an independent atomic safety authority. An authority missing despite the fact that it is required by an important provision of the International Convention on Nuclear Safety, to which the country is a signatory. Safety standards declined further with a governmental directive of April 2000 issued without any public debate.

Before that, a quasi-autonomous Atomic Energy Regulatory Board (AERB) provided some semblance of a watch over the safety standards in the country's nuclear complex. By an order of the Atomic Energy Commission (AEC), the most important component of the complex was taken out of the AERB's purview. The Mumbai-based Bhabha Atomic Research Centre (BARC)—in charge of the main nuclear-weapon-related work as well as spent-fuel reprocessing plants and radioactive waste processing and management—was to be "regulated" in this respect only by an Internal Safety Committee constituted by the BARC itself. The safety of the people was less important than the sanctified secrecy of the nuclear establishment.

The comment of former AERB chairman Adinarayana Gopalakrishnan was candid: "India is a Chernobyl waiting to happen." To him, this was not a fantasy, if "safety norms are not adhered to and new regulations not framed for the ten operating and four under-construction nuclear power reactors." He stressed that the "supremacy of the DAE over the AERB has crippled the regulatory process and compromised safety in the nuclear plants." Similar views were articulated by several other experts. There has been no sign, however, of any official readiness for rethinking on the issue.[2]

* * *

THE nuclear militarists of the subcontinent have, right from Pokharan II and Chagai, argued against any official rethinking on any related subject on the ground of an alleged "national consensus" in their favor in India and Pakistan. The new peace movement began by questioning the "consensus." Sections of people, whose lives and livelihoods were not immediately threatened by the radioactive resurgence, were all expected to join the hawks of either country in hailing it. This did not happen. On the contrary, groups that were supposed to have contributed notably to the "consensus," and to work for the nation's greater nuclear glory, appeared to have their share of dissenters and doubters. There was no stopping the voices of protest from where they were perhaps least expected

Pokharan II startled these groups into action. With the tests, the BJP ceased to appear just a bunch of jokers. Its "hidden agenda" no longer seemed either a really harmless relic of its past, which realpolitik won't let it implement, or a bogey of its opponents' creation. The mushroom cloud parted to reveal a face of fascist militarism that suddenly appeared too close for comfort.

Arundhati Roy, the award-winning author of *The God of Small Things* and the prize exhibit of "patriots" till then, mirrored the mood of the rudely awakened. In The End of Imagination, the essay read out first to an enthralled audience at a Chennai convention organized by the Campaign Committee Against Nuclear Weapons, she started with a confession and a call: "There's nothing new or original left to be said about nuclear weapons: 'There can be nothing more humiliating for a writer of fiction to have to do than restate a case that has, over the years, already been made by other people in other parts of the world...I am prepared to grovel. To humiliate myself abjectly, because, in the circumstances, silence would be indefensible. So those of you who are willing: let's pick our parts, put on these discarded costumes and speak our second-hand lines in this sad second-hand play. But let's not forget that the stakes we're playing for are huge. Our fatigue and our shame could mean the end of us. The end of our children and our children's children. Of everything we love. We have to reach within ourselves and find the strength to think. To fight.'"

She was mocking those who mocked the protesters

and who called them outdated avatars of pristine peace activists. As though the mockers were coming out with refreshingly modern arguments for nuclear militarism, as though the latter-day Nazis represented a shining new age, as though warmongering were the mark of a brave new India making a "bold departure from the past."

It was not without reason that among the very first protesters were working scientists across the country. The peddlers and promoters of Pokharan II were projecting it as an achievement of Indian science and scientists. Lack of pride in the achievement and the achievers, it was suggested, was a new low in anti-national conduct. A nuclear "consensus" among scientists was claimed, as was a national one about the scientific stride that the tests symbolized. Personality cults were built around individual science administrators associated and identified with Pokharan II. They were lionized in well-publicized fora and feted as patriots par excellence. These scientists seized the occasions to make observations of a partisan character and even statements approximating to policy pronouncements.

One of them, A. P. J. Abdul Kalam, to be catapulted to India's Presidency four years later, was quoted as contemptuously directing the opponents of the tests and the nuclear-weaponization program to go stage their protests and demonstrations in Washington and Moscow—as though those against India's Bomb were not opposed to nuclear weapons elsewhere and everywhere. Another eminence of the nuclear establishment, K. Santhanam, declared that India could make the neutron bomb and assured the nation that the scientists were ready to make it. A third, former Atomic Energy Commission chairman R. Chidambaram, pronounced in a press interview: "We are a big country. We must learn to behave like a big country of one billion people. We should constantly remind ourselves of our strength."

T. Jayaraman, whose initiative led to the formation of the increasingly active forum of the Indian Scientists Against Nuclear Weapons (ISANW), also recalled in a paper a pre-Pokharan II interview by Chidambaram. In the interview given on the eve of the formation of a BJP-led government in New Delhi in March 1998, the AEC chief argued that tests were a necessity. In reply to the question whether the country could go nuclear as outlined in the manifesto of the BJP, Chidambaram said: "That the country was technologically ready and the capability was proved long back...this preparedness itself was a testimony to the deterrent capability possessed by the country." Asked whether the country could go ahead only with the help of simulations and by avoiding actual ground experiments, he retorted: "Then what was the use of some countries going for 2,000 explosions?" He added: "If you are weak, people will try to take advantage of it."

Jayaraman's comment: "Clearly the DAE leadership was all set to bury the earlier Indian policy line of conditional self-restraint on the nuclear option. It found in the ascent to power of a government led by the BJP, with its long-standing dream of nuclear weaponization, a congenial political climate." This did not mean a "consensus" in the scientific community that included a significant section on the side of science for peace and development. The ISANW, in alliance with several other groups in the movement, has been campaigning for science policies and programs that give priority for drinking water over diabolical weapons, for malaria eradication over missile development.

The conflict within the community came to the fore, again, with the BJP adopting Kalam as its candidate in the country's presidential election of July 2002. The main opposition Congress and its allies responded exactly the same way as they had to Pokharan II—endorsing the rulers' decision, but demurring a bit about not being consulted and taken into confidence before. It was only the Left that came out in opposition to Kalam. It was the peace movement, however, that posed the questions involved in his candidature with clarity and without any compromise. He had been nominated, the movement pointed out, above all, as a symbol of nuclear militarism.

It was as such a symbol that Kalam has been projected over the past four years. The extraordinary image of the "eminent scientist" was a product of Pokharan II and the pro-nuclear-weaponization propaganda since then. Kalam had conducted himself through all this not as just a working scientist but as a crusader for militarization and nuclear weaponization. His nuclear militarism had been backed up with the same national-chauvinism that the forces behind his candidature flaunted. His victory in the indirect election was, of course, a foregone conclusion, but the much-vaunted "consensus" has again been proved a myth in the process.

Behind the similar myth of a pro-Pokharan II consensus in the media was the other and older myth that the media represented mediapersons. True, exceptions like fortnightly *Frontline* only proved the general rule of media militarism. Despite odd and occasional voices of dissent, allowed in some cases only to keep up liberal appearances, the majority of the mainstream media stood up to be counted among drum-beaters for the warmongers. They, in fact, served the state as the manufacturers and manipulators of the devoutly desired and piously pretended "consensus." But they did not speak for every media person any more than the DAE for all sections of scientists.

In less than three months after the tests, by the end of July 1998, the Chennai-based Journalists Against Nuclear Weapons had come into being and taken on the challenging task of trying and building a wider platform of popular resistance to the ambitious nuclear-weaponization program that New Delhi was expected to announce soon. One of the first projects the JANW took up was a review of media responses to Pokharan II. This was inspired by a message the Chennai group received from a Pakistani journalist, Zaffarullah Khan. He recalled that the Pakistan Federal Union of Journalists and the Indian Journalists' Union "were the first sister organizations in the new nuke states...to issue a joint statement urging both countries 'not to build up tensions in the subcontinent by participating in a senseless arms race towards the end of the twentieth century when the entire world is moving towards a peace-loving society, particularly when both the nations are celebrating the golden jubilee of independence.'" He proceeded to give us a brief but informative review of the reactions of Pakistan's press to the Chagai tests.

Khan and we came to a similar conclusion about an interesting and important aspect of the media role in the entire matter. He found that Pakistan's Urdu press was "extra-jubilant" about Chagai and inelegant in India- and Hindu-bashing. The English-language press offered a "modest space for dissent" but argued for the nation's "divorce" with the policy of "nuclear ambiguity." We found a like division of labor in the pro-Pokharan II media. It was left to the Indian-language media of this camp, especially the print media, to indulge in crudely religious-communal propaganda for the "Hindu Bomb." The non-English-knowing masses were to be served their fascist-militarist fare without frills. The English-language media, however, catered to their educated and elitist clientele in a different manner. They, too, sold the same Pokharan II, but in the name of "national interest," as an "explosion of self-esteem," as the "road to resurgence," as "an end to ambiguity and hypocrisy," as a way out of the Third World, as a corridor to the nuclear club, and as an invitation to the world's high table. There was some tut-tutting about the "communalist" capers but these made no difference to the media's view of the tests.

The world no longer seems to be "moving towards a peace-loving society," but the dominant media in both the countries may be moving in the same direction. Their responses to Kargil and to the standoff have been similar. The Bush war may have elicited very different responses from Pakistan's Urdu press in particular and India's media, but without making a difference to their combined contribution to the cause of peace in the subcontinent. Theirs is a conflict-promoting "consensus" that the movement, including the contingent of media persons, will have to keep countering.

* * *

THE diversity of protest groups to spring up in the wake of Pokharan II and Chagai was bound to inspire moves for their unity within India and Pakistan as an essential condition for their effective functioning in the face of powerful enemy forces. Consolidation at different levels preceded formation of countrywide organizations in both. The founding of the Pakistan Peace Coalition was the culmination of a process that witnessed the formation of the Lahore Peace Forum, the Action Committee Against Arms Race, and the Pakistan Doctors for Peace and Development, among other fora. Under less restrictive conditions, the Indian movement was able to take longer strides, though the advance has been far from adequate.

Over 30 organizations with the anti-nuclear-weapon campaign on their agendas came together in June 2000 in Chennai to form the Movement Against Nuclear Weapons. A similar broad platform against the tests and what they threatened took shape in Bangalore, another city of south India. There were several more initiatives of this kind across the vast country. The nation-level Coalition for Nuclear Disarmament and Peace was created at a convention in New Delhi in November 2000. Over 600 delegates attended the convention, more than 500 from across India. In addition, 50 "solidarity delegates" were present from Pakistan, 15 from Bangladesh and Sri Lanka, and around 20 from other countries including Australia, Canada, France, Japan, New Zealand, South Africa, the UK and the U.S.

The Charter of the CNDP, adopted at the first meeting of its national coordination committee in Chennai on January 19, 2001, declared: "India's self-declared entry into the 'nuclear weapons club' in May 1998, when it conducted five nuclear tests in Pokharan, Rajasthan, is ethically reprehensible as well as socially, politically, and economically ruinous. India and Pakistan have now joined the original five members of the nuclear weapons club and Israel who, unmoved by the horrifying experience of Hiroshima and Nagasaki in 1945, have amassed nuclear weapons. Such a legitimization of nuclear weapons deserves unequivocal condemnation. The [CNDP] was constituted...in response to nuclear weaponization in India and Pakistan against a background of the global amassing of nuclear weapons."

A guiding principle of India's post-Pokharan II peace movement has been that the struggle against nuclear weapons is not one against nuclear weapons alone. The Charter says: "Early nuclear disarmament is essential as a crucial link in the struggle for an egalitarian, just society and world. Thus the struggle for nuclear disarmament must connect with global, regional, national, and local concerns, particularly in the context of internecine conflicts driven by imperialist, fundamentalist and militarist ideologies in the world today." Internal fascism, it has come to be increasingly recognized, heads the list of the implacably hostile forces that the peace camp must encounter in frontal resistance. It was not without reason that the savagery in Gujarat and the border standoff were simultaneous; not without reason, either, that all sections of the movement devoted their campaign time equally to both the dangerous developments during the trying period.

A public awareness campaign for peace and against nuclear madness—the main task before the movement—has not been easy despite India's democracy. The campaign faces obstacles that the country's constitution hardly provides for, as a couple of examples should suffice to show. The first day's proceedings at the CNDP's founding convention—opposing the government's nuclear policy and attended by political leaders and foreign delegates including a large number from Pakistan—went entirely uncovered in all the "national" newspapers from New

Delhi. No mediaperson could dismiss this as a mere accident. The second, and even more shocking, instance was the refusal of a certificate of the official censors to a film on the politics of Pokharan II and Chagai titled War and Peace, a moving documentary by acclaimed film-maker Anand Patwardhan. More shocking because of the reasons cited for the refusal: "objectionable" scenes included one showing Mahatma Gandhi and another of an obscene street celebration of Pokharan II.

The campaign has been more successful when there has been no expectation from any part of the establishment. Or, where it has been conducted with the help of simple campaign tools and aids in places away from prying official eyes or among people beneath official sight. Here, too, there have been contrasting experiences. One is the positive kind, the answer to a peace activist's prayer. For an illustration, I can do no better than to quote a record of my own encounter of a moving kind with an audience that our security experts do not want to waste their technical expertise on. I wrote in the MANW journal, *Suryakanthi* (Sunflower), on the Hiroshima Day (August 6) of 2000:

"It was a rock-side 'residential' area of stone-quarry workers in Tirisoolam, a Chennai suburb. Our slide show 'Hiroshima Can Happen Here' was on, with a small but interested crowd staring at the horrors on the screen on an improvised stand on a bumpy apology for a road. Suddenly, it started raining, and then pouring. We had come armed with umbrellas and these were held over the projector and the script-reader. But, would the audience stay? We could read the worry even in the eyes of the youthful organizers who had brought us there.

"The audience stayed put: including the two topless,

wide-eyed children in the front row, with a tattered guny-bag on their heads. 'Wish we'd brought a camera,' one of us whispered. Yes, that will be an enduring, an inspiring, even if unrecorded-image in our minds, as the show goes on elsewhere."

The other kind of experience was described well by Pakistani activist Pervez Hoodbhoy in an article at the height of the standoff. "…While foreign nationals stream out of both countries and numerous world leaders call for peace and restraint, few Indians or Pakistanis are losing much sleep. Thousands of artillery shells exchanged since the beginning of this year may have changed—or destroyed—the lives of border residents, but elsewhere in both countries the effects are barely perceptible. Stock markets have flickered, but there is no run on the banks or panic buying of necessities. Schools and colleges, which generally close at the first hint of a real crisis, are functioning normally."

Hoodbhoy added: "Nuclear ignorance is almost total, extending even to the educated. Some students at the university in Islamabad where I teach said, when asked, they thought that a nuclear war would be the end of the world. Others thought of nukes as just bigger bombs. Many said it was not their concern, but the army's…. Because nuclear war is considered a distant abstraction, civil defense in both countries is nonexistent….No serious contingency plans have been devised, plans that might save millions of lives by providing timely information… Ignorance and its attendant lack of fear make it easier for leaders to treat their people as pawns in a mad nuclear game." Anti-nuclear-weapon and anti-nuclear-war campaign among the middle class can indeed be an exasperating experience.

Nuclear ignorance can be one of the reasons, but there must be others, considering that the extreme dangers of nuclear militarism are lost even upon several experts. Is it because of the very human hope that Hiroshima cannot happen here? Or, is it all right if Hiroshima happens here, if even a Nagasaki happens to the neighbor? If it is difficult to talk to this class, is it because there is none so deaf as would not hear? Does the class, cultivated as a constituency of fascism, resist the campaign that threatens to rob it of its fond hatred and faith in falsehoods? Answer the questions as we may, no peace campaign can pass over this crucially positioned, opinion-making class.

It is time, too, to tell the entire people involved that the problem of peace in South Asia cannot have a purely South Asian solution. Not after September 11, not after the standoff. The triangle against "global terror" is also the triangle of a grimly nuclear terror. This makes the subcontinent's anti-war struggle a more inextricable part of the international peace movement than ever. The BJP's India prattles about the "pre-emption rights" that the example of the Bush expeditions in Afghanistan, Iraq and elsewhere is going to bestow on it. Pakistan hopes to be protected and pampered further by the Americans as a frontline state. In reality, however, it is in the victory of the larger movement, especially in the West, to end the "war without end" that the region's vital interests lie. No less is the future of world security itself linked to the fading of the hottest of flashpoints that threatens a global nightmare.

CHAPTER 9

A PERMANENT FLASHPOINT?

Has the danger receded? Reports in the United States and elsewhere suggest relations between India and Pakistan are improving. The summer of 2002 was an anomally. Relieved that a disaster has been averted or somehow smug in the knowledge that such a horrifying event as nuclear war could never have happen in this day and age, we can get back to the main event, the war on "terrorism." But this very crusade is linked to rising tensions between India and Pakistan. Now as then, South Asia remains a nuclear flashpoint.

There have been concerted attempts to create a contrary illusion of peace. In April 2003, as the snows started melting in the Kashmir Valley, began the talk of an India-Pakistan thaw. First came a friendly telephone call from Pakistani Prime Minister Mir Zafarullah Khan Jamali (handpicked by President Gen. Musharraf for the post in November 2002) to his Indian counterpart, Vajpayee. Thereupon, Vajpayee dashed to Srinagar and delivered a public speech calling for talks with Pakistan. There have been several such so-advertised "peace signals" sprung upon the people of India and Pakistan ever since. The latest of these was a train ride in August 2003 to Pakistan by a delegation of Indian members of Parliament from the ruling and opposition parties.

That should ring a bell for the readers, as it did for the

observers of the subcontinent. (See Chapter 5.) Yes, there was a famous bus ride to Lahore in February 1999, undertaken by Vajpayee and his entourage. The profusely hailed "peace mission," however, was sandwiched between two major events of precisely the opposite import: the nuclear-weapon tests in Pokharan and the Chagai on one side and the Kargil war on the other. Pakistan struck a similar blow for "peace" when Gen. Musharraf came calling at Agra, but the India-Pakistan summit in the city of Taj Mahal in July 2001 did not see architects of South Asian amity in action. Five months later came the attack on Indian Parliament and then the long India-Pakistan confrontation on the edge of a nuclear catastrophe.

There was much political and media hype in India over Vajpayee's peace overture in April. The limited relief and rejoicing, which his statement may have caused, however, proved short-lived. As soon as he returned from Kashmir, New Delhi reverted to its refrain of years: no talks until the "cross-border terrorism" was ended. A series of official statements to this effect followed. The "parivar," the far-Right "family," growled its warning against going too far with the idea of talks. On May 2, 2003, Vajpayee was really addressing his own political camp, when he told Parliament that this would be his "last attempt" at solving the Kashmir problem though talks. The implication of this assurance was as ominous as it was obvious.

What then prompted his Srinagar statement? Vajpayee, the first Indian Prime Minister to visit the Valley in 15 years even if under heavy security protection, was addressing a war-weary Kashmiri audience from behind a bullet-proof glass shield. He was also sharing the dais with a new Chief Minister of Jammu and Kashmir, Mufti

Mohammed Sayeed, who had come to power with the promise of "a healing touch" in an election (of which more anon). But, there was a more pressing reason for the overture as well. India and Pakistan were both under insistent and increasing pressure from the Bush regime of the U.S., anxious to keep the contradiction and conflict within the South Asian segment of the "anti-terror coalition" under control while the conquest of Iraq was being completed.

Washington had just let it be known that it planned to turn its attention to South Asia once its Middle East job was done. Though both India and Pakistan wanted to turn the new "triangle" against each other, as we have seen, both had reason to be wary in this regard. Allegations of Pakistan's nuclear-technology-sharing with North Korea created anxiety in Islamabad. "It's possible there are signals that Pakistan has to fall in line or it could be the target in future," said A. H. Nayyar of Pakistan's Institute of Sustainable Development in April 2003. As for India, US Secretary of State Colin Powell had thought it fit to warn it in a public statement against equating Pakistan with Iraq. The overtures from Jamali and Vajpayee were, thus, really addressed to Washington and meant to mollify it.

Neither India nor Pakistan, of course, was giving up its attempt to turn the "global war on terror" into its own war against the regional adversary with a superpower as its ally. Neither was going to observe any restraint, including the nuclear, in its preparation for yet another, scary showdown with its putative ally in the avowed world alliance. The U.S., like a boxing referee, might keep asking them to "stop" and "separate," but was clearly letting the bout go on. And the world's leading nuclear power heading the non-proliferation campaign scored a new high in hypocrisy by more than winking at the recklessness of its warring and nuke-flaunting South Asian allies.

* * *

THE most important event of the last year has been the war on Iraq, and its main outcome for South Asia is a worsening of India-Pakistan relations, despite all pretenses about a thaw. The immediate reaction of the government of India to the launch of the war in March 2003 was the same as to the assault on Afghanistan in October 2001, though it was now spelt out even more clearly and strongly. We have seen how gleeful New Delhi was over what struck it as a golden opportunity to get the almighty U.S. on its side against "Pakistan-sponsored cross-border terrorism" impliedly as part of "Islamic terror." We have also seen how the Indian leadership, from the Prime Minister downward, projected India as the worst victim of terrorism in the world and, therefore, the most natural ally of the U.S. in the "global war on terror." New Delhi's calculations were upset, when Gen. Musharraf joined the anti-"terror" bandwagon despite fierce domestic opposition, especially the fundamentalist kind.

New Delhi's reaction to the Iraq war made it appear as though it were waiting for the next opportunity to turn the anti-"terror" strike to its own decisive advantage and against its neighbor and adversary. It could not support the war, which was immediately unpopular and became increasingly so, but could pretend to oppose it—on grounds that implied acceptance of its basis. This translated, in the utterances of several figures of the ruling establishment, into a strident demand for recognition of India's own "right of pre-emption." Former Foreign Minister

Jaswant Singh even spoke about "every country" possessing this supposedly inalienable right.

The ideological guru of the Bharatiya Janata Party, heading the ruling coalition, handed down the line. Rashtriya Swayamsevak Sangh chief K. S. Sudershan said: "If they (the USA) want to fight terrorism, they should look at Pakistan, the epicenter of terrorism. Why Iraq, which has no proven links to international terrorism?" Added Seshadri Chari, editor of RSS's mouthpiece *Organiser*: "I do not support the US action but, at the same time, I believe a nation has a right to act if it perceives a threat to its security."

Officially, however, no clear stand was adopted. It was sustained opposition pressure that brought forth a statement by the Prime Minister on the subject in Parliament in March 2003. Without giving much away, Vajpayee only advocated "a middle path" and refused to elaborate on this. He promised, though, to protest against a "regime change," if effected, in Iraq by external force. It was five months before the promise was kept in a formal, entirely ineffective manner.

For months, the government was in no mood, either, to entertain the opposition plea for a parliamentary resolution to voice disapproval of the war. On March 22, 2003, Vajpayee presented a prepared statement in a meeting with opposition leaders, called in order to work out a consensus on such a resolution. The statement, which received far less notice than it should have had, was about the three considerations India should keep in mind while monitoring developments on the war front.

The first was that "India's attention should remain focused upon its immediate neighborhood." Vajpayee insisted: "We should be careful that neither our internal debate nor our external actions deflect our attention, or that of the world, away from the real source of terrorism in our neighborhood." The allusion to Pakistan was obvious.

The second point he stressed was that "the nexus between international terrorism, fundamentalism and weapons of mass destruction (WMD) is now being strengthened." "The remnants of al-Qaida and the Taliban are being given refuge. There is a real threat of rogue nuclear activity and WMD terrorism. Action against Iraq should not dilute our [main] focus," he added. It is quite clear where the focus should lie in his opinion.

Finally, Vajpayee spoke about the battle lines. Stating that the Iraq crisis had been "very divisive," he added: "The Security Council itself is divided. There are divisions within Europe and within NATO. Most importantly, the Arab world itself is divided. Indeed, many Arab countries are cooperating with the US and Britain." What was left unsaid was quite clear—if these states can cooperate with the US, why can't India?

In other words, as the developments on the Iraq front unfolded, India was prepared to let its stand evolve into support for the Iraq war. This support, however, was conditional. The condition was laid down 18 months earlier and had been reiterated several times since then. The "focus" of Vajpayee's government has remained firmly on "our neighborhood" since 9/11. The government did not hesitate to support the war on Afghanistan. In fact, it argued that the offensive with its aim of targeting terrorist bases would set a precedent for carrying out a similar crusade in Kashmir. This dangerous approach led directly to the military stand-off between India and Pakistan. The 10-

month-long crisis shook the rest of the world.

Promptly and predictably, the BJP's political camp took the cue from the Prime Minister. Human Resources Development Minister Murli Manohar Joshi, the first to react, asked others to be as "pragmatic" as Vajpayee. In an unwittingly Orwellian comment, Joshi said that it would be "hawkish" to "condemn" the war! The External Affair Ministry's response is in the same vein. The Prime Minister's meeting with the opposition leaders might not have produced a "consensus" but that did not prevent the ministry's mandarins from toeing Vajpayee's line.

On March 23, "official sources" told the media that India was "not about to take any initiative, through the Non-Alignment Movement or otherwise, on Iraq, which could jeopardize New Delhi's improved equation with the United States." As one report put it, "sources were also concerned that alienating the U.S. and the U.K. could create problems for India on the Kashmir front. They pointed to the fact that Pakistan had developed a close relationship with the USA by 'cooperating' in nabbing the al-Qaida and Taliban elements."

On March 25, a foreign office spokesperson at a media briefing talked of "the double standards in the war against terrorism following Washington's 'advice' to talk to Islamabad in the wake of the massacre of the Kashmir Pundits (in Jammu)." He added: "If dialogue *per se* is more critical than combating international terrorism with all necessary means, then one can legitimately ask why both in Afghanistan and Iraq military action instead of dialogue has been resorted to."

On April 8, 2003, the Indian Parliament adopted a unanimous resolution deploring the launch of the war of aggression on Iraq and the "regime change" effected in that country by external force. Notable was the fact that, during the discussion on the resolution on the floor of Parliament, External Affairs Minister Yashwant Sinha suggested that Pakistan was a more deserving target for a pre-emptive offensive without United Nations approval than Iraq. Thus, the resolution, which was a result of popular pressure, denounced the professedly pre-emptive strike without denying the right of pre-emption.

The debate on the war in India reached a new phase with the government receiving a request in early May from the U.S. for Indian troops to serve as part of the "stabilization force" in Iraq. Details were not spelt out, but the government assured the nation that it was asking Washington for "clarifications" and that it wanted a "national consensus" on the issue. The Indian public indeed wanted clarifications on several aspects of the proposal—such as the precise role envisaged for the Indian troops and the control and command structure under which they would be required to function. It became increasingly clear that, to the public at large, the idea of Indian soldiers serving the occupation forces in Iraq as mercenaries was anathema. To the government, however, the price that could be extracted for such dubious "peace-keeping" appeared to be a greater concern and consideration. The "consensus"-building was confined to meetings between the Prime Minister and opposition leaders. As on the Iraq war itself, the official attempt was to insist that its main concern was "national interest." This catchphrase could conceal a multitude of sins but meant above all, in this context, an aggravation of regional tensions that was really in the interest of no South Asian nation.

In the second week of June, Deputy Prime Minister L. K. Advani visited the U.S., where he met President Bush, Defense Secretary Donald Rumsfeld and National Security Adviser Condoleezza Rice. He told the media in Washington that the issue of Indian troops for Iraq "surfaced" in all his talks with US officials. Calling opponents of the proposal "uninformed," in an interview from Washington shown on the Indian television on June 11, Advani said the Vajpayee government would take its final decision in "the best national interest." According to a report of Radio Free Europe/Radio Liberty on the same day, "Advani also reportedly has told U.S. officials that before any Indian troops are sent to Iraq, New Delhi wants to see Washington bring pressure on Pakistan to end cross-border incursions into Indian-administered Kashmir by Islamic militants."

This had an undesired impact on Gen. Musharraf. The very next day, on June 12, he told the world media in Islamabad that Pakistan "would like" to send troops to Iraq, if the right conditions were created. This, in turn, made New Delhi even more responsive to Washington's move. The Advani mission was followed by a series of US military initiatives to work out a deal on this issue, which New Delhi did not exactly discourage. On June 16, a team of Pentagon officials held talks with the Indian side including representatives of the Defense Ministry on the troops-for-Iraq proposition. This was the first time the Indian defense establishment interacted with the US Central Command (Centcom), whose area of responsibility had thus far covered the Middle East and Pakistan but excluded India. On July 28, no less a person than Gen. Richard B. Myers, Chairman of Joint Chiefs of Staff of the

US Army, was himself in India's capital.

Gen. Myers told the media before his departure that he did not discuss Indian troops for Iraq. "Oh yeah. Like pigs have wings," sneered Mani Shankar Aiyar of the opposition Congress party in a newspaper column. "Presumably he visited because he wanted to see our monsoon rains pouring down as relief from the sky for the arid wastes of the Iraqi desert." Aiyar added: "The fact is, the Americans have neither given up their desire to get our *jawans* (soldiers) to do their dirty work for them, nor has the Vajpayee government given up its...desire to impale once-independent India in a subsidiary alliance with the United States."

Neither was to give up, even if the increasing internal opposition to a mercenary role for India could not be ignored. The peddlers of the proposal offered an attractive package, which was an open secret though there was no official word about it. Lucrative reconstruction contracts in Iraq were the main ingredient of the package, while the rest of it included assistance to meet the oil price hike expected to be caused by the war, representation for India in the command structure of the envisaged multinational force for the "stabilization" of the occupied country and, thus, an enhanced world status. The "right of pre-emption" did not figure in media reports about the package, but the government spokespersons kept harping on it while US officials continued to talk of India's problem of "cross-border terrorism" in a calculatedly promising tone.

Predictably, the package found its first taker in the corporate sector of the country. An AFP report of June 19 quoted Gautam Mahajan, chairman of the economic relations cell of the Indo-American Chamber of Commerce, as saying: "Political considerations will play a prime role but it makes sound business sense for the Indian government to accede to the US request." Argued Mahajan: "We need to get a stronger presence in Iraq and this might be a way of doing it. Indian companies will find opportunities in Iraq whether we send our soldiers or not but there is no doubt that the paybacks will be much, much higher if we do." "Indian firms have landed small contracts for providing machines, spare parts and services to US and British troops. But there are multimillion-dollar contracts up for grabs," an official from the Indian Machine Tool Manufacturers Association told the agency. "If the government plays its cards right by showing support for the US, the Indian private sector could end up reaping huge benefits," he added. India's US-centric software sector was also reported to be actively lobbying for sending troops to Iraq to thwart US legislative proposals to restrict outsourcing.

Quite a few in the government may not have been convinced that what was good for the corporates was good for the country's economy in this case. New Delhi made known its concern over the cost of complying with US request for nearly 20,000 Indian troops and the maintenance of this force in Iraq, for which it could not seek Washington's assistance without appearing to be a supplier of mercenaries. Monthly "perks" payable to soldiers on a UN mission alone worked out to over U.S. $20 million, and this was in addition to salaries and the transportation and living costs in Iraq. Some in the government may have thought the price worth paying for the privilege of "playing in the big league," while others would settle for nothing less than a superpower recognition of India's "pre-emption right."

Neither the mouth-watering prospect of reconstruction contracts nor the pipedream of militarist power, however, made any difference to the Indian people's opposition to the Iraq war and the idea of India assisting the aggressors. No political party considered it electoral prudence to compromise its stand against both despite all official attempts at a consensus. On July 14, the Vajpayee Cabinet's Committee on Security resolved to say "no" to the US request. But this did not close the chapter, as many reports then sought to make out.

"Were there to be an explicit UN mandate for the purpose, the government of India could consider the deployment of our troops in Iraq," External Affairs Minister Yashwant Sinha said after the cabinet meeting ended. "Our longer-term national interest, our concern for the people of Iraq, our long-standing ties with the Gulf region as a whole as well as our growing dialogue and strengthened ties with the US have been key elements in this consideration," the Cabinet's statement said.

Former Convener of the National Security Advisory Board, chief architect of the country's nuclear doctrine and widely published security analyst K. Subrahmanyam was quick to point out that the statement was "carefully worded" and left other options open. "The US can now go back to the UN and seek a resolution which says that Iraq needs to be stabilized and therefore countries should send troops. Or it can try to get UN recognition for the interim governing council (set up in Iraq). Then there will be no problems and India can send troops," he said. The options have not been abandoned, as New Delhi's regional expectation from the global alliance has not been.

A section of the Establishment, of course, has been open in its support for India abandoning the UN in favor of the Iraq war and the US-led "coalition of the willing." Sample these superiorly servile lines from Shekhar Gupta, chief editor of the *Indian Express*, ridiculing India's expression of commitment to the UN: "While 'we are one with whatever the UN decides' may be a useful line for so many Europeans and others loathe to oppose Bush or to side with him prematurely, it is the one thing we should have avoided. We can choose so many other formulations: That Iraq has to come clean; that the US cannot decide unilaterally and so on. But can't we, please, and in our own supreme interest, go a bit easy in asserting such commitment to the UN?"

He goes on to spell out the "supreme interest": "The danger in this lies not simply in the fact that at some stage Pakistanis could remind us that since we had such faith in the UN, why don't we also express it by implementing the 1947-48 plebiscite resolution on Kashmir. The danger is greater. If the principle that the UN Security Council resolution authorizing intervention in any situation that presents a global danger has universal legitimacy, what is to stop it from passing a similar resolution should Kashmir come to a boil yet again tomorrow? We will defy it, sure enough. But the touching words we speak today, expressing our faith in the Security Council, will come back to haunt us."

The "supreme interest," however, has been firmly kept in the government's mind as it has continued to keep the troops-for-Iraq option open and its acceptance of the proposal conditional. Supporters of the proposal have combined insistence on the "interest" with the absurd argument that India's traditional friendship with the Iraqi people demanded the dispatch of troops to aid the invaders. Illustrative was the official non-response to the arrest of a team of NDTV, a popular Indian television channel conducting an opinion poll in northern Iraq on the proposal, by the Kurdish Security Service on September 4. The poll had shown that Indian troops were not welcome, if sent to help "stabilize" the authority of the occupying forces, to the people of the area. New Delhi took no public note of either the arrests or the findings.

On September 12, it was announced that New Delhi had told US Assistant Secretary of State Christina Rocca, then on a visit to India, that the troops could not be spared because they were required to counter a stepped-up terror campaign in Jammu and Kashmir. The linkage was another way of pleading the "supreme interest." It was a shift from the earlier stand that the parliamentary resolution of April prevented a speedy dispatch of the troops in unconditional compliance with the US request. "Check Pak, we'll send troops" was how the story was headlined in the *Economic Times*, for example, and similar was the manner in which the rest of the officially briefed media read the message. This came on the eve of a meeting of the Cabinet Committee on Security before the Prime Minister's departure for New York.

Islamabad, for its part, has not remained a model of quiet restraint. The Iraq war was, of course, unpopular in Pakistan, but the Musharraf regime continued to be a member of the U.S.-led "alliance against global terror." In the wake of the war, there was some excited talk in the streets and editorial columns of Pakistan as the next possible target of the pre-emptive Bush offensive as it possessed some weapons of mass destruction (WMDs). The "Pakistan next" theory, however, was officially pooh-poohed soon, with Foreign Minister Khurshid Mahmud Kasuri categorically telling the media in the first week of April, "We are not the next target as we are a responsible state." As for India's threat of a pre-emptive strike against Pakistan, Islamabad met it with a counter-offensive.

On April 8, reacting to Yashwant Sinha's description of Pakistan as a "fit case for a pre-emptive strike," Islamabad charged that India was the really "suitable" case for such a strike. Talking to the media, Pakistan's Information and Media Development Minister Sheikh Rasheed Ahmad alleged that, besides harboring WMDs on its own soil, India had also "kept chemical and biological weapons with neighboring countries." This was a grave charge indeed, and could have led to imponderable consequences if Islamabad had persisted with Ahmad's line of argument. The charge, however, was left unelaborated and was not repeated.

Gen. Musharraf and his men preferred not to press on with the charge once its immediate purpose was served. Colin Powell, as we saw before, intervened at this point to admonish India against equating Pakistan with Iraq. New Delhi, of course, has continued to complain about "cross-border terrorism." Islamabad's response has continued to be a package. It has alternated claims to have stopped "cross-border terrorism" with promises to stop it and pleas of inability to stop it fully because of either the terrain or inadequate resources. Washington has continued to assure both the implacable adversaries of its equal sympathy and support.

At the time of writing, the subcontinent has just been

treated once again to the familiar spectacle of an India-Pakistan clash in the United Nations. The drama of the triangle against "global terror," which holds South Asia in terror, was enacted again in the UN General Assembly's annual session in September, which brought Vajpayee, Gen. Musharraf and Bush together. At the end of the session, by all accounts, the so-called India-Pakistan "peace process," announced five months before, lay in a shambles. The "thaw" that had begun with the onset of the Indian summer did not survive the subcontinent's autumn.

The President of Pakistan, answering charges of "cross-border terrorism" in his address to the General Assembly, declared: "India cites "cross-border" terrorism to refuse a dialogue. It knows fully well that the Kashmiri struggle is indigenous. India seeks to exploit the international anti-terrorist sentiment after 9/11, to delegitimize the Kashmiri freedom struggle. On the contrary, it is India which violates international law by refusing to implement Security Council resolutions and perpetrating gross and consistent violations of human rights in Kashmir." He followed this up with a peace formula on Kashmir, envisaging a cease-fire on the Line of Control (LoC) in Kashmir and then a "cessation of violence within India-occupied Kashmir" which Pakistan was "prepared to encourage." The Prime Minister of India was quick to cite this as proof of an open Pakistani "admission" of "cross-border terrorism." In his General Assembly address, Vajpayee proclaimed: "Just as the world did not negotiate with al-Qaida or the Taliban, we shall not negotiate with terrorism." Ruling out any dialogue with Pakistan, in fact, he said: "When the cross-border terrorism stops—or when we eradicate it—we can have a dialogue with Pakistan on the other issues between us."

Vajpayee did not fail to follow this up with a call for a coalition against Pakistan. He said that no state should be allowed to profess partnership with the global coalition against terror while continuing to aid, abet and sponsor terrorism. To condone double standards is to contribute to multiplying terrorism," he remarked. He pursued the same theme in dealing with pressure for dispatch of Indian troops to Iraq. From the US side, it was given out that, after his meeting with the Prime Minister, President Bush had expressed his understanding for Vajpayee's inability to decide on the delicate issue with a national election in India coming up next year. On the Prime Minister's own behalf, however, his External Affairs Minister Sinha para-phrased the response thus given out that "Demands on our own security environment at home has increased. We have to keep this in mind." The allusion to Kashmir and "cross-border terrorism" was obvious.

The sparring in the UN, say both New Delhi and Islamabad, spelt a setback to the pretended "peace process." While the regret sounds far from real, the setback should be no surprise to serious South Asia-watchers. If common partnership in the allegedly "anti-terror" coali-tion has only made India and Pakistan more implacable adversaries, the Iraq war has only intensified the animosi-ty further and made it a greater and graver threat to the entire region than ever before.[1]

* * *

DURING his just cited UN General Assembly address, Gen. Musharraf sounded shockingly like a South Asian peace activist when he declared: "Jammu and

Kashmir has been rightly described as the most dangerous dispute in the world." Neither he nor Vajpayee, of course, was going to do the least about any aspect of the dispute, including the nuclear one that made it so dangerous. Both saw in the danger posed by the dispute an opportunity to draw the attention and support of the US-led West. Islamabad thought the time propitious as never before for US-brokered talks on Kashmir, and New Delhi wanted a Kashmir solution through a pre-emptive strike. What has happened on the Kashmir front, which provided the snow-chill backdrop to the stand-off of the summer of 2002, over the past year?

Here, again, hope of a qualitative advance was claimed—by New Delhi with emphatic US endorsement. The ground for the hope was the State-wide Assembly election in India's Jammu and Kashmir in 2002. The election, held in four phases (on September 16 and 24 and October 1 and 8), was officially hailed as a vindication of India's case on Kashmir and a harbinger of normalcy in the strife-torn State. The polls did usher in a political change. Experience since then, however, has shown that expectations from the change were greatly exaggerated.

The election dislodged Farooq Abdullah and his National Conference (see Chapter 4) from power in the State, and led to the installation on November 2, 2002, of a new government under Mufti Mohammed Sayeed as the Chief Minister. It was a coalition regime of the People's Democratic Party of Sayeed and the Congress (the main opposition party at the national level). New Delhi projected the PDP-Congress victory as proof of the freeness and fairness of the polls. Then US Ambassador Robert D. Blackwill hastened to congratulate India on the conduct of the election, and major Western governments chimed in with their compliments. The Vajpayee government promised support to Sayeed in his policy of "healing touch," the immediate implication of which was the release of quite a few militants from prisons, hailed by human rights activists and harshly criticized by hardliners on Kashmir. All this led inevitably to an end of the political alliance between Abdullah's National Conference and Vajpayee's Bharatiya Janata Party, and exit of the NC (and its representative Omar Abdullah) from the coalition ruling in New Delhi.

It should really be no surprise that the much-advertised change in Kashmir has spelt no advance at all towards a solution to the world's most perilous problem. The relative freeness and fairness of the election, reflected in the results, did not mean that the State had entered a phase of peaceful, democratic politics. In the first place, according to India's Election Commission, despite all the importance officially attached to the event, the voter turnout remained in the vicinity of 42 per cent. A sum-up by quasi-official news agency Press Trust of India on October 12, 2002 (after the fourth and final phase of polling), described the election as the "bloodiest" in the State's history. As many as 400 persons were reported killed during the election period, 284 of them in the Kashmir Valley alone. The official Indian claim was that the turnout would have been much higher but for the Hurriyat boycott of the election and its intimidation of voters. A counter-claim, however, was that Indian security forces engaged in coercing people to vote: Chief Election Commissioner J. M. Lyngdoh's directive against such coercion was deemed an indirect acknowledgement of such an interference with the poll process.

Again, it was the Indian security forces' claim that a majority of those killed during the election, as in any other period, were "foreigners," meaning Pakistan-sent militants. Determined optimists, however, saw an apparent difference this time. On the eve of the election, Vajpayee assured the Kashmiris that "mistakes of the past won't be repeated." This was seen as a departure from the official stand that projected the Kashmir problem as purely a Pakistani creation. It seemed to denote recognition of the indigenous roots of the problem to the extent it recognized the denial of electoral democracy or reasonably free and fair elections to the people of the State in the past. A similarly hopeful shift was sought to be seen in the stand of the Pakistani regime as well. Islamabad still questioned the Indian claim, but without failing to assure Washington from time to time about its steps to stop infiltration of "jihadis" from Pakistan into "India-occupied Kashmir." The steps, including imposition of bans on their organizations and a freeze on their funds, did seem to corroborate the charge of "cross-border terrorism" to some extent. Hopes, based on such seeming changes on both sides, however, were soon to be belied.

The poll-generated violence continued right up to the day of Sayeed's swearing-in, proceeded by the firing of two rifle grenades at his residence in Srinagar. It is not, however, as if peace set in thereafter. As noted before, the election results created exaggerated expectations but, despite Sayeed's "healing touch" and Vajpayees's "hand of friendship" extended with a flourish to Islamabad in April 2003, the Iraq war saw a rapid return of India-Pakistan relations to abnormality. Jammu and Kashmir was bound to bear the brunt of it all again. On July 23, chief of the Indian army's northern command Hari Prasad told a news conference that the security forces had killed more than 700 militants so far in the year, and suggested that the average of 2,000 a year achieved since 1995 would be kept up.

Referring to the suicide attacks by militants on India's armed forces since July 1999, he said: "When a man is prepared to give his life there is very little you can do to stop him. But we will definitely try to bring our casualty level to zero." He added that, in the stepped-up security operations, "six to eight militants" were being killed every day. The State was back to its pre-election state of bloodiness with the claimed killing by India's Border Security Force (BSF) of Ghazi Baba, a leader of militant outfit Jaish-e Mohammed (JeM), in a ten-hour-long encounter on August 30. The Baba, one of the "most wanted men" in India, was officially identified as the "mastermind" behind the attack on Parliament on December 13, 2001, the immediate provocation for the next year's India-Pakistan stand-off. The claim was confirmed, said the BSF, by unnamed, arrested JeM members identifying their slain leader's body.

The claim was not questioned either in the media or in the political arena, as it deserved to be—and not only because the BSF was involved in instances of atrocities, of which the National Human Rights Commission had taken note. The more important reason was the manner in which the investigations into the December 13 incident had been misdirected, as shown up in the cases of one accused. Syed Ahmed Rahman Geelani, a Delhi University teacher, was sentenced to death by a special court in December 2002 on evidence from mobile tele-

phone intercepts. The sentence had to be set aside after a
Supreme Court pronouncement on the inadmissibility of
such evidence, though the case against him on other
grounds remains undecided at the time of writing. Coming
after the acquittal in January 2003 of a young journalist of
the *Kashmir Times*, Iftikar Gilani, who spent seven months
in jail for alleged possession of classified military documents, the case of the Kashmiri teacher only confirmed
apprehensions about official investigations into the attack
on Parliament. It, certainly, did not help implementation
of the 'healing touch' policy.

The Baba's killing triggered off a wave of counter-vio-
lence, which finally erased all hope about the much-hyped
political change in Kashmir marking a turning point. On
September 13, 2003, came the announcement of the
killing of Kuka Parray, a "counter-insurgent" leader in official Indian parlance but known better as a "renegade" in
the Valley, in a village near Baramulla. He did not survive
the bomb blast that greeted his arrival in the village to
inaugurate a cricket match—organized, ironically, in support of the claim that normalcy had returned to the State.
The "renegades" or surrendered militants, rewarded and
re-armed by the Indian security forces, have an unsavory
image and record indeed and, as we have seen before,
human rights organizations and activists have held them
guilty of gross rights violations in several instances. The
tearful coverage of the killing on Indian television channels could have only added to the average Kashmiri's sense
of alienation, as anyone who has been to the sullen State
would vouch.

Killings of a different category, however, were what
dominated the Indian media headlines and comments.

Particularly impactful, in this manner, was the Nadimarg massacre of March 23, 2003, in which unidentified gunmen made a nocturnal raid on a village in the Pulwama district and brutally murdered 24 Kashmiri Pandits (Hindus), including 11 women and two children. This was described widely as the worst of such incidents since the Kalachuk massacre of May 2002 (discussed earlier), but there were a series of other tragedies, taking a heavy toll of innocent civilian lives.

As a Srinagar report of September 4, 2003, in the uninvolved *Washington Post* put it: "After a relatively calm summer, a new wave of violence has spread across Kashmir... Nearly every day brings at least a few attacks: soldiers ambushed, suspected informers tortured and killed, civilians cut down in gun battles. Things had seemed promising after Indian Prime Minister Atal Behari Vajpayee launched a peace initiative in April... But no date for new talks has been set, and peace suddenly seems less likely than ever. Tourists who had begun to return to Kashmir for the first time since the separatist insurgency erupted in 1989 have all left once again." A local tour operator told the newspaper: "In the past couple of weeks, it seems like the old days have returned." The report added: "It remains unclear exactly what touched off the new violence, which began with a gun battle between soldiers and militants the day Vajpayee visited (here)... It has gotten worse everyday since, and more than 90 people have been killed, at least 33 of them civilians."

The governments in New Delhi and Srinagar, the Indian federal and State security forces, and the mainstream Indian media have, routinely and as a rule, depicted these and such other incidents of violence as crimes by militants, particularly the Pakistan-sponsored ones. The claim has always been questioned by militant organizations. The last time they questioned the claim, and could not be entirely ignored by the Indian establishment, was on November 2, 2000, after two officially ordered inquiries blamed state agencies for two cases of group killings. The Hurriyat Conference and the Hizb-ul Mujahideen then demanded a probe into all massacres in the State until then, saying that the inquiries had "proved beyond an iota of doubt that the Indian government has been perpetrating massacres of innocent people in Kashmir in order to give a bad name to the ongoing freedom struggle in the State." The probe was sought, in particular, into killings of Hindus or Kashmiri Pandits in vulnerable areas like Doda, which figures yet again in the list of places affected in the latest spurt of "terrorist strikes." The militant organizations have not stopped making this counter-claim, with the sizeable support of public opinion in the Valley, but this is hardly reported to the rest of India.

Zafarullah Khan Jamali was quoted in August 2003 as noting that a massacre took place in Kashmir every time there was a move for talks (which India refused to have "until cross-border terrorism is stopped"). The Pakistani leader's suggestion was that this was not purely coincidental. The irony may have been more eloquent but for the fact that there were few buyers in Pakistan, too, for Islamabad's claim of no truck with the alleged terrorism. Noted columnist M. B. Naqvi was speaking for many thoughtful Pakistanis, when he wrote in the *News* on September 4, 2003, that "a Pakistan-supported Jihad in Indian-controlled Kashmir has led first to a freeze and then apparently to the cold and hard feeling in India that there is perhaps no option but to go to war." In his column on April 28, talking of Chagai's impact on Pakistan's military rulers, he had said: "Conscious of their nuclear capabilities, they converted Kashmiris' spontaneous and non-violent mass movement in 1989 into an armed insurgency and called it Jihad." By offering in the UN General Assembly to "encourage cessation of hostilities within India-occupied Kashmir," and by saying that sealing the Pakistani border to terrorist traffic is not a "doable job," President Musharraf has only confirmed the complicity of Pakistani hawks in the aggravation and prolongation of the Kashmir problem.

Thus, the much-advertised steps to restore normalcy in Kashmir have proved as misleading as the ones towards India-Pakistan normalization. In this context, the Kashmir counterpart of the resumption of a bus service between the two countries has been the extension of India's mobile phone network to the troubled State from August 21, 2003. Symbolic gestures of this kind, by themselves, can make no serious difference to the situation. One year before the step was taken, journalist Shujaat Bukhari of *The Hindu* told me in Srinagar of the "deep Kashmiri resentment at the denial of the service based on a distrust of the State's people." He compared this with the Kashmiris' resentment at New Delhi's refusal even to consider the unanimous resolution of the elected State Assembly, moved by the "friendly" State government of Farooq Abdullah, demanding "greater autonomy" for the State. In both the cases, the Kashmiris were being treated as second-class citizens or alienated. The manner in which the step on mobile telephones is being implemented can only deepen the sense of distrust and make matters worse.

Days after the inauguration of the service, Pritpal Singh, chief executive officer of the public-sector service provider Bharat Sanchar Nigam Limited, told the media in Srinagar in so many words that "the incoming and outgoing calls on mobile phones will be monitored to prevent any militant activity carried on through cellular phones." Asked if the facility would be withdrawn if misused, he said: "Let people enjoy the facility while it is available."

It may not be available for too long, if the current trend continues. The increasing violence inside the State cannot but vitiate further the border situation, which is fraught with all the dangers of an outbreak of uncontrollable hostilities. The *Hindustan Times*, a national daily, has recently come out with two stories of hate-driven savagery from the Rajouri sector of the Kashmir border. On one of their missions in the sector in September, Pakistani troops were reported to have crossed the border and killed four Indian soldiers in an ambush. They chopped off the head of a dead soldier and carried it back as a "trophy." In grisly retaliation, Indian soldiers "shot dead nine Pakistani soldiers. And, for gruesome impact, [they] brought back the heads of two Pakistani soldiers." The head-hunter's lurid spirit of vendetta does nothing to lighten the threat of a nuclear holocaust looming again over South Asia.

* * *

BEHIND all this lies a brutalizing ideology and politics of hate and lies, of revanchism and reaction in either country (as we saw in Chapter 6). As stated before, an important aim of this book, in fact, is to highlight an internal factor responsible for the seeming race of the subcontinent towards self-destruction. The fascism that has fueled the monstrous growth of nuclear militarism is something that is not recognized for the force it is—even in India or by friends of the Indian peace movement elsewhere, especially in the West. What has happened on this front in the one year since I finished writing the rest of the book? Nothing to warrant any real hope of a halt in the race.

We have talked of the state-aided anti-minority pogrom of Gujarat as the most telling illustration of the fascism that is out to capture untrammeled political power in India. The single most important development from this viewpoint has been the political and electoral victory of fascism in the State that has served as the laboratory of the cult of hate which peddlers of the big lie label "Hindutva." Even while the riots were raging in the streets of the State in the early months of 2002, as noted before, the Bharatiya Janata Party was plotting to make political capital of the so achieved religious-communal polarization. It succeeded in a way that shocked and shamed millions of decent Indians including devout Hindus. On December 15 was announced the BJP's landslide win in the election to the State Assembly, where it grabbed 126 out of a total 182 seats. Narendra Modi, the chief minister who had presided over the pogrom, returned to the post. As Modi and his camp doubtless saw it, he returned with a renewed mandate for a relentless continuation of the anti-minority campaign.

What this has meant within Gujarat is, above all, a delay and a denial of justice to the victims of the pogrom. The state proceeded against those arrested in connection with the Godhra arson under the draconian Prevention of Terrorism Act (POTA), enacted at the post-9/11 call of

Washington for sterner "anti-terrorism" legislation in every willing country. The law, aimed at speedy disposal of cases within its purview, legitimizes detention that would otherwise be deemed arbitrary and conviction on what would otherwise be considered inadequate or inadmissible evidence. Those held in connection with the post-Godhra riots, however, have been spared the terrors of this law. It is not just the slowness of the judicial process that has helped the accused in these cases The regime of Narendra Modi armed with a new electoral mandate has made no secret of its sympathy and support for the forces that set the entire State aflame. The cases have not been able to stand in the courts of law, with several witnesses "turning hostile" during the trial or, in simpler and straighter language, turning tail under dire threats to themselves and their families.

The most infamous illustration has been provided by "the Best Bakery case," about the burning down of a bakery unit of that name along with 14 persons working there in Baroda (a city in Gujarat) on March 1, 2002, at the height of the pogrom. A Gujarat court acquitted all the 21 accused on June 27, 2003, for want of testimony by witnesses. It turned out later that the witnesses including the wife and daughter of the bakery owner went back on their original testimony under "death threats." The daughter, 19-year-old Zahira Sheikh, soon told the country the true story and demanded shifting of the case to a court outside Gujarat. The Narendra Modi regime had no defense left, when the Supreme Court of India in September called a perfunctory governmental appeal against the acquittals "a complete eyewash." Almost identical have been the complaints of the surviving victims of the riots in other cases as well. The country's apex court has been constrained to ask the State government to change the public prosecutors in all these cases as it has become known that quite a few of these worthies are members of the Vishwa Hindu Parishad (VHP), the organization in the vanguard of the war on the State's minorities, especially the Muslims.

It is not only in Gujarat that the course of the cases draws anxious attention. It is not only Gujarat, in fact, that the outcome of the State election is expected to affect. No sooner was the result declared than the BJP and indeed the entire "parivar," the far-Right "family," started proclaiming a resolve to "repeat Gujarat" elsewhere and everywhere in the country. The slogan, clearly, threatened a Gujarat-like pogrom or religious-communal polarization on the eve of every major election for cruelly cynical exploitation. There was no voice of dissent from what media pundits of proximity to powers-that-be describe as the "moderate" section in the BJP. Prime Minister Vajpayee, the supposed symbol and spearhead of this section, had campaigned for Modi in Gujarat despite his earlier demurs about the riots; hailing the election outcome now, he declared that it had defined "secularism" anew. Quick to take the cue, Ashok Singhal and Pravin Togadia of the VHP (whom the readers have met before) announced that the "structure of secularism" would be demolished just the way the Babri Masjid was.

Attempts were made to create situations of conflict in States that awaited elections. In the State of Madhya Pradesh adjoining Gujarat, for example, an Ayodhya-like issue is being sought to be created in a place called Bhojshala with a temple-mosque complex, where Hindus and Muslims have worshipped all these years without any acrimony. What should cause greater and graver concern, however, is the post-Gujarat ambition of the BJP to capture unshared power in New Delhi. It has repeatedly boasted about its ready compliance with the demands and discipline of coalition politics and putting issues of basic importance to it "on the back burner." Now, in the run-up to the next general election, it is raising every one of those issues again. The return of its "hidden agenda" (popular parlance for the list of issues) can have more horrendous consequences than even its complacent political opponents seem to realize. What has never been hidden about the agenda is its objective of promoting hate, the kind that can eventually threaten even a nuclear holocaust.

The first of these issues, which made the BJP a force at the national level in the nineties, is that of Ayodhya. For the past few years, the party had left the demand for raising a temple over the ruins of the Babri Masjid to the VHP and the rest of the "parivar." The Prime Minister's pious protestation had been that he and his party only wanted a settlement of the dispute though a dialogue or a court decision. The Gujarat election result changed all that. The new BJP stand is illustrative of a political and electoral strategy aimed at a mandate for unabashed majoritarianism or anti-minorityism, marching inexorably on to militarism. In July 2003, it was given out that, under pressure from the VHP and Rashtriya Swayamsevak Sangh (RSS), the party had agreed to consider a legislation to facilitate construction of the temple to enshrine religious-communal fascism. Soon, however, the Deputy Prime Minister did some loud thinking to let the country know that the legislation was ruled out for now as the BJP had no majority of its own in Parliament and could not muster enough support for the measure. This was, clearly, an appeal for a majoritarian, anti-minority vote to give the BJP unrestricted power to act on its pre-coalition agenda.

The entire exercise has been accompanied by a shrill and strident "parivar" campaign to keep the anti-Muslim heat relentlessly on. Togadia and his cohorts were back in full battle cry, asking for the temple as a symbol of the "Hindu Rashtra" (Hindu Nation) and demanding India's official declaration as such. The campaign was carried to a shriller pitch after the government-controlled Archaeological Survey of India (ASI) claimed to have unearthed evidence of a Hindu temple under the spot where the Babri Masjid had stood. Flaunting the claim, which reminded historians of Hitler's use of alleged archaeology for promotion of revanchism, the Indian fascists called for an undoing of the "historical wrong." The main objective of the campaign was to deny Indianness to India's largest minority and depict Muslims as second-class citizens or citizens on sufferance. The VHP asked them to be more loyal to Ram, the deity of their Hindu forefathers, than to Babur, a "foreign invader," and threatened "Hindu suicide squads" to "liberate Ayodhya." To the "foreigner" tag was added the frequent taunt about the Indian minority being a fifth column for Pakistan. Togadia even talked of it as a hostage, when he told a public meeting that attacks on Muslims would stop, if the "cross-border terrorism" stopped.

The pattern was repeated also with the other issues of the no longer hidden agenda. Another issue to be similarly retrieved from "the back burner" was one of a uniform civil code (UCC) for all the communities of India. Despite its deceptively progressive appearance, the demand for such a code was always very much a part of the vicious anti-minority offensive of the "parivar." More precisely, the demand is for a uniform personal law, and it is presented mainly as an indictment of Islam and Indian Muslims. The hollowness and hypocrisy of the campaign against Islam as the enemy of women's rights in India need not be dwelt upon here. The more dangerously insidious propaganda is that the Muslim personal law is enabling the "backward" minority to breed at a rate that endangers the majority status of the Hindus! The propaganda persists in the face of the frequently mentioned fact that, even after centuries of Muslim rule over large parts of the country, the minority has remained only 12 per cent of the population. The party has deputed the Deputy Prime Minister himself to voice public concern over "demographic imbalances" allegedly developed over recent years. Closely linked to all this, as seen before, is the campaign against Bangladeshi immigrants routinely described as "infiltrators." And Modi was speaking for his entire political camp and constituency, when he kept speaking from public platforms of the connection between multiplying Indian Muslims and "Mian" Musharraf. On this issue, too, the BJP has taken an Ayodhya-like stance: the party can promise a uniform civil code, but only if it is invested with unencumbered power.

A third issue to be taken off "the back burner" was the one of a ban on cow slaughter. The "parivar" has always pressed the demand for extending the ban, operative in quite a few States, to the rest of India. It is not vegetarianism that inspires the demand but, once again, anti-Muslim virulence. It targets not only the Muslims' beef-eating habit (which they share with several Hindu and tribal communities, especially in East and South India), but also butchery and leather tanning as two of its traditional occupations. The cow-protectors make this clear by crusading only for the female of the Indian bovine species. BJP leader B. P. Singhal, on a television show, in fact, assured the audience that "we don't mind even if millions of tonnes of beef are imported!" Once again, the party is telling its constituency that it cannot enact and enforce the ban without a parliamentary majority of its own.

Many feared that the Gujarat carnage and its aftermath—judicial and political—were bound to invite a minority backlash eventually. Two major massacres since then have been seen as instances of such a strike-back. On September 24, 2002, two unidentified gunmen fired upon a prayer congregation at Gujarat's Akshardham, housing the shrine of a widely revered Hindu sect and mission. The immediate toll was put at 30, including women and children, and more bodies were to be recovered later. The entire nation watched on television the dismal scene of destruction and mourning as well as the army commando operation that ended with the elimination of both the unknown assailants. However, unlike Godhra, to which there was an obviously organized response, Akshardham did not elicit "an equal and opposite reaction" (as Modi had described the Gujarat pogrom). But the "parivar" was anxious not to let go of this opportunity to advance its anti-minority and anti-Pakistan line. Official investigations were still in the initial stages, when Advani (holding the home portfolio as well) descended on Akshardham on September 26. He came, he saw and he was convinced of a Pakistani connection to the crime. The assault on the temple, he pronounced, had the "clear signature" of the Pakistan-based terrorist group, Lashkar-e Toiba (LeT).

With Islamabad denying this with predictable indignation, the tragedy did serve to exacerbate South Asian tensions, thus making up for its failure to trigger off fresh
internal riots.

The second of the suspected backlashes came less
than a year later. On August 26, 2003, two car bombs went
off in Mumbai—one near the well-known Gateway of
India and the other in Zaveri Bazaar, a market with many
Gujarati shops—killing 50 persons and injuring over 150
seriously. The outrage was strongly reminiscent of the seri-
al blasts that rocked the city a decade earlier in what was
seen as a Muslim-terrorist reaction to the demolition of
the Babri Masjid. The mature and quiet response of the
people to the latest blasts disappointed the "parivar" once
again. It was left to Advani, once again, to repeat his
Akshardham act. Air-dashing to Mumbai on the same day,
the Deputy Prime Minister did not wait for any investigation before announcing that "the first impression gathered" pointed to the involvement, again, of the Pakistan-
based LeT, besides the banned Students' Islamic
Movement of India (SIMI). The predictable Islamabad
protest, again, made sure that the potential of the tragedy
for increasing the perils of a South Asian conflict did not
go untapped.

It is to Pakistan, however, that we must turn for an
idea of what the Islamic counterparts of the "parivar"
could contribute to the conflict-promising situation. The
record here for the recent period has been no more reas-
suring. We have seen before that the Musharraf regime's
declaration of war on al-Qaida has meant no decline in
the dangers of "jihadi terrorism." The danger that has
caused the widest concern in the West is the one posed to

the security of the Christian minority of the country. At least 18 attacks have been made on Westerners and churches in Pakistan over a year since September 2002, to go by various reports. Christian rights organizations have complained of atrocities perpetrated on the minority, numbering about 2.5 per cent of the population, the instances including rape, acid-throwing, and destruction of properties. An All-Pakistan Minority Alliance representing Christians and Hindus among others, along with a Christian-Muslim Dialog Group and a National Commission for Peace and Justice, has been campaigning against the atrocities, but without much of an impact on official agencies unwilling to offend the 'jihadi' extremists.

The hate campaign of the "jihadis," however, has received a huge impetus from the unpopular wars on Afghanistan and Iraq. The massive anti-war protest demonstrations in Islamabad, Rawalpindi, Karachi and other cities in February-March 2003, organized by the six-party Islamist combine Muttahida Majlis-e Amal (MMA) were marred, according to reports, by slogans against the country's "infidels" or minorities. The danger the 'jihadis' pose to internal peace and stability is now a matter of concern to all enlightened Pakistanis. One of the many warning signals was the wave of "jihadi" violence that greeted the fourth anniversary of Gen. Musharraf in power on October 12, 2003, when a cinema and a popular market in Islamabad were burnt down. Reacting to the incidents, Lahore-based freelance columnist and former parliamentarian Shafqat Mahmood writes of the "jihad" or "radical groups" that Musharraf has not cared to bring under any control. "Arabs or other foreigners operating in our tribal areas are now and then arrested or shot but the home-grown variety is generally given a free run," says Mahmood, "I wonder if Taliban qualify to be home-grown as they are a product of Pakistani 'madrasaas' (religious schools) but they certainly are being treated as such."

The regional ramifications of the internal, religious-communal violence are clear from the propaganda campaign in Pakistan of the al-Qaida, with which the "home-grown" Taliban have the closest of ties. In a new audiotape released on September 29, 2003, and aired by the Qatar-based al Jazeera Arabic television channel, Osama bin Laden's principal spokesman Ayman al-Zawahiti was heard appealing to Pakistani army officers and soldiers to 'topple' President Musharraf before he "hands you over to the Hindus and flees to enjoy his secret bank accounts" if India attacked their country.

Internal fascism as an increasingly important political factor and force in both India and Pakistan needs to be recalled every time an illusion is sought to be created about an imminent thaw in relations between them. Whenever one hears such deceptive talk of diplomatic initiatives for South Asian peace as assails our ears now, it is good to remember that it has happened before. The initiative in question then must be considered in the light of the politics of hate and lies so successfully practiced in both the countries. Then, at the next "thaw," one may ask oneself, "How likely is it, on the one hand, that such hate-driven men who owe their power in large part to stoking that hatred, will decide to truly come to grips with the problems they themselves have created? How likely is it, on the other hand, that there are alternative explanations such as wanting to please the USA or to be seen as a peace-maker in order to shroud the next phase of nuclear build-up?"

* * *

BOTH India and Pakistan have certainly moved on to the next phase of their military and nuclear build-up through the latest of "thaws." New Delhi took a major stride in this direction on January 4, 2003, when it announced the setting up of a Nuclear Command Authority (NCA). Simultaneously announced was a noticeable departure from India's Draft Nuclear Doctrine (DND) of 1999, analyzed in some detail before. The deciders of the country's nuclear destiny had originally promised that India would not use nuclear weapons against non-nuclear-weapon states, except those allied to nuclear powers. That exception, it seemed, sufficed to make nonsense of the pledge. It was now added that India would "retain the option of retaliating with nuclear weapons" if a biological or chemical weapons attack was made "on India or its forces anywhere." The retaliation or second strike, however, would be "massive and designed to inflict unacceptable damage," just as direly threatened in the draft doctrine. Also proclaimed was the principle that nuclear strikes could be authorized only by the civilian political leadership with the Prime Minister at its helm. This was preferable to handing the ultimate authority in the matter to the top military brass. That, however, is no cause for celebration, as it is the politics of nuclear militarism that has now gained control of the nuclear button.

The announcement came within a week of Gen. Musharraf's startling revelation that he had been all set to unleash "an unconventional war" on India, if a single Indian soldier had crossed the border into Pakistan during the inordinately tense stand-off of 2002. After thus inadvertently testifying to the truth of this book's theme, the

President and his men proceeded to assure his constituency in Pakistan that its own nuclear command structure, set up in February 2000, was superior to India's. The occasion was also taken to emphasize international experts' opinion about Pakistan's superiority also in missile technology or, more precisely, in marrying nuclear warheads to missiles. Originally, Pakistan's nuclear command authority was also to be presided over by the head of the government or the Prime Minister, but the military has clearly retained control of the nuclear program and structure. President Musharraf's status as the country's final nuclear authority is now a proudly acknowledged fact.

The level of nuclear control achieved by New Delhi was brought into serious question, to say the least, by a shocking incident reported in the daily *Hindustan Times* on October 10, 2003. Nineteen computers belonging to "top-secret establishments" of the Defense Research and Development Organization (DRDO), housed in the country's capital, were reported to have been stolen. Subsequently, it was found that the criminals had discarded the computers and made away with the hard discs containing "sensitive data." The report added: "What is worrying the defense establishment is that the DRDO has provided the encryption back-up for protecting strategic communications in the context of India's nuclear arsenal."[2] This would have been greater cause for concern to the common man, if only the media and the political opposition had pursued the matter. As for Pakistan's nuclear control, it hardly seemed assured by the known links between state agencies and "jihadi" forces. Right from 9/11, President Musharraf has been periodically constrained to deny the possibility of Pakistan's nuclear facilities "falling into wrong hands," but he has sounded less and less convincing.

The glaring inadequacies of the command and control structures have not deterred the militarists of either country from going ahead with their nuclear build-up. In the first half of October 2003 alone, Pakistan conducted a series of three missile test flights. Two of the tests, on October 8 and October 14, were on a medium-range 700-kilometer missile called Shaheen-I. On October 2, Pakistan test flew the Ghaznavi (or Hatf-III) with a range of 290 kilometers. Both missiles are capable of carrying nuclear warheads. This was Pakistan's response to India's announcement in September of its plans to deploy and "consolidate its nuclear deterrence." Among these is the formation of a special artillery division to mange nuclear-capable missiles and to integrate the exiting Agni and Prithvi missiles. After a meeting of the NCA, it was also announced that India would soon produce 30 more surface-to-surface, nuclear-capable Prithvi missiles with a range of 150 to 300 kilometers. It was also planned to test-fire the under-construction Agni III with a range of 3,000 kilometers in November, and to deploy two variants of shorter ranges, Agni I and Agni II, sometime in 2003.

All this, obviously, is about war and not "deterrence." As Pakistani journalist and peace activist M. B. Naqvi wrote in the online *News International* on April 28, 2003: "Are the two adequately deterred? Bold will be the man who will answer in the affirmative. Which general or government can miss the fact that a Ghauri will take two to three minutes to reach its target in India? The Indian Prithvi too will take the same time to wreak terrible destruction in Pakistan. No government or army can take a rational or calculated decision or even to pick up the telephone within three minutes, if they do get an inkling. Today, the brutal fact is that both countries are on hair-trigger alert; both will launch on the first indication that the other is activating its missiles. A sadder fact is that they have to remain on this dangerous, instant alert—all the time and always—with its expected accidents and failures."

The "triangle," which played a crucial role in creating the South Asian trauma of 2002, continues to keep the terror-laden situation alive. Neither of the warring allies of Washington in this region has been discouraged in its attempt to turn the "anti-terror" alliance to decisive advantage for itself. The Bush regime of the U.S., in fact, is playing the dishonest broker by dispensing bounteous military assistance and cooperation to both, even while counseling peace to them. And the self-appointed champion of the non-proliferation cause has turned, actually, into an admirer of the knights of nuclear weaponization in the subcontinent.

On his visit to the U.S. in June 2003, President Musharraf succeeded in prizing out of President Bush a pledge of $3-billion assistance "to help advance security and economic opportunity for Pakistan's citizens." On September 25, US Ambassador to Pakistan Nancy J. Powell was reported as saying that the funds would be "split evenly between defense spending and economic assistance." The waiver of post-Chagai US sanctions seemed far away, as Islamabad asked for even more military goods in the "anti-terror" cause. All this, it must be remembered, after Washington was reported to be mightily upset at reports about a Pakistani nuclear deal with North Korea.

Talking of the special US-Pakistan ties, in an article captioned "The thinkable" in the *New York Times Magazine* of May 4, 2003, Bill Keller wrote: "Although we have leaned recently on President Musharraf to make sure Pakistani nuclear capabilities stay home, we are reluctant to lean too hard, because he is now an indispensable ally against terrorists. 'We are doing pretty much what we did in the 80's,' conceded an American official who deals with South Asia. 'The exigencies change, but the dilemma is still the same. You need Pakistan for some reasons, and therefore you cut the Pakistanis more slack than is prudent.'" The result has been nothing for the peace-loving people of South Asia to rejoice over.

Nor is the barrack-room Indo-US bonhomie something to celebrate, especially for Indian peace activists. A new stage in the military relations between the two countries was marked by the three-week joint exercises of special US and Indian forces in Ladakh (of Jammu and Kashmir) that began on September 8, 2003. Such exercises had been held in Agra the previous year, but the US participation in the Ladakh exercises was seen as a semi-official recognition of India's claim on Kashmir. The unstated hope was that this could led to an eventual US recognition of India's right of pre-emption. These exercises were followed by a major Indo-US naval exercise off Kochi on India's southwest coast during October 2-7, with the participation of a US nuclear submarine.

The trouble in the South Asian segment of the "anti-terror" alliance was seriously aggravated in the update-covered period by the emergence of another "anti-terror" axis. The idea of the axis was always part of the ideological package of India's far-Right "parivar." But it was floated afresh by National Security Adviser Brajesh Mishra during his visit to Washington in May 2003. Addressing the 97th annual conference here of the American Jewish Committee, he declared that "a core consisting of democratic societies must emerge, which can take on international terrorism in a holistic and frontal manner to ensure that global terrorism is pursued to its logical conclusion." Identifying India, the U.S., and Israel as three such societies facing "similar threats of terrorism," he called for their strategic partnership. He also announced the proposed visit to India of Israeli Prime Minister Ariel Sharon. Despite the fact that all this marked a sharp departure from India's decades-old policy of support for the Palestinian cause, and despite popular protests, Sharon did arrive in New Delhi on September 9. The BJP-headed Indian government had earlier sought and acquired "anti-terror" Israeli expertise for India's operations in Kashmir. It was the Sharon visit, however, that led to the first sign of the emerging axis in the form of the Phalcon deal.

New Delhi's lobbying for Tel Aviv's sale of the Phalcon air-borne, early warning radar system—jointly developed by the U.S. and Israel—reached an advanced stage rapidly after Mishra's appeal for the axis formation. In about a month, Washington had been persuaded to give a green signal to the sale, which it had earlier opposed strongly citing high tensions in South Asia. Commenting on this in the *Space Daily* on June 25, Pakistani analyst Moieed Wasim Yusuf said: "This will inevitably lead Pakistani strategists to take an even more pessimistic view of the chance of survival of their aircraft in a sustained conflict, in turn leading them to focus more on missile development. The deployment of ballistic missiles, due to the unreliable command and control structure, as mentioned, can be the precursor to a nuclear catastrophe in South Asia."[3] He also made the point that the deal would "increase the likelihood of a nuclear incident (an event short of a nuclear war in which a nuclear device is accidentally or deliberately detonated)." The protests and pleas went unheeded. In October, India signed an agreement with Israel and Russia for the supply of Phalcon, to be mounted on a Russian-made Ilyushin-76 aircraft platform. Pakistan has responded by demanding of the U.S. air-borne radars, F-16s, unmanned drones, and special helicopters "to restore the balance." Yet another round of a dangerous arms race has been launched.

A far graver peril, however, is the near-open, new US advocacy of a free pursuit of nuclear glory by its South Asian allies. This went with the appeal for India's troops for Iraq, according to a leading national daily. The *Indian Express* of July 18, 2003, in a story obviously based on official briefing and not denied since by any concerned party, summarizes the message tendered by officials to visiting Foreign Secretary Kanwal Sibal thus: "Yours is a BJP government, you took the risk in 1998, take the initiative now as well…." That reference is to Pokharan II, and the retrospective, adulatory approval for it can only be read as encouragement to further nuclear folly. The message from the former non-proliferationists, who have switched over to the new line of "usable nukes," could not have been lost on President Musharraf and his Chagai-proud army chums.

The grimness of the situation has found glaring evidence. A major decision of the very first meting of India's

NCA on September 1, 2003, it has been disclosed, was to build bunkers in New Delhi to protect the Union (federal) Cabinet in the event of a nuclear attack. One of these multi-million-rupee shelters is to be located in a building which houses the Prime Minister's Office (PMO) as well as the ministries of defense and external affairs. It was also decided to find a suitable location for back-up bunkers within a radius of 400 km in the States of Uttar Pradesh, Rajasthan or Madhya Pradesh.[4] Obviously, those who took the decisions do not believe what they tell the country: that nuclear weapons mean deterrence and not destruction. Predictably, they did not decide on any steps to protect the people from the same nuclear attack. The decisions of Pakistan's NCA may be better-guarded secrets, but it is a safe bet that the people's protection from the fall-out of nuclear militarism is not within the purview of the august organization.

The people of South Asia must protect themselves. But, hopefully, with the solidarity of the swathe of humanity that has spoken up against the series of wars for world domination since 9/11, that recognizes the larger stakes in averting a nuclear holocaust.

Notes

CHAPTER 1

1 All the four authors of this paper are not only leading anti-nuclear activists but also eminently qualified experts on the subject. Zia Mian, a passionately eloquent critic of Pakistan's nuclear policy, is a physicist at the Princeton University's Center for Energy and Environmental Studies and also a visiting fellow at the Sustainable Development Policy Institute, Islamabad. M. V. Ramana, similarly a strong critic of India's nuclear course, is a physicist at the Princeton University's Center for Energy and Environmental Studies, working on nuclear weapons and nuclear energy in India. Matthew McKinzie, an environmentalist, is a physicist working on nuclear weapons development and its consequences in the Natural Resources Defense Council, a U.S.-based NGO. A. H. Nayyar, working for decades in fields ranging from labor and human rights to nuclear weapons, is an associate professor of physics at the Quaid-e-Azam University, Islamabad.

2 Since those days, there has been a significant change in India's position on the first-strike option. It has now found a way to keep this open without saying so. According to its amended nuclear doctrine announced in October 2003, it reserves the "option of retaliating with nuclear weapons," if a biological or chemical weapons attack is made, in the official Indian judgment, "on India or its forces anywhere." See Chapter 9.

CHAPTER 2

1 Subramania Bharati and Allama Iqbal exemplified the idea of India, of a subcontinental identity, that was to end, ironically, along with colonial rule in the region. Bharati (1882-1921), a Tamil poet from the country's deep South, was a devout Hindu, though also a pioneering social reformer and staunch opponent of obscurantism. Iqbal (1877-1938), a Persian and Urdu poet from Kashmir, was a forward-looking Muslim. Both of them wrote songs of Indian patriotism that bespeak a pride in the composite richness of the country's culture and still evoke a popular emotional response.

2 The Revolt of 1857 was sparked off by the court-martialling of 85 sepoys of a regiment of Meerut (not far from Delhi) for refusing to use greased cartridges. The Hindu and Muslim sepoys were united in refusing to do so. In order to help its passage down the barrel of a rifle, each cartridge was heavily greased with beef or pork fat, which the Hindus and the Muslims were forbidden to eat respectively. A soldier had to bit off the end of a cartridge

before its use. The punishment of imprisonment and shackling awarded to the rebel soldiers provoked a mutiny. The unrest spread far beyond the barracks soon. The Revolt ended with the surrender of Bahadur Shah Zafar in September 1858, followed over the next seven months by the fall of both Hindu and Muslim chieftains who had adopted him as a common symbol and spearhead.

3   Thus it was that the British rulers, through its constitutional reforms of 1909 (known as Morley-Minto Reforms, so named after its authors John Morley and the Earl of Minto, Viceroy Gilbert Elliot), conceded the demand for separate electorates for the Muslims in the proposed provincial assemblies, a demand strongly opposed by the mainstream independence movement led by Mahatma Gandhi. From this demand to that for creation of Pakistan was a logical development.

4   Families with roots in present-day Pakistan, not many generations away from those who had migrated to India during the Partition days, were for decades the mainstay of the Jana Sangh, the parent of the Bharatiya Janata Party. In electoral constituencies where the ex-refugee vote mattered, the JS or the BJP never made any pretence about its politics of revanchism.

CHAPTER 3

1   This region has not been central to the India-Pakistan dispute. It is not, however, as if there were no Kashmiri discontent and unrest in Azad Kashmir or Pak-occupied Kashmir and Pakistan's Northern Areas. Voices have been raised, particularly from the Northern Areas, in protest against denial of democracy and remote Islamabad rule. On May 28, 1999, when Pakistan's rulers were celebrating the first anniversary of the Chagai nuclear-weapon tests, the Supreme Court of Pakistan, in its judgment on a bunch of petitions, was constrained to observe: "It is not understandable on what basis the people of the Northern Areas can be denied the fundamental rights guaranteed in the Constitution (including the right to vote)." On the eve of the third Chagai anniversary, on May 17, 2001, the Jammu and Kashmir Liberation Front (JKLF) launched a public protest against an order by the Pakistan government requiring contestants in the Azad Kashmir assembly elections to declare their support for the accession of the entire State of Jammu and Kashmir to Pakistan. This, the JKLF pointed out, was a denial of the democratic rights of pro-independence candidates, though Islamabad claimed to support the "freedom struggle" of the Kashmiri people.

2   The 776-km-long LoC runs between the Indian State of Jammu and Kashmir (which Pakistan calls Occupied Kashmir) and Pakistan-controlled Azad Kashmir (which India calls Pakistan-occupied Kashmir). It is a product of two wars. The Cease-Fire Line (CFL), drawn after the India-

Pakistan war of 1948, with a few and far-from-major changes, was adopted as the LoC in terms of the Simla Agreement of 1972 after the Bangladesh war. New Delhi has emphasized that the Kargil war of 1999 was provoked by Pakistan's attempt to violate the sanctity of the LoC respected by both the sides for 27 years. India's plea for a "right to pre-emptive strikes" on "terrorist camps inside PoK," however, is evidently incompatible with any idea of the LoC's inviolability.

CHAPTER 4

1 There is a Kashmiri viewpoint that the plebiscite should not be projected as a means to decide Kashmir's accession to either India or Pakistan alone. Official India and Pakistan have continued to interpret only in such terms the first UN resolution on the subject (of January 17, 1948) talking of determining the State's future "in accordance with the will of the people." The Jammu and Kashmir Liberation Front (JKLF) has been speaking for a "third option" of "independence."

2 Muslims, Hindus and Buddhists account for about 65 per cent, 32 per cent, and one per cent respectively of the total population of Jammu and Kashmir. The Hindus and the Buddhists, however, form the majority in the Jammu and Ladakh sections of the State respectively, while the Kashmir Valley is a Muslim-majority area. The Rashtriya Swayamsevak Sangh (RSS) and its allies have for long been campaigning for the State's "trifurcation" as part of their religious-communal politics. The RSS made an effort to intensify the campaign in June 2003. This could have led to a serious aggravation of the situation in the State. Mercifully, the Bharatiya Janata Party (BJP), which has never opposed the demand, has discovered that the trifurcation can only "weaken" New Delhi's case on Kashmir, as Deputy Prime Minister L. K. Advani told the RSS in a public reaction.

3 K. R. Narayanan, then India's Vice-President and earlier a career diplomat, wrote in 1992: "By the middle fifties, the Jammu and Kashmir question had become for the powers a counter on the checkerboard of the Cold War. Pakistan had become a member of great-power military pacts. Besides, in the aftermath of the Hungarian and Suez crises, the Cold War had become even more bitter." (Foreword, Krishna Menon on Kashmir, Speeches at United Nations, ed. E. S. Reddy and A. K. Damodaran, Sanchar, New Delhi, 1992.) It must be noted that the Cold War helped India's Kashmir case, too, in the form of the Soviet Union's support, backed by its veto.

4 According to estimates released in 2003 by the US Committee for Refuges (USCR), a non-governmental organization, Kashmiri Pandits made up most of the about 350,000 Kashmiris displaced since 1990. Of these, about 250,000 stay in and around Hindu-majority Jammu. The remaining 100,000 are refugees in the rest of India, and the bulk of them live on a

government allowance in New Delhi. Their common refrain on media interviews is the hope that the can return someday to Kashmir.

CHAPTER 5

1   Anand Patwardhan won a long-drawn-out battle for peace as well as freedom of expression, when the Bombay High Court delivered a verdict on April 24, 2003, restoring all the 21 cuts imposed by official film censors and annulling their order for an addition to War and Peace.

2   The mainstream Left saw the "option of keeping the nuclear option open" as an anti-imperialist assertion of national sovereignty. Articulating this viewpoint in a signed editorial captioned "The perils of nuclear adventurism" in fortnightly *Frontline* (May 23-June 5, 1998), prominent journalist N. Ram wrote: "Despite the obstructions and pressures and some vacillations over the years (especially during the Prime Ministerships of Morarji Desai and P. V. Narasimha Rao), national policy refused to sign away the sovereignty of decision-making on the nuclear issue while preserving its commitment to the peaceful, non-military uses of nuclear energy." Ram also said that "India's long-standing policy with its twin components – the refusal to surrender the nuclear option by acceding to the NPT regime (or an equivalent option such as "full-scope safeguards" or a "South Asia Nuclear Weapon-Free Zone"), and self-imposed and conditional restraint in not militarizing the option – was eminently sustainable." He added: "Indeed, no other policy could have been considered peace-abiding and responsible under the circumstances. The accomplishment of the BJP-led government, within two months of taking office, has been to undermine this long-standing policy."

CHAPTER 6

1   An attempt was made in 2003 to produce archaeological evidence in support of the claim, though it had all along until then been asserted that a matter of faith needed no such mundane investigation. Following a much-criticized court order, the government-controlled Archaeological Survey of India (ASI) carried out a hurried excavation at the site and claimed to have unearthed evidence of a Hindu temple. Several eminent historians have, since then, rejected the claim and ridiculed the ASI's rationale and methodology. Some observers have also questioned the assumption that archaeology could justify Ayodhya-like agitations, that rediscovery of the past could legitimize Nazi-like revanchism. See J. Sri Raman, "The past as propaganda," *Tribune* (India), July 12, 2003 (www.tribuneindia.com).

2   On April 1, 1933, two months after they captured power in Germany, the Nazis carried out a boycott of Jewish businesses and professionals. The infamous Storm Troopers stood menacingly in front of Jew-owned departmen-

tal stores and shops, while posters screamed. "Don't Buy from Jews," "Jews Are Our Misfortune," "'Jewish store! Whoever buys from here will be photographed," and so on. This, obviously, served as a model for the anti-Muslim campaign in Gujarat. The campaign was helped also by the relative affluence of Bohra Muslim traders who, as moneylenders, were also given a Shylock-like image among the aboriginal people of the State.

3 It was four years and eight months after the murder of Staines and his sons, and following Western pressures for justice in the case, that a lower court delivered a verdict on September 23, 2003, sentencing main accused Dara Singh to death and 12 of his accomplices to life imprisonment. For the victims of the Gujarat violence, a longer wait was inevitable.

4 Sardar Vallabbhai Patel is one of the nationalist leaders whom the far-Right family has tried to adopt and appropriate. It has done so despite the fact that he was the country's Home Minister when the Rashtriya Swayamsevak Sangh was banned in the wake of Mahatma Gandhi's assassination in 1948. Patel's initiative for rebuilding the Somnath temple in Gujarat, which was not preceded by the demolition of any mosque, was claimed to have been part of the inspiration for the Ayodhya campaign.

CHAPTER 7

1 On October 23, 2003, nearly two years after the attack on Parliament, the Delhi High Court set aside the death sentences pronounced by a lower court earlier on two of the accused. One of these was a suspended Delhi University lecturer, S. A. E. Geelani, the charge against whom was based on the inadmissible evidence of a telephonic intercept and had consequently drawn widespread criticism. The other was the wife of an alleged Kashmiri militant, and 'concealment of a conspiracy' was the charge she had faced. The matter, however, has not ended with the verdict. Neither the police nor the other two accused condemned to death have closed the option of an appeal to the Supreme Court.

2 According to official figures, there are about 12,000 "madrassas" in Pakistan today, an unascertained number of which are engaged in making "jihadis" or "holy warriors" of their students including a significant proportion from Arab countries. In an article in the *Washington Post* of January 5, 2001, long before 9/11, Arslan Malik wrote: "until the 1970s, there were less than 1,000 madrassas in Pakistan and they were dedicated primarily to formal instruction in Islamic theology. The decade-long Soviet occupation of Afghanistan starting in 1979 changed this as US policy-makers and their Pakistani allies, convinced that a religious opposition would be well-suited to fight the 'godless communists,' set out to use the seminaries as prep schools for anti-Soviet insurgents. With arms from the United States, support from the Inter-Services Intelligence (ISI), the Pakistani intelligence

agency, and funding from Islamist sources abroad, the madrassas evolved into indoctrination and guerilla training camps."

CHAPTER 8

1   The Movement in India for Nuclear Disarmament (MIND), which had protested against Pokharan I or India's nuclear-weapon tests in 1974 and opposed the policy of "nuclear ambiguity," said of Pokharan II of 1998: "After the five nuclear-weapon tests of May 11 and 13, the BJP-led government has declared India nuclear-weapons power…. These tests were a complete departure from a settled national consensus…there was a national consensus that, in the absence of any tangible movement towards global disarmament, India must keep its nuclear option open." In a document titled "Nuclear India: A Short History," the MIND noted: "Supporters of nuclear weapons argue that India's decision to cross the nuclear threshold is in continuity with New Delhi's policies in the past. They claim that, if there is any policy change under the BJP-led coalition, it is only in response to the altered ground situation…. This is misleading, false and dishonest. May 1998 marks a violent break with India's past postures."

2   Serious questions of nuclear safety and transparency were raised by an accident in the Kalpakkam Atomic Reprocessing Plant (KARP), described as the worst ever in the history of India's Department of Atomic Energy (DAE). The accident took place on January 21, 2003, when six employees of the KARP suffered exposure to very high doses of radiation. It was only in July, following employees' protests and a media outcry, that the plant was shut down, with the DAE announcing that it would be reopened as soon as possible. See Papri Sri Raman, "The Kalpakkam Story," *Peace Now!* (Bulletin of the Coalition for Nuclear Disarmament and Peace, India), Vol. I: Issue II, 2003.

CHAPTER 9

1   The United Nations Resolution on Iraq, dated October 16, 2003, though meant to meet the official condition of countries like India and Pakistan for dispatch of troops to Iraq, did not serve the intended purpose immediately. The unofficial condition of each of the rivals, however, has remained US support against the other: for New Delhi, recognition of its "pre-emption right" and, for Islamabad, intervention for a Kashmir settlement.

2   The government made no statement on the incident. The main opposition Congress, restrained presumably by notions of its national responsibility, did not press its initial demand for such a statement. The truth of the charge that the country's premier intelligence agencies and Ministry of External Affairs were kept in the dark about the incident for some day or

that the nuclear establishment ignored norms of accountability—could not be ascertained.

3   Moieed Wasim Yusuf notes: "An argument has been made that a large number of ballistic missiles can enhance the deterrent effect. This stems from the fact that the inability of the enemy to destroy all delivery systems leaves the enemy concerned about a second strike on its country, thus acting as a self-deterrent." He adds: "However, in the case of South Asia, where reaction times are minimal, and communication channels unreliable, this argument does not hold. During a crisis, both sides will disperse their arsenals as widely as possible. This would mean authorizing low-level personnel to launch nuclear weapons in case of a breakdown in communication channels."

4   A report in *The Hindu* (Delhi edition) of November 6, 1999, said: "The Delhi (State) Government has prepared a Rs. 1,100-crore ($300 million) plan to counter the after-effects of a nuclear attack on the national capital and adjoining areas. The proposal...does not, however, advocate construction of expensive underground shelters.... The proposal has been premised on the assumption that a nuclear attack will not allow survival within a "Dead Zone" radius of around 24 km to 48 km. A "Survival Zone" will begin thereafter and extend to the next 32 km." Quoted in N. D. Jayaprakash's excellent comment titled "Spectre of Armageddon," available on Znet InterActive.

Index

About the Author

A journalist and an activist, J. Sri Raman has been both, through the past three decades that make an especially checkered phase of India's post-Independence history.

Now a freelance journalist based in Chennai (formerly Madras), he has worked as a reporter and a leader-writer (and in sundry other capacities) with major daily newspapers in New Delhi. Through his entire career, which included an earlier phase as a "jobless" journalist, he has contributed to several newspapers including *Patriot*, *Statesman*, the *Indian Express and* the *Hindustan Times* and periodicals including *Sunday*, *This Fortnight*, and the *Week*, besides (very occasionally) to foreign periodicals like *Tribune* (Sri Lanka), *Onze Wereld* (Holland), and *Asiaweek* (Hong Kong).

He has written on a wide range of subjects. He has followed the fortunes of political parties and personalities and, once in the late seventies, the trail of a devastating cyclone on India's southeastern coast. He has covered India's elections at different levels, labor issues and actions, and a UNIDO conference. He has been a critic at national and international film festivals and kept up a non-live commentary on cricket.

There have been more memorable—and meaningful—moments. He was a chronicler in Kabul of the Afghan conflict during 1980-83 when, to the US rulers, the Taliban were freedom fighters fit to receive reckless bounties of arms and funds. A couple of years later, he interviewed secessionist leaders of Sri Lanka's Liberation

Tigers of Tamil Eelam (LTTE) in their Chennai hideout, taken there in a car with dark-tinted windows, when they enjoyed the hospitality of India's rulers who were to turn against them soon. He now testifies professionally to the contradictions and the crying hypocrisy of current "anti-terror" campaigns. He has written a large number of opinion pieces, directed increasingly against the domestic far Right allied to the warmongering forces of the world.

Now, he writes regularly for the Chandigarh-based newspaper *Tribune* and a fortnightly column for the Lahore-based *Daily Times*. He likes to think of himself as an Indo-Pakistan journalist.

On the activist front, he started as a trade unionist among journalists and print workers in the seventies. He has ended up as a peace campaigner. Soon after India's nuclear-weapon tests in 1998, he founded the Journalists Against Nuclear Weapons (JANW) and is now the Convener of the Movement Against Nuclear Weapons (MANW) representing several organizations (including the JANW). As such, he has been in the forefront of the campaign in India aimed at averting an India-Pakistan war and a nuclear holocaust. He is on the Advisory Board of the Global Network Against Weapons and Nuclear Power in Space.

He has edited, and contributed the main essay to, *The Media Bomb*, a critique of Indian media reactions to India's nuclear-weapon tests. He is also the author of a sheaf of poems under the title *At Gunpoint*.

He lives with his wife Papri and daughters (also fellow-activists) Taranga and Varna.